W9-AHB-493

Lauren Darcey
Shane Conder

Sams **Teach Yourself**

Android™

Application Development

in **24** **Hours**

800 East 96th Street, Indianapolis, Indiana 46240 USA

Sams Teach Yourself Android™ Application Development in 24 Hours

Visible Earth images owned by NASA, http://visibleearth.nasa.gov/.

ISBN-13: 978-0-321-67335-0
ISBN-10: 0-321-67335-2

Library of Congress Cataloging-in-Publication Data

Darcey, Lauren, 1977-

   Sams teach yourself Android application development in 24 hours / Lauren Darcey, Shane Conder.

      p. cm. — (Sams teach yourself in 24 Hours)

   Includes index.

   ISBN 978-0-321-67335-0 (pbk.)

   1. Application software—Development. 2. Android (Electronic resource) 3. Mobile computing. I. Conder, Shane, 1975- II. Title.

   QA76.76.A65D26 2010

   005.1—dc22

                                2010011663

Printed in the United States of America

Third Printing January 2011

Trademarks

Warning and Disclaimer

Bulk Sales

Sams Publishing offers excellent discounts on this book when ordered in quantity for bulk purchases or special sales. For more information, please contact

U.S. Corporate and Government Sales
1-800-382-3419
corpsales@pearsontechgroup.com

For sales outside of the U.S., please contact

International Sales
international@pearson.com

Editor-in-Chief
Mark Taub

Acquisitions Editor
Trina MacDonald

Development Editor
Michael Thurston

Managing Editor
Kristy Hart

Project Editor
Betsy Harris

Copy Editor
Kitty Wilson

Indexer
Erika Millen

Proofreader
Sheri Cain

Technical Editor
Jonathan Jackson

Publishing Coordinator
Olivia Basegio

Book Designer
Gary Adair

Senior Compositor
Gloria Schurick

Contents at a Glance

Table of Contents

Part II: Building an Application Framework

Part VI: Appendixes

About the Authors

Lauren Darcey is responsible for the technical leadership and direction of a small software company specializing in mobile technologies, including Android, iPhone, Blackberry, Palm Pre, BREW, and J2ME. With more than two decades of experience in professional software production, Lauren is a recognized authority in enterprise architecture and the development of commercial-grade mobile applications. Lauren received a B.S. in Computer Science from the University of California, Santa Cruz.

She spends her copious free time traveling the world with her geeky mobile-minded husband and is an avid nature photographer. Her work has been published in books and newspapers around the world. In South Africa, she dove with 4-meter-long great white sharks and got stuck between a herd of rampaging hippopotami and an irritated bull elephant. She's been attacked by monkeys in Japan, gotten stuck in a ravine with two hungry lions in Kenya, gotten thirsty in Egypt, narrowly avoided a coup d'état in Thailand, geocached her way through the Swiss Alps, drank her way through the beer halls of Germany, slept in the crumbling castles of Europe, and gotten her tongue stuck to an iceberg in Iceland (while being watched by a herd of suspicious wild reindeer).

Shane Conder has extensive development experience and has focused his attention on mobile and embedded development for the past decade. He has designed and developed many commercial applications for BREW, J2ME, Palm, Windows Mobile, and Android— some of which have been installed on millions of phones worldwide. Shane has written extensively about the mobile industry and evaluated mobile development platforms on his tech blogs and is well known within the blogosphere. Shane received a B.S. in Computer Science from the University of California.

A self-admitted gadget freak, Shane always has the latest phone or laptop. He can often be found fiddling with the latest technologies, such as Amazon Web Services, Android, iPhone, Google App Engine, and other exciting, state-of-the-art technologies that activate the creative part of his brain. He also enjoys traveling the world with his geeky wife, even if she did make him dive with 4-meter-long great white sharks and almost get eaten by a lion in Kenya. He admits that it was his fault they got attacked by monkeys in Japan, that he snickered and whipped out his Android phone to take a picture when Laurie got her tongue stuck to that iceberg in Iceland, and that he still hasn't learned his lesson about writing his own bio.

Other Publications by the Authors

The authors have also published *Android Wireless Application Development*, part of the Addison-Wesley *Developer's Library* series, as well as numerous online technical articles for http://developer.com, http://informIT.com, and their own Android blog, http://android-book.blogspot.com.

Dedication

To grandparents the world over, especially those who are kind and generous, bake awesome pecan pies, and like to watch *America's Most Wanted*. You are **not** a bother but a blessing. And if you don't remember us telling you so, don't you worry, because we'll just tell you again tomorrow.

Acknowledgments

This book would never have been written without the guidance and encouragement we received from a number of very patient and supportive people, including our editorial team, coworkers, friends, and family.

Throughout this project, our editorial team at Pearson (Sams Publishing) was top notch. Special thanks go to Trina MacDonald, Olivia Basegio, and Betsy Harris. Our fantastic technical reviewer, Jonathan Jackson, helped us ensure that this book provides true, correct, and high-quality technical information. Finally, we'd like to thank many of our friends and family members who supported us during some difficult times, when we needed to make our book deadlines despite a very serious family illness that required us to write the book from Grandma's kitchen table. (Yes, you can develop Android apps *anywhere*.) We would like to specifically single out Liz Reid, Guy Grayson, the Lenz family (especially Thomas and Patrick), Shoshi Brown and family (especially Jacob), the Badger family (especially Wi-Vi and Nolia), Richard deCastongrene, Asher Siddiqui, Anthony Shaffer, Spencer Nassar, and Mary Thompson for their support and encouragement.

We Want to Hear from You!

As the reader of this book, *you* are our most important critic and commentator. We value your opinion and want to know what we're doing right, what we could do better, what areas you'd like to see us publish in, and any other words of wisdom you're willing to pass our way.

You can email or write me directly to let me know what you did or didn't like about this book—as well as what we can do to make our books stronger.

Please note that I cannot help you with technical problems related to the topic of this book, and that due to the high volume of mail I receive, I might not be able to reply to every message.

When you write, please be sure to include this book's title and author as well as your name and phone or email address. I will carefully review your comments and share them with the author and editors who worked on the book.

Email: feedback@samspublishing.com

Mail: Mark Taub
            Editor-in-Chief
            Sams Publishing
            800 East 96th Street
            Indianapolis, IN 46240 USA

Reader Services

Visit our website and register this book at http://informit.com/register for convenient access to any updates, downloads, or errata that might be available for this book.

Introduction

The Android platform is packing some serious heat these days in the mobile marketplace and gaining traction worldwide. The platform has seen numerous advancements in terms of SDK functionality, handset availability, and feature set. A wide diversity of Android handsets and devices are now shipping and (finally) in consumers' hands—and we're not just talking about phones: Android has begun to ship on netbooks, Internet tablets (such as the ARCHOS 5), ebook readers (like the Barnes & Noble nook), digital photo frames, and a variety of other consumer electronics. There are even proof-of-concept appliances such as an Android microwave and washer/dryer combo. (Hey, why not? See http://bit.ly/bGqmZp.) Mobile operators and carriers are taking the platform seriously and spending gazillions on ad campaigns for Android phones—like Verizon's Droid campaign.

In the past year or so, the Android platform has transitioned from a "gearheads-only" platform to providing some serious competition to more established platforms. (Yes, we're talking about platforms such as the iPhone.)

But let's not digress into an argument over whose platform is better so early, okay? Because, honestly, you're wasting your time if you think there's one platform to rule them all. The reality is, people the world over use different phones in different places (CDMA, GSM) and for different reasons (price, availability, coverage quality, feature set, design, familiarity, compatibility). There is no one-size-fits-all answer to this debate.

Having developed for just about every major mobile platform out there, we are keenly aware of the benefits and drawbacks of each platform. We do not presume to claim that one platform is better than another in general; each platform has distinct advantages over the rest, and these advantages can be maximized.

The trick is to know which platform to use for a given project. Sometimes, the answer is to use as many platforms as possible. Lately, we've been finding that the answer is the Android platform: It's inexpensive and easy to develop for, it's available to millions of potential users worldwide, and it has fewer limitations than other platforms.

Still, the Android platform is relatively young and has not yet reached its full-fledged potential. This means frequent SDK updates, an explosion of new devices on the market, and a nearly full-time job keeping track of everything going on in the Android world.

In other words, it may be a bit of a bumpy ride, but there's still time to jump on this bandwagon, write some kick-butt applications, and make a name for yourself.

So let's get to it.

Who Should Read This Book?

There's no reason anyone with an Android handset and a good idea for a mobile application couldn't put this book to use for fun and profit. Whether you're a programmer looking to break into mobile technology or an entrepreneur with a cool app idea, this book is for you.

We make very few assumptions about you as a reader of this book. You may have a basic understanding of the Java programming language (understanding classes, methods, basic inheritance, and so on), but Android makes a fantastic platform for learning Java as well. We have avoided using any fancy or confusing Java in this book, so if you're just getting started with programming, you should be able to read the first few chapters of any introductory Java book or do an online tutorial and have enough Java knowledge to make it through this book alive.

We do assume that you're somewhat comfortable installing applications on a computer (for example, Eclipse, the Java JDK, and the Android SDK) and tools and drivers (for USB access to a phone), and we assume that you can navigate your way around an Android handset well enough to launch applications and such. No wireless development experience is necessary.

How This Book Is Structured

In 24 easy one-hour lessons, you'll design and develop a fully functional network- and LBS (Location-Based Services)-enabled Android application, complete with social features. Each lesson builds on your knowledge of newly introduced Android concepts, and you'll iteratively improve your application from chapter to chapter.

This book is divided into six parts:

▶ **Part I: Android Fundamentals**

In Part I, you'll get an introduction to Android, become familiar with the Android SDK and tools, install the development tools, and write your first Android application. Part I also introduces the design principles necessary to write Android applications, including how Android applications are structured and configured, as well as how to incorporate application resources such as strings, graphics, and user interface components into your projects.

▶ **Part II: Building an Application Framework**

In Part II, you'll begin developing an application framework that will serve as primary teaching-tool for the rest of the book. You'll start by developing an animated splash screen, followed by screens for main menu, settings, help, and scores. You'll learn basic user interface design principles, how to collect input from the user, and how to display dialogs to the user. Finally, you'll implement the core application logic of the game screen.

▶ **Part III: Enhancing Your Application with Powerful Android Features**

In Part III, you'll dive deeper into the Android SDK, adding more specialized features to the Been There, Done That! application. You'll learn how to work with graphics and the built-in camera, how to leverage LBS, how to network-enable your application, and how to enhance your application with social features.

▶ **Part IV: Adding Polish to Your Android Application**

In Part IV, you'll learn how to customize your application for different handsets, screen sizes, and foreign languages. You'll also learn about different ways to test mobile applications.

▶ **Part V: Publishing Your Application**

In Part V, you'll learn what you need to do to prepare for and publish your Android applications to the Android Market.

▶ **Part VI: Appendixes**

In Part VI, you'll find several helpful references for setting up your Android development environment, using the Eclipse IDE, and accessing supplementary book materials, like the book websites and downloadable source code.

What Is (and Isn't) in This Book

While we specifically targeted Android SDK Version 2.1 in this book, many of the examples were tested on handsets running a variety of Android SDK versions.

The Android SDK is updated *very* frequently (every few months). We kept this in mind when choosing which features of the SDK to highlight to ensure maximum forward and backward compatibility. When necessary, we point out areas where the Android SDK version affects the features and functionality available to the developer.

This book is written in a beginner's tutorial style. If you're looking for an exhaustive reference on Android development, with cookbook-style code examples and a more thorough examination of all the features of the Android platform, we recommend our other, more advanced Android book, *Android Wireless Application Development*, which is part of the Addison-Wesley *Developer's Library* series.

What Development Environment Is Used?

The code in this book was written using the following development environments:

- ▶ Windows 7 and Mac OS X 10.6

- ▶ Eclipse Java IDE Version 3.5 (Galileo)

- ▶ Eclipse JDT plug-in and Web Tools Platform (WTP)

- ▶ Sun Java SE Development Kit (JDK) 6 Update 18

- ▶ Android SDK Version 2.1 (Primary target, developed and tested on a variety of SDK versions)

- ▶ Various Android handsets (Android SDK 1.6, 2.0.1, and 2.1)

What Conventions Are Used in This Book?

This book presents several types of sidebars for special kinds of information:

- ▶ **Did You Know?** messages provide useful information or hints related to the current text.

- ▶ **By the Way** messages provide additional information that might be interesting or relevant.

- ▶ **Watch Out!** messages provide hints or tips about pitfalls that may be encountered and how to avoid them.

This book uses the following code-related conventions:

- ▶ Code and programming terms are set in a monospace font.

- ▶ ➡ is used to signify that the code that follows should appear on the same line as the preceding code.

- ▶ Exception handling and error checking are often removed from printed code samples for clarity and to keep the book a reasonable length.

This book uses the following conventions for step-by-step instructions and explanations:

- ▶ The core application developed in this book is developed iteratively. Generally, this means that the first time a new concept is explained, every item related to the new concept is discussed in detail. As we move on to more advanced topics in later lessons, we assume that you have mastered some of the more rudimentary aspects of Android development from previous chapters, and we do not repeat ourselves much. In some cases, we instruct you to implement something in an early lesson and then help you improve it in a later chapter.

▶ We assume that you'll read the chapters of this book in order. As you progress through the book, you'll note that we do not spell out each and every step that must be taken for each and every feature you implement to follow along in building the core application example. For example, if three buttons must be implemented on a screen, we walk you step-by-step through the implementation of the first button but leave the implementation of the other two buttons as an exercise for you. In a later chapter on a different topic, we might simply ask you to implement some buttons on another screen.

▶ Where we tell you to navigate through menu options, we separate options using commas. For example, if we told you to open a new document, we'd say "Select File, New Document."

Getting Started with Android

What You'll Learn in This Hour:

▶ A brief history of the Android platform

▶ Familiarizing yourself with Eclipse

▶ Creating Android projects

▶ Running and debugging applications

Android is the first *complete*, *open*, and *free* mobile platform. Developers enjoy a comprehensive software development kit, with ample tools for developing powerful, feature-rich applications. The platform is open source, relying on tried-and-true open standards developers will be familiar with. And best of all, there are no costly barriers to entry for developers: no required fees. (A modest fee is required to publish on third-party distribution mechanisms such as the Android Market.) Android developers have numerous options for distributing and commercializing their applications.

Introducing Android

To understand where Android fits in with other mobile technologies, let's take a minute to talk about how and why this platform came about.

Google and the Open Handset Alliance

In 2007, a group of handset manufacturers, wireless carriers, and software developers (notably, Google) formed the Open Handset Alliance, with the goal of developing the next generation of wireless platform. Unlike existing platforms, this new platform would be nonproprietary and based on open standards, which would lead to lower development costs and increased profits. Mobile software developers would also have unprecedented access to the handset features, allowing for greater innovation.

As proprietary platforms such as RIM BlackBerry and Apple iPhone gained traction, the mobile development community eagerly listened for news of this potential game-changing platform.

Android Makes Its Entrance

In 2008, the Open Handset Alliance announced the Android platform and launched a beta program for developers. Android went through the typical revisions of a new platform. Several prerelease revisions of the Android Software Development Kit (SDK) were released. The first Android handset (the T-Mobile G1) began shipping in late 2008. Throughout 2009, more Android handsets and diverse types of devices powered by Android reached world markets. As of this writing, there are more than 36 Android phones available from carriers around the world. This number does not include the numerous Android tablet and e-book readers also available, nor the dozens of upcoming devices already announced, nor the consumer electronics running Android. The rate of new Android devices reaching the world markets has continued to increase. In the United States, all major carriers now include Android phones in their product lines.

Google has been a contributing member of the Open Handset Alliance from the beginning. The company hosts the Android open source project as well as the Android developer program at http://developer.android.com. This developer website is your go-to site for downloading the Android SDK, getting the latest platform documentation, and browsing the Android developer forums. Google also runs the most popular service for selling Android applications to end users: the Android Market. The Android mascot is the little green robot shown in Figure 1.1.

FIGURE 1.1
The Android mascot.

The Android Developer Challenge

Google has hosted several contests, called Developer Challenges, to encourage developers to write Android applications. The first two rounds saw $10 million in prize money awarded!

Cheap and Easy Development

If there's one time when "cheap and easy" is a benefit, it's with mobile development. Wireless application development, with its ridiculously expensive compilers and preferential developer programs, has been notoriously expensive to break into compared to desktop development. Here, Android breaks the proprietary mold. Unlike with other mobile platforms, there are virtually no costs to developing Android applications.

The Android SDK and tools are freely available on the Android developer website, http://developer.android.com. The freely available Eclipse program has become the most popular integrated development environment (IDE) for Android application development; there is also a powerful plug-in available on the Android developer site for facilitating Android development.

So we've covered cheap; now let's talk about why Android development is easy. Because Android applications are written in Java, developers will be familiar with many of the packages provided as part of the Android SDK, such as `java.net`. Developers will be pleased to find that the learning curve for Android is quite reasonable.

So let's get started!

Familiarizing Yourself with Eclipse

Let's begin by writing a simple Android "Hello, World" application that displays a line of text to the user. As you do so, you will also be taking a tour through the Eclipse environment. Specifically, you will learn about the features offered by the Android Development Tools (ADT) plug-in for Eclipse. The ADT plug-in provides functionality for developing, compiling, packaging, and deploying Android applications. Specifically, it provides the following:

- ▶ The Android project wizard, which generates all the required project files
- ▶ Android-specific resource editors
- ▶ The Android SDK and AVD (Android Virtual Devices) Manager

► The Eclipse DDMS perspective for monitoring and debugging Android applications

► Integration with Android LogCat logging

► Automated builds and application deployment to Android emulators and handsets

► Application packaging and code signing tools for release deployment

Installing the Android SDK and Tools

You will find all the details of how to install and configure your computer for Android application development in Appendix A, "Configuring Your Android Development Environment." You will need to install and configure Eclipse, the Android SDK, and the ADT plug-in for Eclipse. You may also need to install the USB drivers for any Android handsets you will be using for development.

Now let's take some of these features for a spin.

Creating Android Projects

The Android Project Wizard creates all the required files for an Android application. Open Eclipse and follow these steps to create a new project:

1. Choose File, New, Android Project or click the Android Project creator icon, which looks like a folder (with the letter *a* and a plus sign:) on the Eclipse toolbar.

Watch Out!

The first time you try to create an Android Project, you might need to choose File, New, Project and then select the Android, Android Project. After you have done this once, it appears in the Eclipse project types and you can use the method described in Step 1.

2. Choose a project name. In this case, name the project Droid1.

3. Choose a location for the project. Because this is a new project, select the Create New Project in Workspace radio button. Check the Use Default Location check box.

Did you Know?

If you prefer to store your project files in another location, simply uncheck the Use Default Location check box and browse to the directory of your choice.

4. Select a build target for your application. For most applications, you want to select the version of Android most appropriate for the devices used by your target audience and the needs of your application. If you will be using the Google add-ons (for example, Google Maps), be sure to choose the Google APIs version for your target platform. For this example, the Android 2.1 (API level 7) build target is sufficient.

5. Specify an application name. This name is what users will see. In this case, call the application Droid #1.

6. Specify a package name, following standard package namespace conventions for Java. Because all code in this book falls under the com.androidbook.* namespace, use the package name com.androidbook.droid1.

7. Check the Create Activity check box. This will instruct the wizard to create a default launch Activity class for the application. Call your activity DroidActivity.

What Is an Activity?

An activity is a core component of the Android platform. Each activity represents a task the application can do, often tied to a corresponding screen in the application user interface.

The Droid #1 application has a single activity, called DroidActivity, which has a single responsibility: to display a String to the user. We will talk more about activities in Hour 3, "Building Android Applications."

Your project settings will look as shown in Figure 1.2.

8. Confirm that the Min SDK Version field is correct. This field will be set to the API level of the build target by default (Android 2.1 is API level 7). If you want to support older versions of the Android SDK, you need to change this field. However, in this case, we can leave it as its default value.

9. Click the Next button.

10. The Android project wizard allows you to create a test project in conjunction with your Android application. For this example, a test project is unnecessary. However, you can always add a test project later by clicking the Android Test Project creator icon, which is to the right of the Android project wizard icon (with the letter *a*, letter *J* and letter *u*: [JU]) on the Eclipse toolbar. Test projects are discussed in detail in Hour 22, "Testing Android Applications."

11. Click the Finish button.

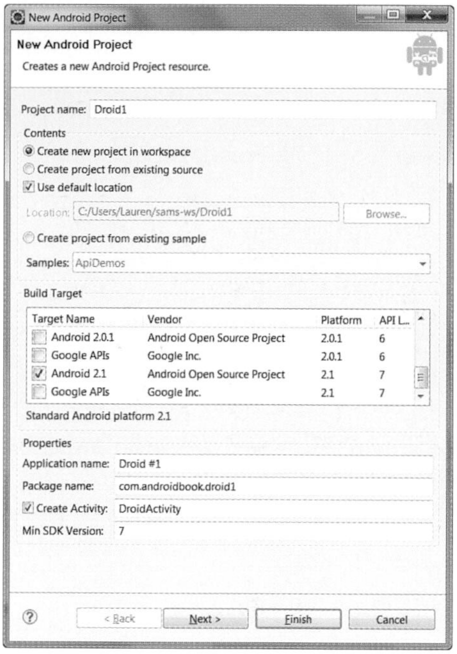

FIGURE 1.2
The Android
Project Wizard
in Eclipse.

Exploring the Android Project Files

You will now see a new Android project called Droid1 in the Eclipse File Explorer. In addition to linking the appropriate Android SDK jar file, the following core files and directories are created:

▶ **AndroidManifest.xml**—The central configuration file for the application.

▶ **default.properties**—A generated build file used by Eclipse and the Android ADT plug-in. Do not edit this file.

▶ **/src folder**—Required folder for all source code.

▶ **/src/com.androidbook.droid1/DroidActivity.java**—Main entry point to this application, named DroidActivity. This activity has been defined as the default launch activity in the Android manifest file.

▶ **/gen/com.androidbook.droid1/R.java**—A generated resource management source file. Do not edit this file.

▶ **/assets folder**—Required folder where uncompiled file resources can be included in the project.

▶ **/res folder**—Required folder where all application resources are managed. Application resources include animations, drawable graphics, layout files, data-like strings and numbers, and raw files.

▶ **/res/drawable**—Application icon graphic resources are included in several different sizes.

▶ **/res/layout/main.xml**—Layout file used by `DroidActivity` to draw onscreen.

▶ **/res/values/strings.xml**—The path where string resources are defined.

You can also add existing Android projects to Eclipse by using the Android Project Wizard. To do this, simply select Create Project from Existing Source instead of the default Create New Project in Workspace in the New Android Project dialog (refer to Figure 1.2). Several sample projects are provided in the `/samples` directory of the Android SDK, under the specific platform they support. For example, the Android SDK sample projects are found in the directory `/platforms/android-xxx/samples` (where xxx is the platform version number).

You can also select a third option: Create Project from Existing Sample, which will do as it says. However, make sure you choose the build target first option to get the list of sample projects you can create.

Did you Know?

Editing Project Resources

By default, the Android manifest file resource editor is opened when you create a new Android project. If you have clicked away from this screen to check out the various project files, simply double-click the `AndroidManifest.xml` file within your new project to return to the Android manifest file resource editor (see Figure 1.3).

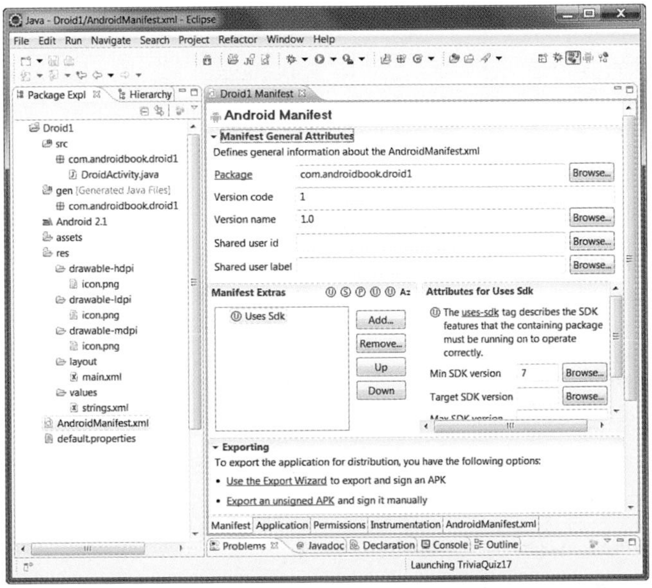

FIGURE 1.3
Editing an Android resource file in Eclipse.

Editing the Android Manifest File

The Android manifest file is the central configuration file for an Android application. The editor organizes the manifest information into a number of tabs:

▶ **Manifest**—This tab, shown in Figure 1.3, is used for general application-wide settings such as the package name and application version information (used for installation and upgrade purposes).

▶ **Application**—This tab is used to define application details such as the name and icon the application displays, as well as the "guts" of the application, such as what activities can be run (including the default launch `DroidActivity`) and other functionality and services that the application provides.

▶ **Permissions**—This tab is used to define the application's permissions. For example, if the application requires the ability to read the contacts from the phone, then it must register a `Uses-Permission` tag within the manifest, with the name `android.permission.READ_CONTACTS`.

▶ **Instrumentation**—This tab is used for unit testing, using the various instrumentation classes available within the Android SDK.

▶ **AndroidManifest.xml**—This tab provides a simple XML editor to edit the manifest file directly.

If you switch to the AndroidManifest.xml tab, your manifest file will look something like this:

```xml
<?xml version="1.0" encoding="utf-8"?>
<manifest
    xmlns:android="http://schemas.android.com/apk/res/android"
    package="com.androidbook.droid1"
    android:versionCode="1"
    android:versionName="1.0">
    <application
        android:icon="@drawable/icon"
        android:label="@string/app_name">
        <activity
            android:name=".DroidActivity"
            android:label="@string/app_name">
            <intent-filter>
                <action
                    android:name="android.intent.action.MAIN" />
                <category
                    android:name="android.intent.category.LAUNCHER" />
            </intent-filter>
        </activity>
    </application>
    <uses-sdk
        android:minSdkVersion="7" />
</manifest>
```

Try It Yourself ▼

Edit the Android Manifest File

Now let's edit the Android manifest file. One setting you're going to want to know about is the debuggable attribute. You will not be able to debug your application until you set this value, so follow these steps:

1. Open the `AndroidManifest.xml` file in the resource editor.

2. Navigate to the Application tab.

3. Pull down the drop-down for the debuggable attribute and choose true.

4. Save the manifest file.

If you switch to the AndroidManifest.xml tab and look through the XML, you will notice that the application tag now has the debuggable attribute:

```
android:debuggable="true"
```

▲

Editing Other Resource Files

Most Android application resources are stored under the /res subdirectory of the project. The following subdirectories are also available:

▶ /drawable-ldpi, /drawable-hdpi, /drawable-mdpi—These subdirectories store graphics and drawable resource files for different screen densities and resolutions. If you browse through these directories using the Eclipse Project Explorer, you will find the icon.png graphics file in each one; this is your application's icon. You'll learn more about the difference between these directories in Hour 20, "Developing for Different Devices."

▶ /layout—This subdirectory stores user interface layout files. Within this subdirectory you will find the main.xml screen layout file that defines the user interface for the default activity.

▶ /values—This subdirectory organizes the various types of resources, such as text strings, color values, and other primitive types. Here you find the strings.xml resource file, which contains all the resource strings used by the application.

If you double-click on any of resource files, the resource editor will launch. Remember, you can always edit the XML directly.

▼   ## Try It Yourself

Edit a String Resource

If you inspect the main.xml layout file of the project, you will notice that it displays a simple layout with a single TextView control. This user interface control simply displays a string. In this case, the string displayed is defined in the string resource called @string/hello.

To edit the string resource called @string/hello, using the string resource editor, follow these steps:

1. Open the strings.xml file in the resource editor.

2. Select the String called hello and note the name (hello) and value (Hello World, DroidActivity!) shown in the resource editor.

3. Within the Value field, change the text to Hello, Dave.

4. Save the file.

If you switch to the strings.xml tab and look through the raw XML, you will notice that two string elements are defined within a <resources> block:

```
<?xml version="1.0" encoding="utf-8"?>
<resources>
    <string name="hello">Hello, Dave</string>
    <string name="app_name">Droid #1</string>
</resources>
```

The first is the string @string/hello. The second is @string/app_name, which contains the name label for the application. If you look at the Android manifest file again, you will see @string/app_name used in the application configuration.

▲

We will talk much more about project resources in Hour 4, "Managing Application Resources." For now, let's move on to compiling and running the application.

Running and Debugging Applications

To build and debug an Android application, you must first configure your project for debugging. The ADT plug-in enables you to do this entirely within the Eclipse development environment. Specifically, you need to do the following:

▶ Configure an Android Virtual Device (AVD) for the emulator

▶ Create a debug configuration for your project

▶ Build the Android project and launch the debug configuration

When you have completed each of these tasks, Eclipse will attach its debugger to the Android emulator (or handset), and you are free to debug the application as needed.

Managing Android Virtual Devices

To run an application in the Android emulator, you must configure an Android Virtual Device (AVD). The AVD profile describes the type of device you want the emulator to simulate, including which Android platform to support. You can specify different screen sizes and orientations, and you can specify whether the emulator has an SD card and, if so, its capacity. In this case, an AVD for the default installation of Android 2.1 will suffice. Here are the steps for creating a basic AVD:

1. Launch the Android SDK and AVD Manager from within Eclipse by clicking on the little green Android icon with the arrow (🤖) on the toolbar. You can also launch the manager by selecting Window, Android SDK and AVD Manager in Eclipse.

2. Click the Virtual Devices menu item on the left menu. The configured AVDs will be displayed as a list.

3. Click the New button to create a new AVD.

4. Choose a name for the AVD. Because you are going to take all the defaults, name this AVD VanillaAVD.

5. Choose a build target. For example, to support Android 2.1, choose the item build target called *Android 2.1 – API Level 7* from the drop-down.

6. Choose an SD card capacity, in either kibibytes or mibibytes. This SD card image will take up space on your hard drive, so choose something reasonable, such as a 1024MiB or less. (The minimum is 9MiB, but keep in mind that the full size of the SD card is stored on your machine.)

7. Choose a skin. This option controls the different visual looks of the emulator. In this case, go with the default HVGA screen, which will display in portrait mode.

   Your project settings should look as shown in Figure 1.4.

8. Click the Create AVD button and wait for the operation to complete.

9. Click Finish.

> Because the Android Virtual Devices Manager formats the memory allocated for SD card images, creating AVDs with SD cards may take a few moments.

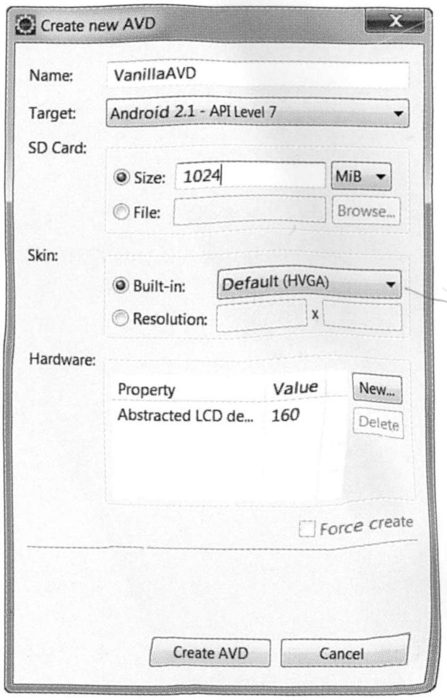

FIGURE 1.4
Creating a new AVD in Eclipse.

Creating Debug and Run Configurations in Eclipse

You are almost ready to launch your application. You have one *last* task remaining: You need to create a Debug configuration (or a Run configuration) for your project. To do this, take the following steps:

1. In Eclipse, choose Run, Debug Configurations.

2. Double-click the Android Application item to create a new entry.

3. Choose that new entry, called New_configuration.

4. Change the name of the entry to DroidDebug.

5. Choose the Droid1 project by clicking the Browse button.

6. On the Target tab, check the box next to the AVD you created.

Did you Know?

> If you choose Manual on the Target tab, instead of choosing Automatic and selecting an AVD, you will be prompted to choose a target each time you launch this configuration. This is useful when you're testing on a variety of handsets and emulator configurations. See "Launching Android Applications on a Handset," later in this hour, for more information.

7. Apply your changes by clicking the Apply button. Your Debug Configurations dialog should look as shown in Figure 1.5.

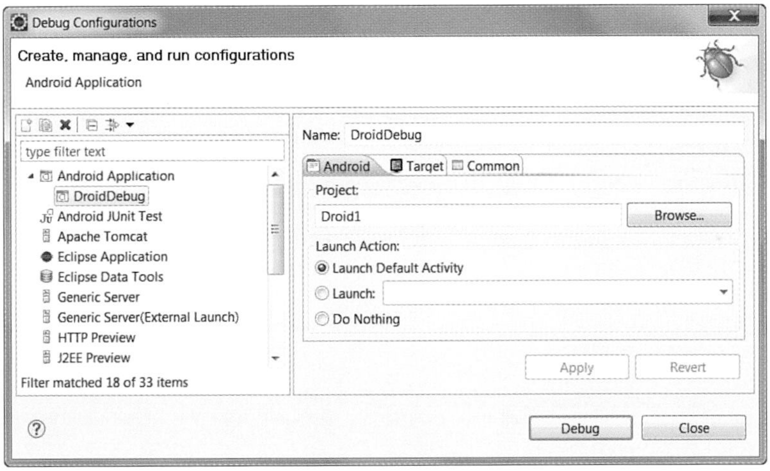

FIGURE 1.5
The DroidDebug debug configuration in Eclipse.

Launching Android Applications Using the Emulator

It's launch time, and your droid is ready to go! To launch the application, you can simply click the Debug button from within the Launch Configuration screen, or you can do it from the project by clicking the little green bug icon (🐞) on the Eclipse toolbar. Then select DroidDebug Debug Configuration from the list.

By the Way

> The first time you try to select DroidDebug debug configuration from the little green bug drop-down, you have to navigate through the configuration manager. Future attempts will show this configuration for convenient use under the bug drop-down.

After you click the Debug button, the emulator screen will launch. This can take some time, so be patient. You may need to click the Menu button on the emulator when you come to the Screen Locked view (see Figure 1.6).

FIGURE 1.6
An Android emu-
lator launching
(Screen Locked
view).

Now the Eclipse debugger is attached, and your application runs, as shown in Figure 1.7.

FIGURE 1.7
The Droid #1
Android applica-
tion running in
the emulator.

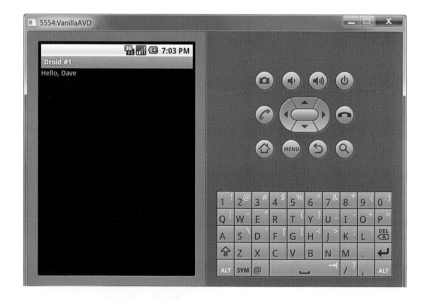

As you can see, the application is very simple. It displays a single `TextView` control, with a line of text. The application does nothing else.

Debugging Android Applications Using DDMS

In addition to the normal Debug perspective built into Eclipse for stepping through code and debugging, the ADT plug-in adds the DDMS perspective. While you have the application running, take a quick look at this perspective in Eclipse. You can get to the DDMS perspective (see Figure 1.8) by clicking the Android DDMS icon ( )) in the top-right corner of Eclipse. To switch back to the Eclipse Project Explorer, simply choose the Java perspective from the top-right corner of Eclipse.

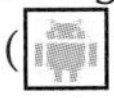

> **By the Way**
>
> If the DDMS perspective is not visible in Eclipse, you can add it to your workspace by clicking the Open Perspective button in the top right next to the available perspectives (or, alternately, choose Window, Open Perspective). To see a complete list of available perspectives, select the Other option from the Open Perspective drop-down menu. Select the DDMS perspective and press OK.

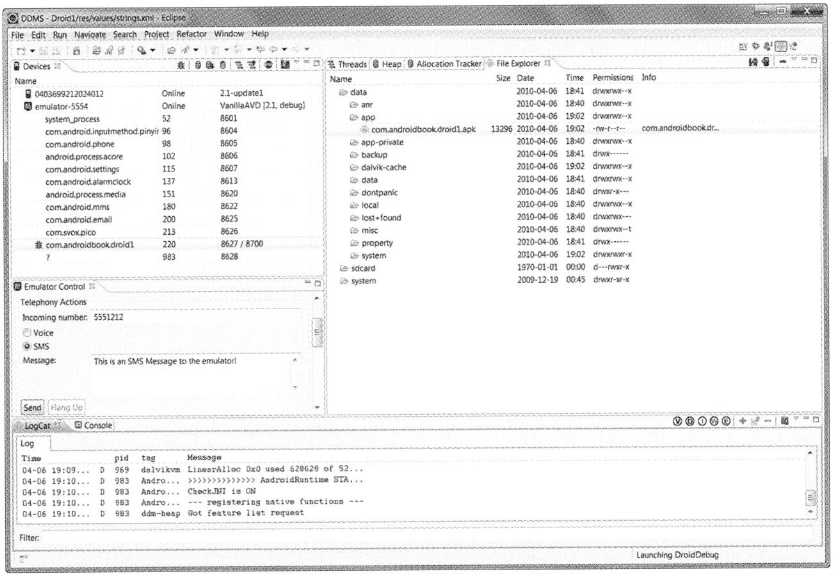

FIGURE 1.8
The DDMS perspective in Eclipse.

The DDMS perspective can be used to monitor application processes, as well as interact with the emulator. You can simulate voice calls and send SMS messages to the emulator. You can send a mock location fix to the emulator to mimic location-based services. You will learn more about DDMS and the other tools available to Android developers in Hour 2, "Mastering the Android Development Tools."

The LogCat logging tool is displayed on both the DDMS perspective and the Debug Perspective. This tool displays logging information from the emulator or the handset, if a handset is plugged in.

Launching Android Applications on a Handset

It's time to load your application onto a real handset. To do this, you need to plug a handset into your computer, using the USB data cable.

To ensure that you debug using the correct settings, follow these steps:

1. In Eclipse, choose Run, Debug Configurations.

2. Double-click DroidDebug Debug Configuration.

3. On the Target tab, set Deployment Target Selection Mode to Manual. You can always change it back to Automatic later, but choosing Manual will force you to choose whether to debug within the emulator (and choose an AVD) or a device, if one is plugged in, whenever you choose to debug.

4. Apply your changes by clicking the Apply button.

5. Plug an Android device into your development computer, using a USB cable.

6. Click the Debug button within Eclipse.

   A dialog (Figure 1.9) appears, showing all available configurations for running and debugging your application. All physical devices are listed, as are existing emulators that are running. You can also launch new emulator instances by using other AVDs you have created.

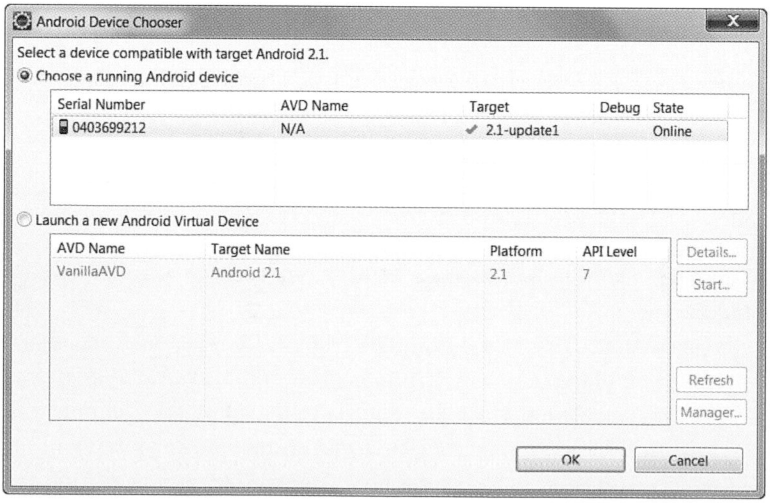

FIGURE 1.9
The Eclipse dialog for choosing an application deployment target.

7. Double-click one of the running Android devices. There should be one listed for each handset plugged into the machine, in addition to one for each emulator instance running. If you do not see the handset listed, check your cables and make sure you installed the appropriate drivers, as explained in Appendix A.

Download software @ samsung site

Eclipse now installs the Android application on the handset, attaches a debugger, and runs the application. Your handset now shows a screen very similar to the one you saw in the emulator. If you look at the DDMS perspective in Eclipse, you see that logging information is available, and many features of the DDMS perspective work with real handsets as well as the emulator.

New to Eclipse?

If you're still learning the ropes of the Eclipse development environment, now is a great time to check out Appendix B, "Eclipse IDE Tips and Tricks."

Summary

Congratulations! You are now an Android developer. You are starting to learn your way around the Eclipse development environment. You created your first Android project. You reviewed and compiled working Android code. Finally, you ran your newly created Android application on the Android emulator as well as on a real Android device.

Q&A

Q. *What programming languages are supported for Android development?*

A. Right now, Java is the only programming language fully supported for Android development. Other languages, such as C++, may be added in the future. Although applications must be Java, C and C++ can be used for certain routines that need higher performance by using the Android NDK. For more information about using the Android NDK, see http://developer.android.com/sdk/ndk.

Q. *Why would I want to create AVDs for Android 1.1 (or any older firmware) when newer versions of the Android SDK are available?*

A. Although handset firmware may be updated over-the-air, not every Android device will support every future firmware version. Check the firmware available on each of your target handsets carefully before choosing which version your application will support and be tested on.

Q. *The Android resource editors can be cumbersome for entering large amounts of data, such as many string resources. Is there any way around this?*

A. Android project files, such as the Android manifest, layout files, and resource values (for example, /res/values/strings.xml), are stored in specially formatted XML files. You can edit these files manually by clicking on the XML tab of the resource editor. We will talk more about the XML formats in Hour 4.

Workshop

Quiz

1. Who are the members of the Open Handset Alliance?

    A. Handset manufacturers

    B. Wireless operators and carriers

    C. Mobile software developers

    D. All of the above

2. True or False: You can simply launch the Android emulator to use default settings right after the SDK is installed.

3. What is the most popular IDE for Android development?

    A. Eclipse

    B. IntelliJ

    C. Emacs

4. True or False: You can use Eclipse for handset debugging.

Answers

1. D. The Open Handset Alliance is a business alliance that represents all levels of the handset supply chain.

2. False. You must first create an AVD.

3. A. Eclipse is the most popular IDE for Android development. Other IDEs can be used, but they will not enable you to use the ADT plug-in that is integrated with Eclipse.

4. True. Eclipse supports debugging within the emulator and on the handset.

Exercises

1. Visit http://developer.android.com and take a look around. Check out the online Developer's Guide and reference materials. Check out the Community tab and considering signing up for the Android Beginners and Android Developers Google Groups.

2. Add more text to the Droid #1 application. To do this, first add another String resource to the strings.xml resource file and save this file. Next, use the layout resource editor to modify the main.xml layout file to add a second TextView control. Set the text attribute of the TextView control to your newly created String resource. Finally, rerun the application in the emulator to see the results.

3. Add to your Eclipse workspace one of the Android sample projects provided with the Android SDK. Browse through the project files and then create a run configuration and launch the sample application in the emulator.

HOUR 2

Mastering the Android Development Tools

What You'll Learn in This Hour:

▶ Using the Android documentation
▶ Debugging applications with DDMS
▶ Working with the Android Emulator
▶ Using the Android Debug Bridge (ADB)
▶ Working with Android virtual devices

Android developers are lucky to have more than a dozen development tools at their disposal to help facilitate the design of quality applications. Understanding what tools are available and what they can be used for is a task best done early in the Android learning process, so that when you are faced with a problem, you have some clue as to which utility might be able to help you find a solution. The Android development tools are found in the /tools subdirectory of the Android SDK installation. During this hour, we walk through a number of the most important tools available for use with Android. This information will help you develop Android applications faster and with fewer roadblocks.

Using the Android Documentation

Although it is not a tool, per se, the Android documentation is a key resource for Android developers. An HTML version of the Android documentation is provided in the /docs subfolder of the Android SDK documentation, and this should always be your first stop when you encounter a problem. You can also access the latest help documentation online at the Android Developer website, http://developer.android.com.

The Android documentation is divided into six sections (see Figure 2.1):

▶ **SDK**—This tab provides important information about the SDK version installed on your machine. One of the most important features of this tab is the release notes, which describe any known issues for the specific installation. This information is also useful if the online help has been upgraded but you want to develop to an older version of the SDK.

▶ **Dev Guide**—This tab links to the Android Developer's Guide, which includes a number of FAQs for developers, as well as step-by-step examples and a useful glossary of Android terminology for those new to the platform.

▶ **Reference**—This tab includes a searchable package and class index of all Android APIs provided as part of the Android SDK.

▶ **Blog**—This tab links to the official Android developer blog. Check here for the latest news and announcements about the Android platform. This is a great place to find how-to examples, learn how to optimize Android applications, and hear about new SDK releases and Android Developer Challenges.

▶ **Videos**—This tab, which is available online only, is your resource for Android training videos. Here, you'll find videos about the Android platform, developer tips, and the Google I/O conference sessions.

▶ **Community**—This tab is your gateway to the Android developer forums. There are a number of Google groups you can join, depending on your interests.

FIGURE 2.1
Android developer documentation (online version).

Now is a good time to get to know your way around the Android SDK documentation. First, try the local documentation and then check out the online documentation.

Debugging Applications with DDMS

The Dalvik Debug Monitor Service (DDMS) is a debugging utility that is integrated into Eclipse through the DDMS perspective. The DDMS perspective provides a number of useful features for interacting with emulators and handsets (see Figure 2.2).

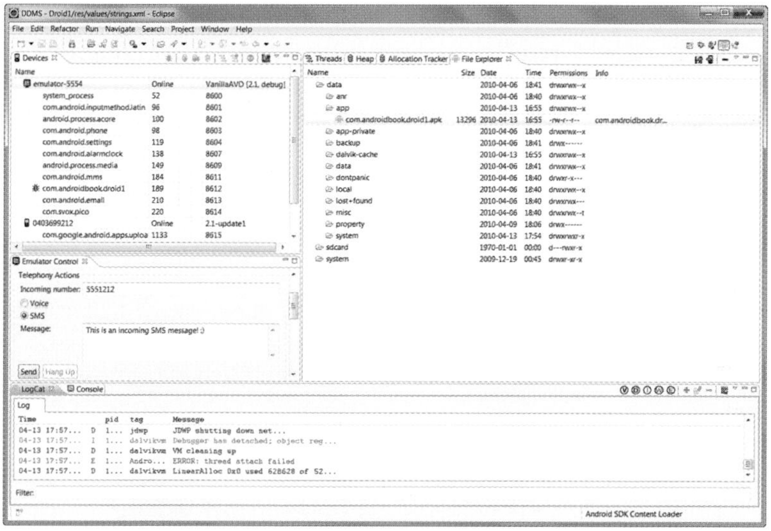

FIGURE 2.2
The DDMS perspective, with one emulator and one Android device connected.

The features of DDMS are roughly divided into five functional areas:

▶ Task management

▶ File management

▶ Emulator interaction

▶ Logging

▶ Screen captures

DDMS and the DDMS perspective are essential debugging tools. Now let's take a look at how to use these features in a bit more detail.

> The DDMS tool can be launched separately from Eclipse. You can find it in the Android SDK /tools directory.

Managing Tasks

The top-left corner of the DDMS lists the emulators and handsets currently connected. You can select individual instances and inspect processes and threads. You can inspect threads by clicking on the device process you are interested in—for example, com.androidbook.droid1—and clicking the Update Threads button ( ), as shown in Figure 2.3. You can also prompt garbage collection on a process and then view the heap updates by clicking the green cylinder button ( ). Finally, you can stop a process by clicking the button that resembles a stop sign ( ).

FIGURE 2.3
Using DDMS to examine thread activity for the Droid1 application.

Debugging from the DDMS Perspective

Within the DDMS perspective, you can choose a specific process on an emulator or a handset and then click the little green bug ( ) to attach a debugger to that process. You need to have the source code in your Eclipse workspace for this to work properly. This works only in Eclipse, not in the standalone version of DDMS.

Browsing the Android File System

You can use the DDMS File Explorer to browse files and directories on the emulator or a device (see Figure 2.4). You can copy files between the Android file system and your development machine by using the push (![push icon]) and pull (![pull icon]) icons.

![DDMS File Explorer screenshot showing devices list and file explorer with system fonts]

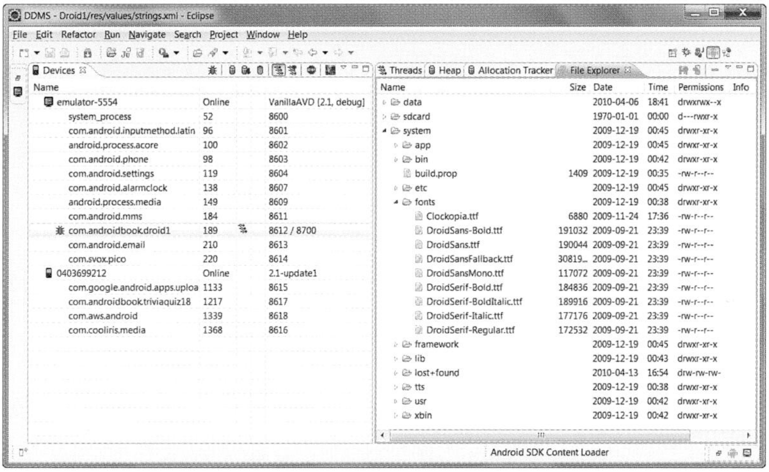

FIGURE 2.4
Using the DDMS File Explorer to browse system fonts on the handset.

You can also delete files and directories by using the minus button (![minus icon]) or just pressing Delete. There is no confirmation for this Delete operation, nor can it be undone.

Interacting with Emulators

DDMS can send a number of events, such as simulated calls, SMS messages, and location coordinates, to specific emulator instances. These features are found under the Emulator Control tab in DDMS. These events are all "one way," meaning that they can be initiated from DDMS, not from the emulator to DDMS.

> These features work for emulators only, not for handsets. For handsets, you must use real calls and real messages.

By the Way

Simulating Incoming Calls to the Emulator

You can simulate incoming voice calls by using the DDMS Emulator Control tab (see Figure 2.5). This is not a real call; no data (voice or otherwise) is transmitted between the caller and the receiver.

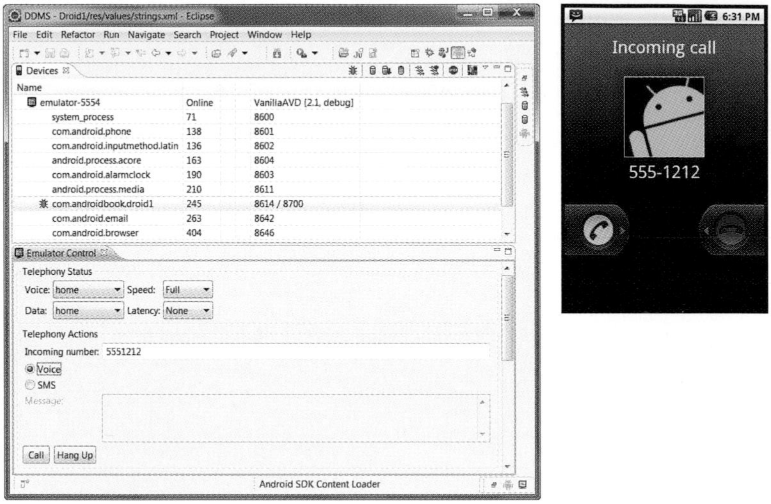

FIGURE 2.5
Using the
DDMS Emulator
Control tab (left)
to place a call
to the emulator
(right).

▼ **Try It Yourself**

Simulate an Incoming Call to an Emulator

To simulate an incoming call to an emulator running on your machine, follow these steps:

1. In DDMS, choose the emulator you want to call.

2. On the Emulator Control tab, input the incoming phone number (for example, 5551212) in the Telephony Actions section.

3. Select the Voice radio button.

4. Click the Call button.

5. In the emulator, you should see an incoming call. Answer the call by clicking the Send button in the emulator.

6. End the call at any time by clicking the End button in the emulator or by clicking the Hang Up button on the DDMS Emulator Control tab.

▲

Simulating Incoming SMS Messages to the Emulator

You can simulate incoming SMS messages by using the DDMS Emulator DDMS (see Figure 2.6). You send an SMS much as you initiate a voice call.

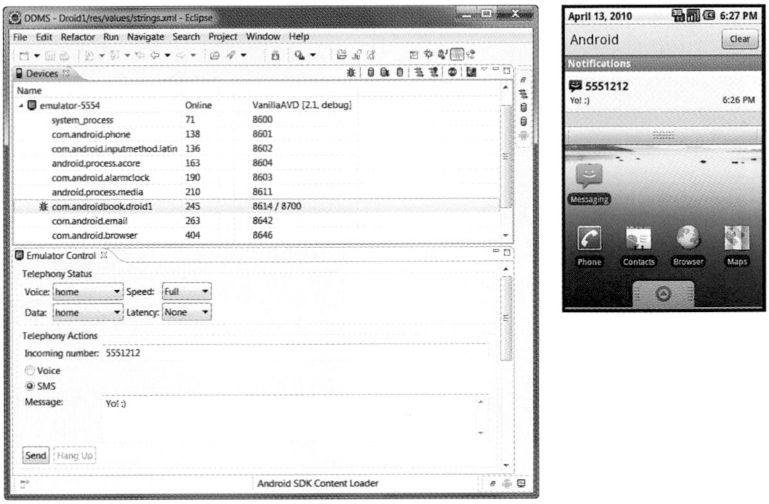

FIGURE 2.6
Using the DDMS Emulator Control tab (left) to send an SMS message to the emulator (right).

Try It Yourself ▼

Send an SMS to the Emulator

To send an SMS message to an emulator running on your machine, follow these steps:

1. In DDMS, choose the emulator you want a send an SMS to.

2. On the Emulator Control tab, input the Incoming phone number (for example, 5551212) in the Telephony Actions section.

3. Select the SMS radio button.

4. Type an SMS message.

5. Click the Send button. In the emulator, you should see an incoming SMS notification. ▲

Taking Screenshots of the Emulator or Handset

One feature that can be particularly useful for debugging both handsets and emulators is the ability to take screenshots of the current screen (see Figure 2.7).

FIGURE 2.7
Using the
DDMS Screen
Capture button
to take a
screenshot of
the handset.

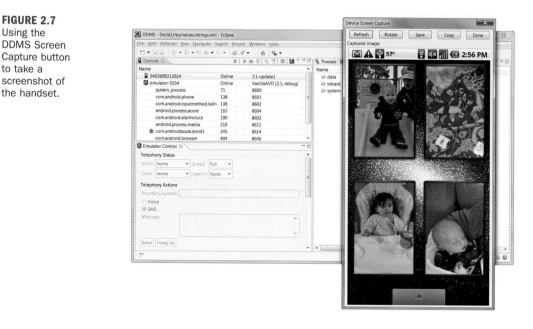

▼   **Try It Yourself**

Take a Screen Capture

The screenshot feature is particularly useful when used with true handsets. To take a
screen capture, follow these steps:

1. In DDMS, choose the device (or emulator) you want a screenshot of.

2. On that device or emulator, make sure you have the screen you want.
   Navigate to it, if necessary.

3. Choose the multicolored square picture icon (▨) to take a screen capture.
   This launches a capture screen dialog.

4. Within the capture screen, click Save to save the screenshot to your local hard
   drive.

Viewing Log Information

The LogCat logging utility that is integrated into DDMS allows you to view the Android logging console. You may have noted the LogCat logging tab, with its diagnostic output, in many of the figures shown so far in this chapter. We will talk more about how to implement your own custom application logging in Hour 3, "Building Android Applications."

Filtering Log Information

Eclipse has the ability to filter logs by log severity. You can also create custom log filters by using tags. For more information on how to do this, see Appendix B, "Eclipse IDE Tips and Tricks."

Working with the Android Emulator

The Android emulator is probably the most powerful tool at a developer's disposal. It is important for developers to learn to use the emulator and understand its limitations.

The Android emulator is integrated with Eclipse, using the ADT plug-in for the Eclipse IDE.

Emulator Limitations

The Android emulator is a convenient tool, but it has a number of limitations:

▶ The emulator is not a device. It simulates general handset behavior, not specific hardware implementations.

▶ Sensor data, such as satellite location information, battery and power settings, and network connectivity, are all simulated using your computer.

▶ Peripherals such as camera hardware are not fully functional.

▶ Phone calls cannot be placed or received but are simulated. SMS messages are also simulated and do not use a real network.

▶ No USB or Bluetooth support is available.

Using Android emulator is not a substitute for testing on a true target handset or device.

Providing Input to the Emulator

As a developer, you can provide input to the emulator in a number of ways:

▶ Use your computer mouse to click, scroll, and drag items (for example, side volume controls) onscreen as well as on the emulator skin.

▶ Use your computer keyboard to input text into controls.

▶ Use your mouse to simulate individual finger presses on the soft keyboard or physical emulator keyboard.

▶ Use a number of emulator keyboard commands to control specific emulator states.

▼   **Try It Yourself**

Try out some of the methods of interacting with the emulator:

1. In Eclipse, launch the Droid1 application you created in Hour 1, "Getting Started with Android."

2. While your application is running, press the control-F11 and control-F12 keys to toggle the emulator orientation. Note how your application redraws the simple screen in portrait and landscape modes.

3. Press Alt+Enter to enter full screen mode with the emulator. Then press Alt+Enter again to return to normal mode.

Many useful commands are available. For an exhaustive list, see the official emulator documentation that was installed with the Android SDK documentation and is also available online, at http://developer.android.com/guide/developing/tools/emulator.html.

▲

Exploring the Android System

If you're not already familiar with Android devices, now is a good time to learn your way around the Android system as users see it. Table 2.1 lists some important features of Android.

TABLE 2.1   Android System Screens and Features

Feature	Description	Appearance
Home screen	Default screen. This is a common location for app widgets and live folders.	
Dialer application	Built-in application for making and receiving phone calls. Note that the emulator has limited phone features.	
Messaging application	Built-in application for sending and receiving SMS messages. Note that the emulator has limited messaging features.	
Browser application	Built-in web browser. Note that the emulator has an Internet connection, provided that your machine has one.	
Contacts application	Database of contact information.	
Application sliding drawer	Shows all installed applications. From the Home screen, pull the gray sliding drawer tab to see all installed applications.	

TABLE 2.1   continued

Feature	Description	Appearance
Settings application	Built-in application to configure a wide variety of "phone" settings for the emulator, such as application management, sound and display settings, and localization.	
Dev Tools application	Built-in application to configure configure development tool settings.	

Using Emulator Skins

Emulator features such as screen size, screen orientation, and whether the emulator has a hardware or soft keyboard are dictated by the emulator skin. The Android SDK supports a number of different skins which emulate various handset screen resolutions (the default being HVGA). The specific skins available depends on the target build platform. Determining the appropriate skin is part of the AVD configuration process.

Using SD Card Images with the Emulator

To save data with the emulator, there must be an SD card image configured. For example, you must have a properly configured SD card image to save media files like camera graphics and sound files to the emulator.

The most convenient way to create SD card images for use with the emulator is to create them as part of the AVD process, as you did in Hour 1. SD card images should be at least 9 MiB.

Using Other Android Tools

Although we've already covered the most important tools, a number of other special-purpose utilities are included with the Android SDK:

> ▶ **Android Hierarchy Viewer**—Allows developers to inspect application user interface components such as View Properties while the application is running.

▶ **Draw 9-Patch tool**—Helps developers design stretchable PNG files.

▶ **AIDL Compiler**—Helps developers create remote interfaces to facilitate inter-process communication (IPC) on the Android platform.

▶ mksdcard **command-line utility**—Allows developers to create stand-alone SD card images for use within AVDs and the emulator.

Developing Android Applications Without Eclipse

Eclipse is the preferred development environment for Android, but it is not required for development. The ADT plug-in for Eclipse provides a convenient entry point for many of the underlying development tools for creating, debugging, packaging, and signing Android applications.

Developers who do not use Eclipse or require some of the more powerful debugging features not available in the Eclipse ADT plug-in can access these underlying tools directly from the command line. Tools such as the following are found in the /tools directory of the Android SDK:

▶ android—Creates Android project files and to manage AVDs.

▶ aapt **(Android Asset Packaging Tool)**—Packages Android project files into .apk files for installation on the emulator and handset.

▶ ddms **(Dalvik Debug Monitor Service)**—Has a user interface of its own, which resembles the Eclipse DDMS perspective.

▶ adb **(Android Debug Bridge)**—Has a command-line interface for interacting with the emulator and the device.

Summary

The Android SDK ships with a number of powerful tools to help with common Android development tasks. The Android documentation is an essential reference for developers. The DDMS debugging tool, which is integrated into the Eclipse development environment, is useful for monitoring emulators and devices. The Android emulator can be used for running and debugging Android applications virtually, without the need for an actual device. There are also a number of other tools for interacting with handsets and emulators at the command-line level, as well as specialized utilities for designing Android application user interfaces and graphics, as well as packaging applications.

Q&A

Q. *Is the Android documentation installed with the Android SDK the same as the documentation found at http://developer.android.com?*

A. No. The documentation installed with the SDK was "frozen" at the time the SDK was released, which means it is more specific to the version of the Android SDK you installed. The online documentation will always be the latest version of the Android SDK. We recommend using the online documentation, unless you are working offline or have a slow Internet connection, in which case the local SDK documentation will suffice.

Q. *Do the different emulator skins have different features?*

A. Yes. The emulator skins correspond to different screen sizes and orientations. They also have keypads and buttons. Some have hardware keyboards, and others rely on soft keyboard support.

Q. *Is testing your application on the emulator alone sufficient?*

A. No. The Android emulator simulates the functionality of a real device and can be a big time- and cost-saving tool for Android projects. It is a convenient tool for testing, but it can only pretend at real device behavior. The emulator cannot actually determine your real location or make a phone call. Also, the emulator is a generic device and does not attempt to simulate any quirky details of a specific handset. Just because your application runs fine on the emulator does not guarantee that it will work on the device.

Workshop

Quiz

1. Which features are available in the DDMS perspective?

    A. Taking screenshots of emulator and handset screens

    B. Browsing the file system of the emulator or handset

    C. Monitoring thread and heap information on the Android system

    D. Stopping processes

    E. Simulating incoming phone calls and SMS messages to emulators

    F. All of the above

2. True or False: You must use the Android emulator for debugging.

3. Which target platforms can Android applications be written for?

4. True or False: The Android emulator is a generic device that supports only one screen configuration.

Answers

1. F. All of the above. The DDMS perspective can be used to monitor, browse, and interact with emulators and handsets in a variety of ways.

2. False. The Android emulator is useful for debugging, but you can also connect the debugger to an actual device and debug directly.

3. There are a number of target platforms available and more are added with each new SDK release. Some important platform targets include Android 1.1, Android 1.5, Android 1.6, Android 2.0., Android 2.0.1, and Android 2.1. Targets higher than Android 1.1 can include the Google APIs, if desired. These targets map to the AVD profiles you must create in order to use the Android emulator.

4. False. The Android emulator is a generic device, but it can support several different skins. For a complete list of skins supported, see the Android SDK and AVD Manager in Eclipse.

Exercises

1. Launch the Android emulator and browse the settings available. Change the language settings. Uninstall an application.

2. Launch the Android emulator and customize your home screen. Change the wallpaper. Install an AppWidget. Get familiar with how the emulator tries to mimic a real handset. Note the limitations, such as how the dialer works.

3. Try launching the Hierarchy Viewer tool with the Droid1 project you created in Hour 1. Note how you can drill down to see the TextView_controls you created.

HOUR 3

Building Android Applications

What You'll Learn in This Hour:

▶ Designing a typical Android application
▶ Using the application context
▶ Working with activities, intents, and dialogs
▶ Logging application information

Every platform technology uses different terminology to describe its application components. The three most important classes on the Android platform are `Context`, `Activity`, and `Intent`. While there are other, more advanced, components developers can implement, these three components form the building blocks for each and every Android application. In this hour, we focus on understanding how Android applications are put together. We also take a look at some handy utility classes that can help developers debug applications.

Designing a Typical Android Application

An Android application is a collection of tasks, each of which is called an activity. Each activity within an application has a unique purpose and user interface. To understand this more fully, imagine a theoretical game application called Chippy's Revenge.

Designing Application Features

The design of the Chippy's Revenge game is simple. It has five screens:

▶ **Splash**—This screen acts as a startup screen, with the game logo and version. It might also play some music.

▶ **Menu**—On this screen, a user can choose from among several options, including playing the game, viewing the scores, and reading the help text.

▶ **Play**—This screen is where game play actually takes place.

▶ **Scores**—This screen displays the highest scores for the game (including high scores from other players), providing players with a challenge to do better.

▶ **Help**—This screen displays instructions for how to play the game, including controls, goals, scoring methods, tips, and tricks.

Starting to sound familiar? This is the prototypical design of just about any mobile application, game or otherwise, on any platform.

> Certainly, you are free to implement any kind of user interface you desire. There are no real user interface requirements on the Android platform, other than that the application must be stable, responsive, and play nice with the rest of the Android system. That said, the best and most popular applications leverage the users' existing experience with user interfaces. It's best to improve upon those features, when necessary, rather than reinvent them, so you don't force the user to exert time and effort to learn your application in order to use it properly.

Determining Application Activity Requirements

You need to implement five activity classes, one for each feature of the game:

▶ `SplashActivity`—This activity serves as the default activity to launch. It simply displays a layout (maybe just a big graphic), plays music for several seconds, and then launches `MenuActivity`.

▶ `MenuActivity`—This activity is pretty straightforward. Its layout has several buttons, each corresponding to a feature of the application. The `onClick()` handlers for each button trigger cause the associated activity to launch.

▶ `PlayActivity`—The real application guts are implemented here. This activity needs to draw stuff onscreen, handle various types of user input, keep score, and generally follow whatever game dynamics the developer wants to support.

▶ `ScoresActivity`—This activity is about as simple as `SplashActivity`. It does little more than load a bunch of scoring information into a `TextView` control within its layout.

▶ `HelpActivity`—This activity is almost identical to `ScoresActivity`, except that instead of displaying scores, it displays help text. Its `TextView` control might possibly scroll.

Each activity class should have its own corresponding layout file stored in the application resources. You could use a single layout file for ScoresActivity and HelpActivity, but it's not necessary. If you did, though, you would simply create a single layout for both and set the image in the background and the text in the TextView control at runtime, instead of within the layout file.

Figure 3.1 shows the resulting design for your game, Chippy's Revenge Version 0.0.1 for Android.

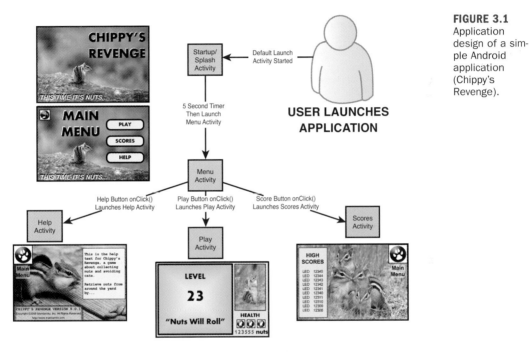

FIGURE 3.1
Application design of a simple Android application (Chippy's Revenge).

Implementing Application Functionality

Now that you understand how a typical Android application might be designed, you're probably wondering how to go about implementing that design.

We've talked about how each activity has its own user interface, defined within a separate layout resource file. You might be wondering about implementation hurdles such as the following:

▶ How do I control application state?

▶ How do I save settings?

▶ How do I launch a specific activity?

With our theoretical game application in mind, it is time to dive into the implementation details of developing an Android application. A good place to start is the application context.

Using the Application Context

The application context is the central location for all top-level application functionality. You use the application context to access settings and resources shared across multiple activity instances.

You can retrieve the application context for the current process by using the getApplicationContext() method, like this:

```
Context context = getApplicationContext();
```

Because the `Activity` class is derived from the `Context` class, you can use `this` instead of retrieving the application context explicitly.

Once you have retrieved a valid application context, you can use it to access application-wide features and services.

Retrieving Application Resources

You can retrieve application resources by using the getResources() method of the application context. The most straightforward way to retrieve a resource is by using its unique resource identifier, as defined in the automatically generated R.java class. The following example retrieves a String instance from the application resources by its resource ID:

```
String greeting = getResources().getString(R.string.hello);
```

Accessing Application Preferences

You can retrieve shared application preferences by using the getSharedPreferences() method of the application context. You can use the SharedPreferences class to save simple application data, such as configuration settings. Each SharedPreferences object can be given a name, allowing you can organize preferences into categories or store preferences all together in one large set.

For example, you might want to keep track of each user's name and some simple game state information, such as whether the user has credits left to play. The following code creates a set of shared preferences called GamePrefs and saves a few such preferences:

```
SharedPreferences settings = getSharedPreferences("GamePrefs", MODE_PRIVATE);
SharedPreferences.Editor prefEditor = settings.edit();
prefEditor.putString("UserName", "Spunky");
prefEditor.putBoolean("HasCredits", true);
prefEditor.commit();
```

To retrieve preference settings, you simply retrieve SharedPreferences and read the values back out:

```
SharedPreferences settings = getSharedPreferences("GamePrefs", MODE_PRIVATE);
String userName = settings.getString("UserName", "Chippy Jr. (Default)");
```

Accessing Other Application Functionality Using Contexts

The application context provides access to a number of top-level application features. Here are a few more things you can do with the application context:

▶ Launch Activity instances

▶ Retrieve assets packaged with the application

▶ Request a system-level service provider (for example, location service)

▶ Manage private application files, directories, and databases

▶ Inspect and enforce application permissions

The first item on this list—launching Activity instances—is perhaps the most common reason you will use the application context.

Working with Activities

The Activity class is central to every Android application. Much of the time, you'll define and implement an activity for each screen in your application.

In the Chippy's Revenge game application, you have to implement five different Activity classes. In the course of playing the game, the user transitions from one activity to the next, interacting with the layout controls of each activity.

Launching Activities

There are a number of ways to launch an activity, including the following:

- ▶ Designating a launch activity in the manifest file
- ▶ Launching an activity using the application context
- ▶ Launching a child activity from a parent activity for a result

Designating a Launch Activity in the Manifest File

Each Android application must designate a default activity within the Android manifest file. If you inspect the manifest file of the Droid1 project, you will notice that DroidActivity is designated as the default activity.

> Other Activity classes might be designated to launch under specific circumstances. You manage these secondary entry points by configuring the Android manifest file with custom filters.

In Chippy's Revenge, SplashActivity would be the most logical activity to launch by default.

Launching Activities Using the Application Context

The most common way to launch an activity is to use the startActivity() method of the application context. This method takes one parameter, called an intent. We will talk more about the intent in a moment, but for now, let's look at a simple startActivity() call.

The following code calls the startActivity() method with an explicit intent:

```
startActivity(new Intent(getApplicationContext(), MenuActivity.class));
```

This intent requests the launch of the target activity, named MenuActivity, by its class. This class must be implemented elsewhere within the package.

Because the MenuActivity class is defined within this application's package, it must be registered as an activity within the Android manifest file. In fact, you could use this method to launch every activity in your theoretical game application; however, this is just one way to launch an activity.

Launching an Activity for a Result

Sometimes an activity wants to launch a related activity and get the result, instead of launching an entirely independent activity. In this case, you can use the

`Activity.startActivityForResult()` method. The result will be returned in the `Intent` parameter of the calling activity's `onActivityResult()` method. We will talk more about how to pass data using an `Intent` parameter in a moment.

Managing Activity State

Applications can be interrupted when various higher-priority events, such as phone calls, take precedence. There can be only one active application at a time; specifically, a single application activity can be in the foreground at any given time.

Android applications are responsible for managing their state, as well as their memory, resources, and data. The Android operating system may terminate an activity that has been paused, stopped, or destroyed when memory is low. This means that any activity that is not in the foreground is subject to shutdown. In other words, an Android application must keep state and be ready to be interrupted and even shut down at any time.

Using Activity Callbacks

The `Activity` class has a number of callbacks that provide an opportunity for an activity to respond to events such as suspending and resuming. Table 3.1 lists the most important callback methods.

TABLE 3.1 Key Callback Methods of Android Activities

Callback Method	Description	Recommendations
`onCreate()`	Called when an activity starts or restarts.	Initializes static activity data. Binds to data or resources required. Sets layout with `setContentView()`.
`onResume()`	Called when an activity becomes the foreground activity.	Acquires exclusive resources. Starts any audio, video, or animations.
`onPause()`	Called when an activity leaves the foreground.	Saves uncommitted data. Deactivates or releases exclusive resources. Stops any audio, video, or animations.
`onDestroy()`	Called when an application is shutting down.	Cleans up any static activity data. Releases any resources acquired.

The main thread is often called the *UI thread*, because this is where the processing for drawing the UI takes place internally. An activity must perform any processing that takes place during a callback reasonably quickly, so that the main thread is not blocked. If the main UI thread is blocked for too long, the Android system will shut down the activity due to a lack of response. This is especially important to respond quickly during the onPause() callback, when a higher-priority task (for example, an incoming phone call) is entering the foreground.

Figure 3.2 shows the order in which activity callbacks are called.

FIGURE 3.2
Important callback methods of the activity life cycle.

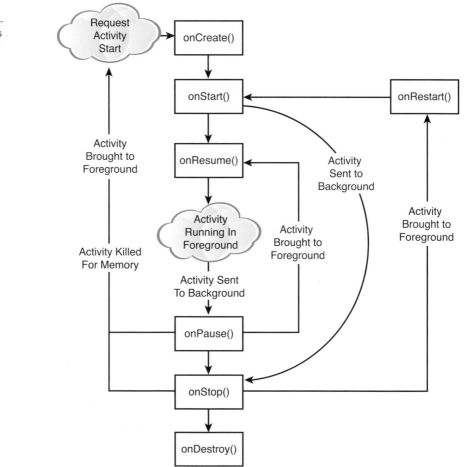

Saving Activity State

An activity can have private preferences—much like shared application preferences. You can access these preferences by using the getPreferences() method of the activity. This mechanism is useful for saving state information. For example, PlayActivity for your game might use these preferences to keep track of the current level and score, player health statistics, and game state.

Shutting Down Activities

To shut down an activity, you make a call to the finish() method. There are several different versions of this method to use, depending whether the activity is shutting itself down or shutting down another activity.

Within your game application, you might return from the Scores, Play, and Help screens to the Menu screen by finishing ScoresActivity, PlayActivity, or HelpActivity.

Working with Intents

An Intent object encapsulates a task request used by the Android operating system. When the startActivity() method is called with the Intent parameter, the Android system matches the Intent action with appropriate activity on the Android system. That activity is then launched.

The Android system handles all intent resolution. An intent can be very specific, including a request for a specific activity to be launched, or somewhat vague, requesting that any activity matching certain criteria be launched. For the finer details on intent resolution, see the Android documentation.

Passing Information with Intents

Intents can be used to pass data between activities. You can use an intent in this way by including additional data, called extras, within the intent.

To package extra pieces of data along with an intent, you use the putExtra() method with the appropriate type of object you want to include. The Android programming convention for intent extras is to name each one with the package prefix (for example, com.androidbook.chippy.NameOfExtra).

For example, the following intent includes an extra piece of information, the current game level, which is an integer:

```
Intent intent = new Intent(getApplicationContext(), HelpActivity.class);
intent.putExtra("com.androidbook.chippy.LEVEL", 23);
startActivity(intent);
```

When the HelpActivity class launches, the getIntent() method can be used to retrieve the intent. Then the extra information can be extracted using the appropriate methods. Here's an example:

```
Intent callingIntent = getIntent();
int helpLevel = callingIntent.getIntExtra("com.androidbook.chippy.LEVEL", 1);
```

This little piece of information could be used to give special Help hints, based on the level.

For the parent activity that launched a subactivity using the startActivityForResult() method, the result will be passed in as a parameter to the onActivityResult() method with an Intent parameter. The intent data can then be extracted and used by the parent activity.

Using Intents to Launch Other Applications

Initially, an application may only be launching activity classes defined within its own package. However, with the appropriate permissions, applications may also launch external activity classes in other applications.

There are well-defined intent actions for many common user tasks. For example, you can create intent actions to initiate applications such as the following:

- ▶ Launching the built-in web browser and supplying a URL address
- ▶ Launching the web browser and supplying a search string
- ▶ Launching the built-in Dialer application and supplying a phone number
- ▶ Launching the built-in Maps application and supplying a location
- ▶ Launching Google Street View and supplying a location
- ▶ Launching the built-in Camera application in still or video mode
- ▶ Launching a ringtone picker
- ▶ Recording a sound

Here is an example of how to create a simple intent with a predefined action (ACTION_VIEW) to launch the web browser with a specific URL:

```
Uri address = Uri.parse("http://www.perlgurl.org");
Intent surf = new Intent(Intent.ACTION_VIEW, address);
startActivity(surf);
```

This example shows an intent that has been created with an action and some data. The action, in this case, is to view something. The data is a uniform resource identifier (URI), which identifies the location of the resource to view.

For this example, the browser's activity then starts and comes into foreground, causing the original calling activity to pause in the background. When the user finishes with the browser and clicks the Back button, the original activity resumes.

Applications may also create their own intent types and allow other applications to call them, allowing for tightly integrated application suites.

> The OpenIntents.org website keeps a list of intent actions at www.openintents.org/en/intentstable. This list includes those built into Android as well as those available from third-party applications.

Working with Dialogs

Handset screens are small, and user interface real estate is valuable. Sometimes you want to handle a small amount of user interaction without creating an entirely new activity. In such instances, creating an activity dialog can be very handy. Dialogs can be helpful for creating very simple user interfaces that do not necessitate an entirely new screen or activity to function. Instead, the calling activity dispatches a dialog, which can have its own layout and user interface, with buttons and input controls.

Table 3.2 lists the important methods for creating and managing activity dialog windows.

TABLE 3.2   Important Dialog Methods of the `Activity` **Class**

Method	Purpose
`Activity.showDialog()`	Shows a dialog, creating it if necessary.
`Activity.onCreateDialog()`	Is a callback when a dialog is being created for the first time and added to the activity dialog pool.
`Activity.onPrepareDialog()`	Is a callback for updating a dialog on-the-fly. Dialogs are created once and can be used many times by an activity. This callback enables the dialog to be updated just before it is shown for each `showDialog()` call.
`Activity.dismissDialog()`	Dismisses a dialog and returns to the activity. The dialog is still available to be used again by calling `showDialog()` again.
`Activity.removeDialog()`	Removes the dialog completely from the activity dialog pool.

Activity classes can include more than one dialog, and each dialog can be created and then used multiple times.

There are quite a few types of ready-made dialog types available for use in addition to the basic dialog. These are `AlertDialog`, `CharacterPickerDialog`, `DatePickerDialog`, `ProgressDialog`, and `TimePickerDialog`.

You can also create an entirely custom dialog by designing an XML layout file and using the `Dialog.setContentView()` method. To retrieve controls from the dialog layout, you simply use the `Dialog.findViewById()` method.

Logging Application Information

Android provides a useful logging utility class called `android.util.Log`. Logging messages are categorized by severity (and verbosity), with errors being the most severe. Table 3.3 lists some commonly used logging methods of the Log class.

TABLE 3.3   Commonly Used Log Methods

Method	Purpose
`Log.e()`	Logs errors
`Log.w()`	Logs warnings
`Log.i()`	Logs informational messages
`Log.d()`	Logs debug messages
`Log.v()`	Logs verbose messages

> Excessive use of the Log utility can result in decreased application performance. Debug and verbose logging should be used only for development purposes and removed before application publication.

The first parameter of each Log method is a string called a tag. One common Android programming practice is to define a global static string to represent the overall application or the specific activity within the application such that log filters can be created to limit the log output to specific data.

For example, you could define a string called TAG, as follows:

```
private static final String TAG = "MyApp";
```

Now anytime you use a Log method, you supply this tag. An informational logging message might look like this:

```
Log.i(TAG, "In onCreate() callback method");
```

Summary

In this hour, you've seen how different Android applications can be designed using three application components: `Context`, `Activity`, and `Intent`. Each Android application comprises one or more activities. Top-level application functionality is accessible through the application context. Each activity has a special function and (usually) its own layout, or user interface. An activity is launched when the Android system matches an intent object with the most appropriate application activity, based on the action and data information set in the intent. Intents can also be used to pass data from one activity to another.

In addition to learning the basics of how Android applications are put together, you've also learned how to take advantage of useful Android utility classes, such as application logging, which can help streamline Android application development and debugging.

Q&A

Q. *How do I design a responsive application that will not be shut down during low-memory conditions?*

A. Applications can limit (but never completely eradicate) the risk of being shut down during low-memory situations by prudently managing activity state. This means using the appropriate activity callbacks and following the recommendations. Most importantly, applications should acquire resources only when necessary and release those resources as soon as possible.

Q. *How should I design an input form for an Android application?*

A. Mobile applications need to be ready to pause and resume at any time. Typical web form style—with various fields and Submit, Clear, and Cancel buttons—isn't very well suited to mobile development. Instead, consider committing data as it is entered. This will keep data housekeeping to a minimum as activity state changes, without frustrating users.

Workshop

Quiz

1. Which of these screens does it make the most sense to show to a user first?

   A. Menu screen

   B. Splash screen

   C. Play screen

2. True or False: Android provides a simple method for storing application settings.

3. What is the recommended way to get a context instance, required by many Android calls?

   A. `Context context = (Context) this;`

   B. `Context context = getAndroidObject(CONTEXT);`

   C. `Context context = getApplicationContext();`

4. True or False: The `android.util.Log` class supports six types of logging.

Answers

1. B. The splash screen shows the game logo before the user starts to play.

2. True. Simply use the `SharedPreferences` class to store simple settings.

3. C. This retrieves the context tied to your application. Using the activity context, as shown in A, works but is not recommended.

4. False. The `Log` class supports five log types: error, warning, informational, debug, and verbose.

Exercises

1. Add a logging tag to your Droid1 project. Within the `onCreate()` callback method, add an informational logging message, using the `Log.i()` method. Run the application and view the log results.

2. Implement some of the `Activity` callback methods in addition to `onCreate()`, such as `onStart()`, `onRestart()`, `onResume()`, `onPause()`, `onStop()`, and `onDestroy()`. Add a log message to each callback method and then run the application normally. View the log results to trace the application life cycle. Next, try some other scenarios, such as pausing or suspending the application and then resuming. Simulate an incoming call. Watch the application log to see how the activity responds to such events.

HOUR 4

Managing Application Resources

What You'll Learn in This Hour:

- ▶ Using application and system resources
- ▶ Working with simple resource values
- ▶ Working with drawable resources
- ▶ Working with layouts
- ▶ Working with files
- ▶ Working with other types of resources

Android applications rely upon strings, graphics, and other types of resources to generate robust user interfaces. Android projects can include these resources, using a well-defined project resource hierarchy. In this hour, we review the most common types of resources used by Android applications, how they are stored, and how they can be accessed programmatically.

Using Application and System Resources

Resources are broken down into two types: application resources and system resources. Application resources are defined by the developer within the Android project files and are specific to the application. System resources are common resources defined by the Android platform and accessible to all applications through the Android SDK.

You can access both types of resources at runtime. You can also access resources from within other compiled resources, such as XML layout files, to define attributes of specific controls.

Working with Application Resources

Application resources are created and stored within the Android project files under the /res directory. Using a well-defined but flexible directory structure, resources are organized, defined, and compiled with the application package. Application resources are not shared with the rest of the Android system.

Storing Application Resources

Defining application data as resources is a good programming practice. Grouping application resources together and compiling them into the application package has the following benefits:

▶ Code is cleaner and easier to read, leading to fewer bugs.

▶ Resources are organized by type and guaranteed to be unique.

▶ Resources are conveniently located for handset customization.

▶ Localization and internationalization are straightforward.

The Android platform supports a variety of resource types (see Figure 4.1), which can be combined to form different types of applications.

Android applications can include many different kinds of resources. The following are some of the most common resource types:

▶ Strings, colors, and dimensions

▶ Drawable graphics files

▶ Layout files

▶ Raw files of all types

Resource types are defined with special XML tags and organized into specially named project directories. Some /res subdirectories, such as the /drawable, /layout, and /values directories, are created by default when a new Android project is created, while others must be added by the developer when required.

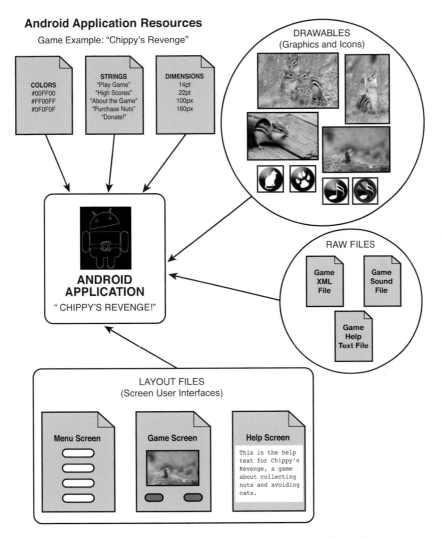

FIGURE 4.1
Android applications can use a variety of resources.

Resource files stored within /res subdirectories must abide by the following rules:

- ▶ Resource filenames must be lowercase.

- ▶ Resource filenames may contain letters, numbers, underscores, and periods only.

- ▶ Resource filenames (and XML name attributes) must be unique.

> When resources are compiled, their name dictates their variable name. For exam-
> ple, a graphics file saved within the /drawable directory as mypic.jpg is refer-
> enced as @drawable/mypic. It is important to name resource names intelligently.

Consult the Android documentation for specific project directory naming conventions.

Referencing Application Resources

All application resources are stored within the /res project directory structure and
are compiled into the project at build time. Application resources can be used programmatically. They can also be referenced in other application resources.

> Each time you save a resource file (that is, copy a resource file such as a graph-
> ics file into the appropriate directory) within Eclipse, the R.java class file is
> recompiled to incorporate your changes. If you have not used the correct directory-
> or file-naming conventions, you see a compiler error in the Eclipse Problems tab.

Application resources can be accessed programmatically using the generated class
file called R.java. To reference a resource, you must retrieve the application's
Resources object using the getResources() method and then make the appropriate method call, based on the type of resource you wish to retrieve.

For example, to retrieve a string named hello defined in the strings.xml resource
file, you would use the following method call:

```
String greeting = getResources().getString(R.string.hello);
```

We will talk more about how to access different types of resources later in this hour.

To reference an application resource from another compiled resource, such as a layout file, use the following format:

```
@[resource type]/[resource name]
```

For example, the same string used earlier would be referenced as follows:

```
@string/hello
```

We will talk more about referencing resources later in the hour, when we talk about
layout files.

Working with System Resources

Developers can access, in addition to application resources, Android system resources. You can share many system resources across multiple applications for a common look and feel. For example, the Android system string resource class (`android.R.string`) contains strings for words such as OK, Cancel, Yes, No, Cut, Copy, and Paste.

System resources are stored within the `android` package. There are classes for each of the major resource types.

For example, the `android.R.string` class contains the system string resources. To retrieve a system resource string for ok, for example, you first need to use the static method of the `Resources` class called `getSystem()` to retrieve the global system `Resource` object. Then you can call the `getString()` method with the appropriate string resource name, like this:

```
String confirm = Resources.getSystem().getString(android.R.string.ok);
```

To reference a system resource from another compiled resource, such as a layout file, use the following format:

```
@android:[resource type]/[resource name]
```

For example, you could use the system string for ok by setting the appropriate string attribute as follows:

```
@android:string/ok
```

Working with Simple Resource Values

Simple resources such as string, color, and dimension values should be defined in XML files under the `/res/values` project directory in XML files. These resource files use special XML tags that represent name/value pairs. These types of resources are compiled into the application package at build time.

Working with Strings

You can use string resources anywhere your application needs to display text. You tag string resources with the <string> tag and store them in the resource file /res/values/strings.xml.

Here is an example of a string resource file:

```
<?xml version="1.0" encoding="utf-8"?>
<resources>
    <string name="app_name">Name this App</string>
    <string name="hello">Hello</string>
</resources>
```

String resources have a number of formatting options. Table 4.1 shows some simple examples of well-formatted string values.

> Strings that contain apostrophes or single straight quotes must be escaped or wrapped within double straight quotes.

TABLE 4.1   String Resource Formatting Examples

String Resource Value	Will Be Displayed As
Hello, World	Hello, World
"Hello, World"	Hello, World
Mother\'s Maiden Name:	Mother's Maiden Name:
He said, \"No.\"	He said, "No."

There are several ways to access a string resource programmatically. The simplest way is to use the getString() method:

```
String greeting = getResources().getString(R.string.hello);
```

Working with Colors

You can apply color resources to screen controls. You tag color resources with the <color> tag and store them in the file /res/values/colors.xml. This XML resource file is not created by default and must be created manually.

> You can add a new XML file, such as this one, by choosing File, New, Android XML File and then fill out the resulting dialog with the type of file (such as values). This will automatically set the expected folder and type of file for the Android project.

Here is an example of a color resource file:

```xml
<?xml version="1.0" encoding="utf-8"?>
<resources>
    <color name="background_color">#006400</color>
    <color name="app_text_color">#FFE4C4</color>
</resources>
```

The Android system supports 12-bit and 24-bit colors in RGB format. Table 4.2 lists the color formats that the Android platform supports.

TABLE 4.2   Color Formats Supported in Android

Format	Description	Example
#RGB	12-bit color	#00F (blue)
#ARGB	12-bit color with alpha	#800F (blue, alpha 50%)
#RRGGBB	24-bit color	#FF00FF (magenta)
#AARRGGBB	24-bit color with alpha	#80FF00FF (magenta, alpha 50%)

The following code retrieves a color resource named app_text_color using the getColor() method:

```java
int textColor = getResources().getColor(R.color.app_text_color);
```

> There are lots of color pickers on the web. For example, http://html-color-codes.info provides a simple color chart as well as a clickable color picker.

Did you Know?

Working with Dimensions

To specify the size of a user interface control such as a Button or TextView control, you need to specify different kinds of dimensions. You tag dimension resources with the <dimen> tag and store them in the resource file /res/values/dimens.xml. This XML resource file is not created by default and must be created manually.

Here is an example of a dimension resource file:

```xml
<?xml version="1.0" encoding="utf-8"?>
<resources>
    <dimen name="thumbDim">100px</dimen>
</resources>
```

Each dimension resource value must end with a unit of measurement. Table 4.3 lists the dimension units that Android supports.

TABLE 4.3   Dimension Unit Measurements Supported in Android

Type of Measurement	Description	Unit String
Pixels	Actual screen pixels	px
Inches	Physical measurement	in
Millimeters	Physical measurement	mm
Points	Common font measurement	pt
Density-independent pixels	Pixels relative to 160dpi	dp
Scale-independent pixels	Best for scalable font display	sp

The following code retrieves a dimension resource called `thumbDim` using the `getDimension()` method:

```
float thumbnailDim = getResources().getDimension(R.dimen.thumbDim);
```

Working with Drawable Resources

Drawable resources, such as image files, must be saved under the `/res/drawable` project directory. These types of resources are then compiled into the application package at build time and are available to the application.

> You can drag and drop image files into the `/res/drawable` directory by using the Eclipse Project Explorer. Again, remember that filenames must be lowercase and contain only letters, numbers, and underscores.

Working with Images

The most common drawable resources used in applications are bitmap-style image files, such as PNG and JPG files. These files are often used as application icons and button graphics but may be used for a number of user interface components.

As shown in Table 4.4, Android supports many common image formats.

TABLE 4.4   Image Formats Supported in Android

Supported Image Format	Description	Required Extension
Portable Network Graphics (PNG)	Preferred format (lossless)	`.png`
Nine-Patch Stretchable Images (PNG)	Preferred format (lossless)	`.9.png`

TABLE 4.4   Continued

Supported Image Format	Description	Required Extension
Joint Photographic Experts Group (JPEG/JPG)	Acceptable format (lossy)	.jpg
Graphics Interchange Format (GIF)	Discouraged but supported	.gif

Using Image Resources Programmatically

Images resources are encapsulated in the class BitmapDrawable. To access a graphic resource file called /res/drawable/logo.png, you would use the getDrawable() method, as follows:

```
BitmapDrawable logoBitmap =
    (BitmapDrawable)getResources().getDrawable(R.drawable.logo);
```

Most of the time, however, you don't need to load a graphic directly. Instead, you can use the resource identifier as an attribute on a control such as an ImageView control. The following code, for example, sets and loads the logo.png graphic into an ImageView control named LogoImageView, which must be defined within the layout:

```
ImageView logoView = (ImageView)findViewById(R.id.LogoImageView);
logoView.setImageResource(R.drawable.logo);
```

Working with Other Types of Drawables

In addition to graphics files, you can also create specially formatted XML files to describe other Drawable subclasses, such as ShapeDrawable. You can use the ShapeDrawable class to define different shapes, such as rectangles and ovals. See the Android documentation for the android.graphics.drawable package for further information.

Working with Layouts

Most Android application user interfaces are defined using specially formatted XML files called *layouts*. Layout resource files are included in the /res/layout directory. You compile layout files into your application as you would any other resources.

> Layout files often define an entire screen and are associated with a specific activity, but they need not be. Layout resources can also define part of a screen and can be included within another layout.

Did you Know?

Here is an example of a layout resource file:

```xml
<?xml version="1.0" encoding="utf-8"?>
<LinearLayout
    xmlns:android="http://schemas.android.com/apk/res/android"
    android:orientation="vertical"
    android:layout_width="fill_parent"
    android:layout_height="fill_parent">
    <TextView
        android:layout_width="fill_parent"
        android:layout_height-"wrap_content"
        android:text="@string/hello" />
</LinearLayout>
```

You might recognize this layout: It is the default layout, called `main.xml`, created with any new Android application. This layout file describes the user interface of the only activity within the application. It contains a `LinearLayout` control that is used as a container for all other user interface controls—in this case, a single `TextView` control.

The `main.xml` layout file also references another resource: the string resource called `@string/hello`, which is defined in the `strings.xml` resource file.

Did you Know?

> Layouts can also be created, modified, and used at runtime. However, in most cases, using the XML layout files greatly improves code clarity and reuse.

There are two ways to format layout resources. The simplest way is to use the layout resource editor in Eclipse to design and preview layout files. You can also edit the XML layout files directly.

Designing Layouts Using the Layout Resource Editor

You can design and preview layouts in Eclipse by using the layout resource editor (see Figure 4.2). If you click on the project file `/res/layout/main.xml`, you see a Layout tab, which shows you the preview of the layout. You can add and remove layout controls by using the Outline tab. You can set individual properties and attributes by using the Properties tab.

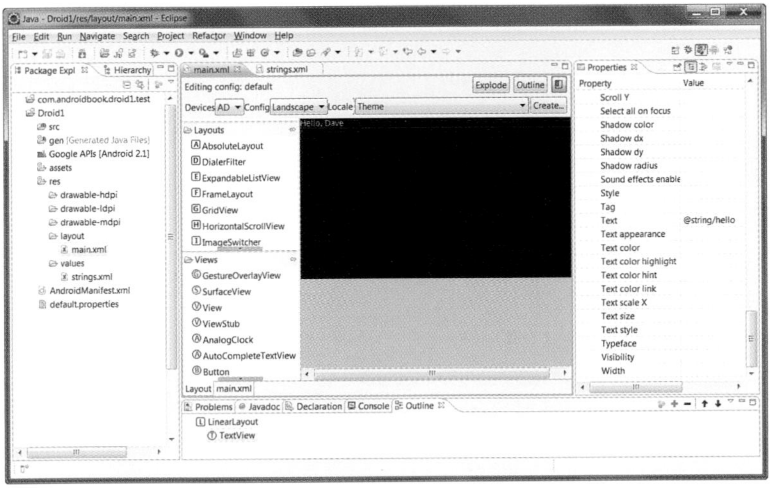

FIGURE 4.2
The layout
resource editor
in Eclipse.

Like most other user interface designers, the layout resource editor works well for basic layout design. However, the layout resource editor does not fully support all View controls. For some of the more complex user interface controls, you might be forced to edit the XML by hand. You might also lose the ability to preview your layout if you add any of these controls to your layout. In such a case, you can still view your layout by running your application in the emulator or on a handset. Displaying an application correctly on a handset, rather than the Eclipse layout editor, should be a developer's primary objective.

Designing Layouts Using XML

You can edit the raw XML of a layout file directly. If you click on the project file /res/layout/main.xml, you see the main.xml tab, which shows you the raw XML of the layout file.

> As you gain experience developing layouts, you should familiarize yourself with the XML layout file format. Switch to the XML view frequently and accustom yourself to the XML generated by each type of control. Do not rely on the Eclipse layout resource editor alone.

By the Way

▼ Try It Yourself

Give the Eclipse Layout editor a spin:

1. Open the Droid1 Android project you created earlier.

2. Navigate to the /res/layout/main.xml layout file and double-click the file to open it in the Eclipse layout resource editor.

3. Switch to the Layout tab, and you should see the layout preview in the main window.

> The two most important tabs for the layout resource editor are the Outline tab and the Properties tab. If you drag the Properties tab up to the right side of the Eclipse Java perspective, you can simultaneously view the main layout resource editor in the middle of the screen, the Project Explorer to the left, the Properties tab to the right (to fully use the vertical space it needs), and Outline mode along the bottom (which is usually shorter and doesn't need the vertical space of the Properties tab).

4. Click the Outline tab. This outline is the XML View hierarchy of this layout file. In this case, you have a LinearLayout control. If you expand it, you see that it contains a TextView control.

5. Select the TextView control on the Outline tab. You see a red box highlight this control in the layout preview.

6. Click the Properties tab. This tab displays all the properties and attributes that can be configured for the TextView control you selected. Scroll down to the property called Text and note that it has been set to a string resource variable called @string/hello.

7. Click the Text property called @string/hello on Properties tab. You can now modify the field. Each time you change this field, note how the layout preview changes. You can type in a string directly, type a different string resource (@string/app_name, for example), or click the little button with the three dots and choose an appropriate resource from the list of string resources available to your application.

8. Switch to the main.xml tab and note the XML. If you save and run your project in the emulator, you should see results similar to those displayed in the preview.

▼

Feel free to continue to explore. You might want to try adding controls, such as an ImageView control or another TextView control, to your layout. We cover designing layouts in much more detail later in this book.

Using Layout Resources Programmatically

If and when you need to access an entire layout programmatically, you can use a LayoutInflater class to inflate the layout file into a View object, as in the following example:

```
LayoutInflater inflater = getLayoutInflater();
View layout = inflater.inflate(R.layout.main, null);
```

However, in most instances, you do not need to load the layout itself, but you need to interact with specific controls within the layout, such as the TextView control in the main.xml layout file. Layout contents, whether Button, ImageView, or TextView controls, are derived from the View class.

The default layout file created with the Droid1 project contains a TextView control. However, this TextView control does not have a default name attribute. The easiest way to access the right View control is by name, so take a moment and set the id attribute of the TextView control, using the layout resource editor: Call it @+id/TextView01.

Here's how you would retrieve a TextView object named TextView01 that has been defined in the layout resource file:

```
TextView txt = (TextView)findViewById(R.id.TextView01);
```

Working with Files

In addition to string, graphic, and layout resources, Android projects can contain files as resources. These files may be in any format. However, some formats are more convenient than others.

Working with XML Files

The XML file format is well supported on the Android platform. Arbitrary XML files can be included as resources. These XML files are stored in the /res/xml directory. XML file resources are the preferred format for any structured data your application requires.

How you format your XML resource files is up to you. A variety of XML utilities (shown in Table 4.5) are available as part of the Android platform.

TABLE 4.5   XML Utility Packages

Package	Description
android.sax.*	Framework to write standard SAX handlers
android.util.Xml.*	XML utilities, including the XMLPullParser
org.xml.sax.*	Core SAX functionality (see www.saxproject.org)
javax.xml.*	SAX and limited DOM, Level 2 core support
org.w3c.dom	Interfaces for DOM, Level 2 core
org.xmlpull.*	XmlPullParser and XMLSerializer interfaces (see www.xmlpull.org)

To access an XML file called /res/xml/default_values.xml programmatically, you could use the getXml() method, like this:

```
XmlResourceParser defaultDataConfig = getResources().getXml(R.xml.default_values);
```

Working with Raw Files

An application can include raw files as resources. Raw files your application might use include audio files, video files, and any other file formats you might need. All raw resource files should be included in the /res/raw directory.

There are no rules or restrictions for formatting raw files (aside from the resource filenames rules discussed earlier). If you plan to include media file resources, you should consult the Android platform documentation to determine what media formats and encodings are supported on your application's target handsets. The same goes for any other file format you want to include as an application resource. If the file format you plan on using is not supported by the native Android system, your application will be required to do all file processing internally.

To access a raw file resource programmatically, simply use the openRawResource() method. For example, the following code would create an InputStream object to access to the resource file /res/raw/file1.txt:

```
InputStream iFile = getResources().openRawResource(R.raw.file1);
```

By the Way

All raw file resources must have unique names, excluding the file suffix, so file1.txt and file1.dat would conflict.

There are times when you might want to include files within your application but not have them compiled into application resources. Android provides a special project directory called /assets for this purpose. This project directory resides at the same level as the /res directory. Any files included in this directory are included as binary resources, along with the application installation package, and are not compiled into the application.

Uncompiled files, called *application assets*, are not accessible through the getResources() method. Instead, you must use AssetManager to access files included in the /assets directory.

Did you Know?

Working with Other Types of Resources

We have covered the most common types of resources you might need in an application. There are numerous other types of resources available as well. These resource types may be used less often and may be more complex. However, they allow for very powerful applications. Some of the other types of resources you can take advantage of include:

- ▶ String arrays
- ▶ Menus
- ▶ Animation sequences
- ▶ Shape drawables
- ▶ Styles and themes
- ▶ Custom layout controls

When you are ready to use these other resource types, consult the Android documentation for further details. You will also want to consider reading a more advanced book on Android development. There are several available, including the Developer's Library book *Android Wireless Application Development*. Written by yours truly, this complete Android reference includes an exhaustive explanation of application resources types, with accompanying source code sample projects.

Summary

Android applications can use many different types of resources, including application-specific resources and system-wide resources. The Eclipse resource editors facilitate resource management, but XML resource files can also be edited manually. Once defined, resources can be accessed programmatically as well as referenced, by name, by other resources. String, color, and dimension values are stored in specially formatted XML files, and graphic images are stored as individual files. Application user interfaces are defined using XML layout files. Raw files, which can include custom data formats, may also be included as resources for use by the application. Finally, applications may include uncompiled binary files, which are called application assets.

Q&A

Q. *Can I tell what all the system resources are, just by their names?*

A. Sometimes you can't. The official documentation for the Android system resources does not describe each resource. If you are confused about what a specific system resource is or how it works, you can either experiment with it or examine its resource definition. Android system resources are defined in the `/tools/lib/res/default` directory of the Android SDK.

Q. *Must string, color, and dimension resources be stored in separate XML files?*

A. Technically, no. However, it is highly recommended. For example, localization and internationalization may require different strings, but the dimensions might remain the same ones. Keeping the resource types separate keeps them organized.

Q. *Which XML parser should I use?*

A. Our tests have shown that the SAX parser is the most efficient XML parser (closely followed by XMLPullParser), and we recommend this parser for most purposes. However, the choice is yours, and you should test your specific XML implementation to determine the appropriate parser for your application's needs.

Q. *What is the difference between project resources and project assets?*

A. Project resources are compiled into the application and easily accessed using the `getResources()` method. Application assets are used less frequently to store uncompiled files within the application package file that is installed on the handset. Assets are accessed using the `getAssets()` method.

Workshop

Quiz

1. What color formats are supported for color resources?

    A. 12-bit color

    B. 24-bit color

    C. 64-bit color

2. True or False: You can include files of any format as a resource.

3. Which graphics formats are supported and encouraged on Android?

    A. Joint Photographic Experts Group (JPG)

    B. Portable Network Graphics (PNG)

    C. Graphics Interchange Format (GIF)

    D. Nine-Patch Stretchable Images (.9.PNG)

4. True or False: Resource filenames can be uppercase.

5. True or False: Naming resources is arbitrary.

Answers

1. A and B. Both 12-bit and 24-bit color are supported.

2. True. Simply include a file as a raw resource.

3. B and D. Although all four formats are supported, they are not all encouraged. PNG graphics, including Nine-Patch Stretchable graphics, are highly encouraged for Android development because they are lossless and efficient. JPG files are acceptable but lossy, and GIF file use is outright discouraged.

4. False. Resource filenames may contain letters, numbers, and underscores and must be lowercase.

5. False. The resource names dictate the variable names used to reference the resources programmatically.

Exercises

1. Add a new color resource with a value of `#00ff00` to your Droid1 project. Within the layout file, change the `textColor` attribute of the `TextView` control to the color resource you just created. Rerun the application and view the result.

2. Add a new dimension resource with a value of 22pt to your Droid1 project. Within the layout file, change the `textSize` attribute of the `TextView` control to the dimension resource you just created. Rerun the application and view the result.

3. Add a new drawable graphics file resource to your Droid1 project. Within the layout file, add an `ImageView` control and set its `src` attribute to the drawable resource you just created. Rerun the application and view the result.

4. Add a raw text file resource to the Droid1 project. Use the `openRawResource()` method to create an `InputStream` object and read the file. Output the contents of the file to the log by using the `Log.v()` method. Rerun the application and view the result.

HOUR 5

Configuring the Android Manifest File

What You'll Learn in This Hour:

▶ Exploring the Android manifest file

▶ Configuring basic application settings

▶ Defining activities

▶ Managing application permissions

▶ Managing other application settings

Every Android project includes a special file called the Android manifest file. The Android system uses this file to determine application configuration settings, including the application's identity as well as what permissions the application requires to run. In this hour, we will examine the Android manifest file in detail and look at how different applications use its features.

Exploring the Android Manifest File

The Android manifest file, named `AndroidManifest.xml`, is an XML file that must be included at the top level of any Android project. The Android system uses the information in this file to do the following:

▶ Install and upgrade the application package

▶ Display application details to users

▶ Launch application activities

▶ Manage application permissions

▶ Handle a number of other advanced application configurations, including acting as a service provider or content provider.

> If you use Eclipse with the ADT plug-in for Eclipse, the Android project wizard will create the initial `AndroidManifest.xml` file with default values for the most important configuration settings.

You can edit the Android manifest file by using the Eclipse manifest file resource editor or by manually editing the XML.

The Eclipse manifest file resource editor organizes the manifest information into categories presented on five tabs:

▶ Manifest

▶ Application

▶ Permissions

▶ Instrumentation

▶ AndroidManifest.xml

Using the Manifest Tab

The Manifest tab (see Figure 5.1) contains package-wide settings, including the package name, version information, and minimum Android SDK version information. You can also set any hardware configuration requirements here.

Using the Application Tab

The Application tab (see Figure 5.2) contains application-wide settings, including the application label and icon, as well as information about application components such as activities, intent filters, and other application functionality, including configuration for service and content provider implementations.

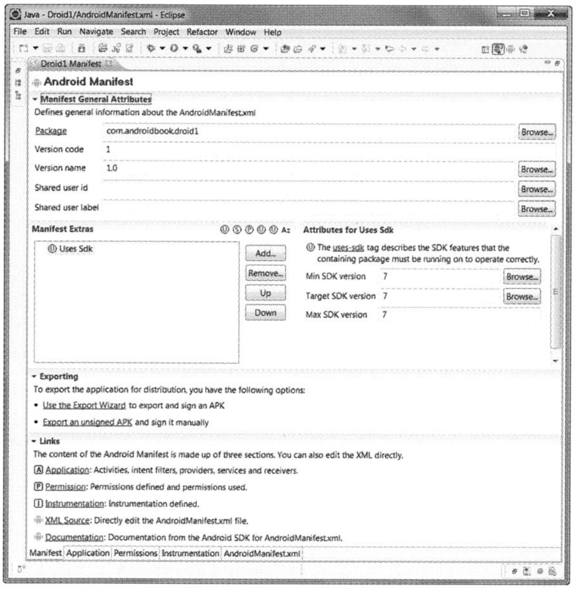

FIGURE 5.1
The Manifest tab of the Eclipse manifest file resource editor.

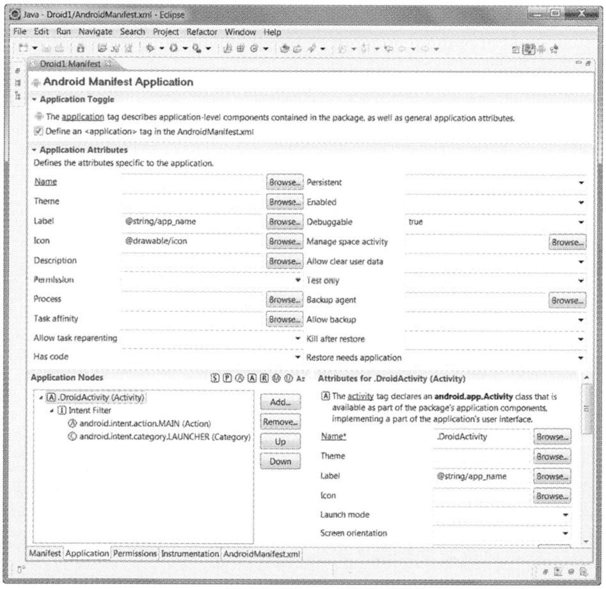

FIGURE 5.2
The Application tab of the Eclipse manifest file resource editor.

Using the Permissions Tab

The Permissions tab (see Figure 5.3) contains any permission rules required by the application. This tab can also be used to enforce custom permissions created for the application.

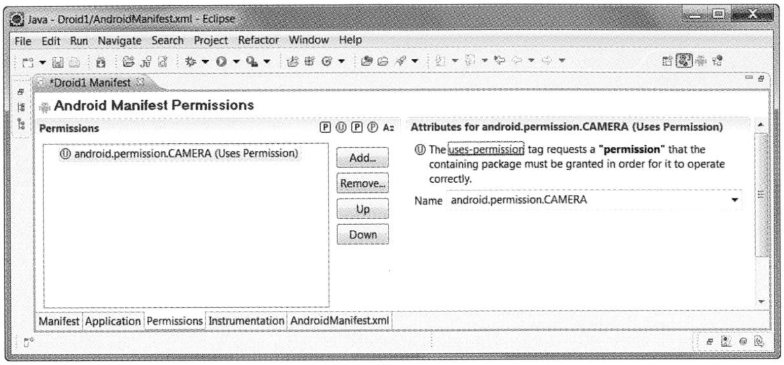

FIGURE 5.3
The Permissions tab of the Eclipse manifest file resource editor.

Watch Out!

Do not confuse the application Permission field (a drop-down list on the Application tab) with the Permissions tab features. Use the Permissions tab to define the permissions required for the application to access the resources or APIs it needs. The other is for defining permissions required by other applications to access exposed resources and APIs in your application.

Using the Instrumentation Tab

You can use the Instrumentation tab (see Figure 5.4) to declare any instrumentation classes for monitoring the application. In the Name field, you fill in the fully qualified class name of the `Instrumentation` subclass for your application, and for Target Package, you provide the name of the package whose manifest file contains the `<application>` tag for the application to be monitored. We will talk more about instrumentation and testing in a later chapter.

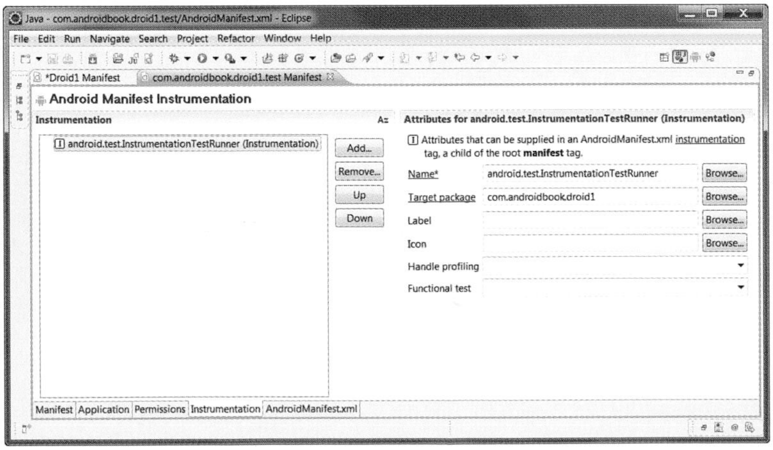

FIGURE 5.4
The Instrumentation tab of the Eclipse manifest file resource editor.

Using the AndroidManifest.xml Tab

The Android manifest file is a specially formatted XML file. You can edit the XML manually in the AndroidManifest.xml tab of the manifest file resource editor (see Figure 5.5).

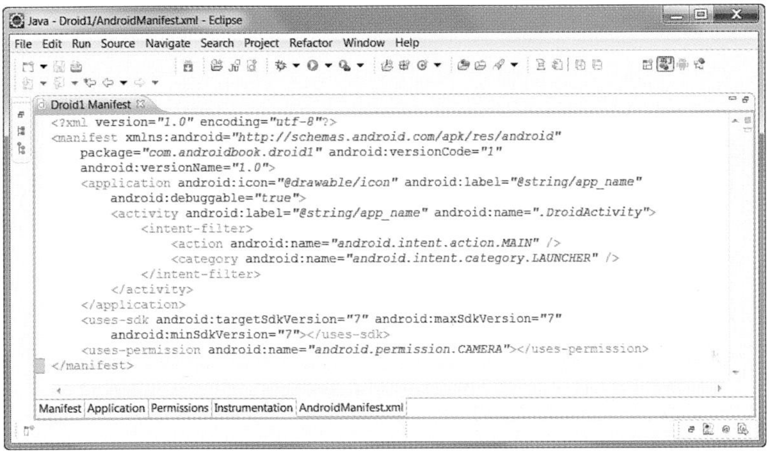

FIGURE 5.5
The AndroidManifest .xml tab of the Eclipse manifest file resource editor.

Figure 5.5 shows the Android manifest file for the Droid1 project you created in the first hour, which has fairly simple XML.

Note that the file has a single <manifest> tag, within which all the package-wide settings appear. Within this tag is one <application> tag, which defines the specific application, with its single activity, called DroidActivity, with an Intent filter. In addition, the <uses-sdk> tag is set to 3.

Now let's talk about each of these settings in a bit more detail.

Configuring Basic Application Settings

Many of the most important settings your application requires are set using attributes and child tags of the <manifest> and <application> blocks.

Naming Android Packages

You define the package within the Android manifest file in the `<manifest>` tag, using the `package` attribute, as follows:

```
<manifest
    xmlns:android="http://schemas.android.com/apk/res/android"
    package="com.androidbook.droid1"
    android:versionCode="1"
    android:versionName="1.0">
```

By the Way

If you use the Android project wizard in Eclipse to create a project, you must fill in the package name at that time. That package name is used in the default Android manifest file.

Linking Secondary Libraries

Applications can use the `<uses-library>` tag to link to other libraries in addition to the standard Android packages. This feature is available on the Application tab of the resource editor. Here's an example:

```
<uses-library
    android:name="com.company.sharedutilities" />
```

Versioning an Application

Manifest version information is used for two purposes:

▶ To organize and keep track of application features

▶ To manage application upgrades

For this reason, the `<manifest>` tag has two separate version attributes: a version name and a version code.

Setting the Version Name

The version name is the traditional versioning information, used to keep track of application builds. Smart versioning is essential when publishing and supporting applications. The `<manifest>` tag `android:versionName` attribute is a string value provided to keep track of the application build number. For example, the Droid1 project has the version name 1.0. The format of the version name field is up to the developer. However, note that this field is visible to the user.

Setting the Version Code

The version code allows the Android platform to programmatically upgrade and downgrade an application. The `<manifest>` tag `android:versionCode` attribute is an integer value that the Android platform and Android marketplaces use to manage application upgrades and downgrades. android:versionCode generally starts at a value of 1. This value should be incremented with each new version of the application deployed to users. The version code field is not visible to the user and need not stay in sync with the version name.

Setting the Minimum Android SDK Version

Android applications can be compiled for compatibility with several different SDK versions. You use the <uses-sdk> tag to specify the minimum SDK required on the handset in order for the application to build and run properly. The android:minSdkVersion attribute of this tag is an integer representing the minimum Android SDK version required. Table 5.1 shows the Android SDK versions available for shipping applications.

TABLE 5.1   Android SDK Versions Available

Android SDK Version	Value
Android 1.0 SDK	1
Android 1.1 SDK	2
Android 1.5 SDK	3
Android 1.6 SDK	4
Android 2.0 SDK	5
Android 2.0.1 SDK	6
Android 2.1 SDK	7

For example, in the Droid1 project, you specified that the minimum SDK as Android 2.1 SDK:

```
<uses-sdk
    android:minSdkVersion="7" />
```

Naming an Application

The <application> tag android:label attribute is a string representing the application name. You can set this name to a fixed string, as in the following example:

```
<application
    android:label="My application name">
```

You can also set the android:label attribute to a string resource. In the Droid1 project, you set the application name to the string resource as follows:

```
<application
    android:label="@string/app_name">
```

In this case, the resource string called app_name in the strings.xml file supplies the application name.

Providing an Icon for an Application

The <application> tag attribute called android:icon is a Drawable resource representing the application. In the Droid1 project, you set the application icon to the Drawable resource as follows:

```
<application
    android:icon="@drawable/icon">
```

▼   **Try It Yourself**

Although you will place just a single icon reference in the <application> tag attribute android:icon, you will need to create three different icons. These will represent the three default icons for low pixel density screens (ldpi), high pixel density screens (hdpi), and medium pixel density screens (mdpi). The Android system will automatically choose the appropriate graphic based upon the capabilities of the device the application is running on. You will learn more about this topic in Hour 20, "Developing for Different Devices." For now, you can just create a single graphic and then resize it for the three different resolutions.

To make your own custom application icons, perform the following steps:

1. Design a 48×48 pixel graphic with your favorite graphics program. This is the icon for medium pixel density screens.

2. Save the graphic in PNG format, using the filename myicon.png.

3. Add the graphic file as a Drawable resource to your application, in the /res/drawable-mdpi directory.

4. Repeat steps 1–3, but resize the graphic to 72×72 pixels and place it in the `/res/drawable-hdpi` directory. This is the icon for high pixel density screens.

5. Repeat steps 1–3, but resize the graphic to 36×36 pixels and place it in the `/res/drawable-ldpi` directory. This is the icon for low pixel density screens.

6. Set the `android:icon` property to the resource name of your new icon, `@drawable/myicon`. This will pick one of the three graphics you created based on the pixel density of the handset (or emulator) that the application is running on.

The end result will be the same graphic found in three differently sized files in three different resource directories. Typically, a graphic may be further optimized for each resolution.

Providing an Application Description

The `<application>` tag `android:description` attribute is a string representing a short description of the application. You can set this name to a string resource:

```
<application
    android:label="My application name"
    android:description="@string/app_desc">
```

The Android system and application marketplaces use the application description to display information about the application to the user.

Setting Debug Information for an Application

The `<application>` tag `android:debuggable` attribute is a Boolean value that indicates whether the application can be debugged using a debugger such as Eclipse. You will not be able to debug your application until you set this value. You will also want to reset this value to `false` before you publish your application.

Setting Other Application Attributes

There are a number of other settings on the Application tab, but they generally apply only in very specific cases, such as when you want to apply a theme other than the default to your application. There are also settings for handling how the application interacts with the Android operating system. For most applications, the default settings are acceptable.

You will be spending a lot of time on the Application tab in the Application Nodes box, where you can register application components—most commonly, each time you register a new activity.

Defining Activities

Recall that Android applications comprise a number of different activities. Every activity must be registered within the Android manifest file before it can be used. You need to update the manifest file each time you add a new activity to an application.

Each activity represents a specific task to be completed, often with its own screen. Activities are launched in different ways, using the Intent mechanism. Each activity can have its own label (name) and icon but uses the application's generic label and icon by default.

Registering Activities

You can register each new activity in the Application Nodes section of the Application tab. Each new activity has its own <activity> tag in the resulting XML. For example, the following XML excerpt defines an activity class called DroidActivity:

```
<activity
    android:name=".DroidActivity" />
```

This activity must be defined as a class within the application package.

Try It Yourself

To register a new activity in the Droid1 project, follow these steps:

1. Open the Droid1 project in Eclipse.

2. Right-click /src/com.androidbook.droid1 and choose New Class. The New Java Class window opens.

3. Name your new class DroidActivity2.

4. Click the Browse button next to the Superclass field and set the superclass to android.app.Activity.

5. Click the Finish button. You see the new class in your project.

6. Make a copy of the main.xml layout file in the /res/layout resource directory for your new activity and name it second.xml. Modify the layout so that you know it's for the second activity. For example, you could change the text string shown. Save the new layout file.

7. Open the `DroidActivity2` class. Right-click within the class and choose Source-Override/Implement Methods.

8. Check the box next to the `onCreate(Bundle)` method. This method is added to your class.

9. Within the `onCreate()` method, set the layout to load for the new activity by adding and calling the `setContentView(R.layout.second)` method. Save the class file.

10. Open the Android manifest file and click the Application tab of the resource editor.

11. In the Application Nodes section of the Application tab, click the Add button and choose the Activity element. The attributes for the activity are shown in the right side of the screen.

> If you have an existing Activity selected, you'll be adding to that. Instead, select None or choose the Create a New Element at the Top Level, in Application radio button at the top of the dialog.

Watch Out!

12. Click the Browse button next to the activity Name field. Choose the new activity you created, `DroidActivity2`.

13. Save the manifest file. Switch to the AndroidManifest.xml tab to see what the new XML looks like.

You now have a new, fully registered `DroidActivity2` activity that you can use in your application.

Designating the Launch Activity

You can use an `Intent` filter to designate an activity as the primary entry point of the application. The `Intent` filter for launching an activity by default must be configured using an `<intent-filter>` tag with the MAIN action type and the LAUNCHER category. In the Droid1 project, the Android project wizard set `DroidActivity` as the primary launching point of the application:

```
<activity
    android:name=".DroidActivity"
    android:label="@string/app_name">
    <intent-filter>
        <action
            android:name="android.intent.action.MAIN" />
```

```
    <category
        android:name="android.intent.category.LAUNCHER" />
    </intent-filter>
</activity>
```

This `<intent-filter>` tag instructs the Android system to direct all application launch requests to the `DroidActivity` activity.

Managing Application Permissions

The Android platform is built on a Linux kernel and leverages its built-in system security as part of the Android security model. Each Android application exists in its own virtual machine and operates within its own Linux user account (see Figure 5.6).

Applications that want access to shared or privileged resources on the handset must declare those specific permissions in the Android manifest file. This security mechanism ensures that no application can change its behavior on-the-fly or perform any operations without the user's permission.

By the Way

> Because each application runs under a different user account, each application has its own private files and directories, just as a Linux user would.

Android applications can access their own private files and databases without any special permissions. However, if an application needs to access shared or sensitive resources, it must declare those permissions using the `<uses-permission>` tag within the Android manifest file. These permissions are managed on the Permissions tab of the Android manifest file resource editor.

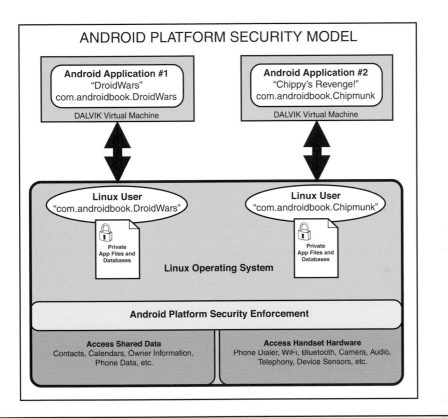

FIGURE 5.6
Simplified Android platform architecture from a security perspective.

Try It Yourself

To give your application permission to access the built-in camera, use the following steps:

1. Open the Droid1 project in Eclipse.

2. Open the Android manifest file and click the Permissions tab of the resource editor.

3. Click the Add button and choose Uses Permission. The Name attribute for the permission is shown in the right side of the screen as a drop-down list.

4. Choose android.permission.CAMERA from the drop-down list.

5. Save the manifest file. Switch to the AndroidManifest.xml tab to see what the new XML looks like.

You have now registered the camera permission. Your application will be able to access the camera without security exceptions.

During the application installation process, the user is shown exactly what permissions the application uses. The user must agree to install the application after reviewing these permissions.

Table 5.2 lists some of the most common permissions used by Android applications.

TABLE 5.2   Common Permissions Used by Android Applications

Permission Category	Useful Permissions
Location-based services	android.permission.ACCESS_COARSE_LOCATION android.permission.ACCESS_FINE_LOCATION
Accessing contact database	android.permission.READ_CONTACTS android.permission.WRITE_CONTACTS
Accessing calendars	android.permission.READ_CALENDAR android.permission.WRITE_CALENDAR
Changing general phone settings	android.permission.SET_ORIENTATION android.permission.SET_TIME_ZONE android.permission.SET_WALLPAPER
Making calls	android.permission.CALL_PHONE android.permission.CALL_PRIVILEGED
Sending and receiving messages	android.permission.READ_SMS android.permission.RECEIVE_MMS android.permission.RECEIVE_SMS android.permission.RECEIVE_WAP_PUSH android.permission.SEND_SMS android.permission.WRITE_SMS
Using network sockets	android.permission.INTERNET
Accessing audio settings	android.permission.RECORD_AUDIO android.permission.MODIFY_AUDIO_SETTINGS
Accessing network settings	android.permission.ACCESS_NETWORK_STATE android.permission.CHANGE_NETWORK_STATE
Accessing Wi-Fi settings	android.permission.ACCESS_WIFI_STATE android.permission.CHANGE_WIFI_STATE
Accessing phone hardware	android.permission.BLUETOOTH android.permission.CAMERA android.permission.FLASHLIGHT android.permission.VIBRATE android.permission.BATTERY_STATS
Account services	android.permission.GET_ACCOUNTS android.permission.MANAGE_ACCOUNTS

Permission Category	Useful Permissions

Synchronization	`android.permission.READ_SYNC_SETTINGS`
	`android.permission.READ_SYNC_STATS`
	`android.permission.WRITE_SYNC_SETTINGS`

For a complete list of the permissions used by Android applications, see the `android.Manifest.permission` class documentation.

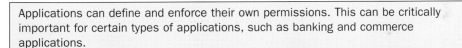

Some permissions are not enforced yet by the Android system. An application should still request these permissions anyway, for compatibility reasons.

Applications can define and enforce their own permissions. This can be critically important for certain types of applications, such as banking and commerce applications.

Managing Other Application Settings

In addition to the features already discussed in this hour, a number of other specialized features can be configured in the Android manifest file. For example, if your application requires a hardware keyboard or a touch screen, you can specify these hardware configuration requirements in the Android manifest file.

You must also declare any other application components—such as whether your application acts as a service provider, content provider, or broadcast receiver—in the Android manifest file.

Summary

The Android manifest file (`AndroidManifest.xml`) exists at the root of every Android project. It is a required component of any project. The Android manifest file uses a simple XML schema to describe what the application is, what its components are, and what permissions it has. The Android platform uses this information to manage the application. Eclipse has a handy resource editor for managing Android manifest files.

Q&A

Q. *Can application names be internationalized?*

A. Yes. You simply define the `android:label` attribute as a string resource and create resource files for each locale you want to support. We will talk more about localizing resources later in this book.

Q. *If permissions are not being enforced, why should I include them in the Android manifest file?*

A. While your application might function even if you don't declare certain permissions, this is dangerous behavior. Firmware upgrades can result in the Android system enforcing these permissions at a future date, causing your application to stop functioning properly.

Q. *I added a new* `Activity` *class to my project, and my application keeps crashing. What did I do wrong?*

A. Chances are, you forgot to register the activity in the Android manifest file. If you don't register the activity by using an `<activity>` tag, your application may crash upon launch.

Q. *If I can use the Eclipse resource editor to edit the Android manifest file, why do I need to know about the raw XML?*

A. When making straightforward configuration changes to the manifest file, using the resource editor is the most straightforward method. However, when bulk changes must be made, editing the XML directly can be much faster.

Q. *Why do I need read permission to shared resources such as contacts?*

A. To protect the privacy of the user, applications must register permission to read sensitive data. While applications cannot do any direct harm to the Android system with just read access, the information extracted from contacts or the calendar could theoretically be used for nefarious purposes. Thus, permission is required to access this information.

Workshop

Quiz

1. True or False: Every Android application needs an Android manifest file.

2. True or False: The `android:versionCode` numbers must correspond with the application `android:versionName`.

3. What is the permission for using the camera?

    A. `android.permission.USE_CAMERA`

    B. `android.permission.CAMERA`

    C. `android.permission.hardware.CAMERA`

4. True or False: When installing an application, the user is shown the permissions requested in the Android manifest file.

Answers

1. True. The Android manifest file is an essential part of every Android project. This file defines the application's identity, settings, and permissions.

2. False. The `android:versionCode` attribute must be incremented each time the application is deployed, and it can be upgraded. This number need not match the `android:versionName` setting.

3. B. You use the `android.permission.CAMERA` permission to access the camera.

4. True. This way, the user knows what the application might attempt to do, such as take a picture or access the user's contacts.

Exercises

1. Create a new icon for the Droid1 project.

2. Create another `Activity` class. Edit the permissions to use a permission of your choice. Also, try to use feature without requesting the appropriate permission and observe the results.

3. Perform a modification to the manifest file using the manifest file editor. Observe the changes made by looking at the XML. Attempt to do the same by just editing the XML.

HOUR 6

Designing an Application Framework

What You'll Learn in This Hour:

▶ Designing an Android trivia game
▶ Implementing an application prototype
▶ Running the game prototype

It's time to put the skills you have learned so far to use. In this hour, you design an Android application prototype, a basic framework on which you will build in the future. You will add many exciting features to this application over the course of this book.

Designing an Android Trivia Game

Because social trivia games are so popular right now, you want to implement one. In your soon-to-be-viral game, the user will be asked random questions about travel and related experiences, such as these:

▶ Have you ever visited the pyramids in Egypt?

▶ Have you ever milked a cow?

▶ Have you ever gone diving with great white sharks?

▶ Have you climbed a mountain?

The user with the highest score is the most well traveled and well seasoned. You'll call the game *Been There, Done That!*.

Determining High-Level Game Features

Try to imagine what features a good game application should have. In addition to the game question screen itself, you need the following:

▶ A startup screen

▶ A way to view scores

▶ An explanation of the game rules

▶ A way to store game settings

You also need a way to transition between these different features. One way to do this is to create a main menu screen that the user can use to navigate the application features.

Reviewing the requirements, we find that we need six primary screens within the Been There, Done That! application. They are the following:

▶ A startup screen

▶ A main menu screen

▶ A game play screen

▶ A settings screen

▶ A scores screen

▶ A help screen

These screens will make up the core user interface for the application.

Determining Activity Requirements

Each screen of the Been There, Done That! application will have its own `Activity` class. Figure 6.1 shows the six activities required, one for each screen.

A good design practice is to implement a base `Activity` class with shared components, which we'll simply call `QuizActivity`. You will employ this practice as you define the activities needed by the Been There, Done That! game:

▶ `QuizActivity`—Derived from `android.app.Activity`, this is the base class. Here, you will define application preferences and other application-wide settings and features.

▶ `QuizSplashActivity`—Derived from `QuizActivity`, this class represents the splash screen.

▶ QuizMenuActivity—Derived from QuizActivity, this class represents the main menu screen.

▶ QuizHelpActivity—Derived from QuizActivity, this class represents the help screen.

▶ QuizScoresActivity—Derived from QuizActivity, this class represents the scores screen.

▶ QuizSettingsActivity—Derived from QuizActivity, this class represents the settings screen.

▶ QuizGameActivity—Derived from QuizActivity, this class represents the game screen.

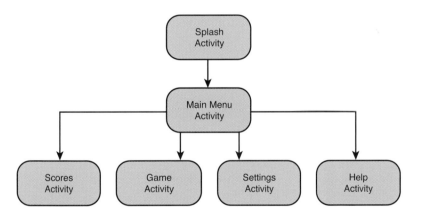

FIGURE 6.1
A rough design of the activity workflows in the Been There, Done That! application.

Determining Screen-Specific Game Features

Now it's time to define the basic features of each activity in the Been There, Done That! application.

Defining Splash Screen Features

The splash screen serves as the initial entry point for the Been There, Done That! game. Its functionality should be encapsulated within the QuizSplashActivity class. This screen should do the following:

▶ Display the name and version of the application

▶ Display an interesting graphic or logo for the game

▶ Transition automatically to the main menu screen after a period of time

Figure 6.2 shows a mockup of the splash screen.

FIGURE 6.2
The Been There, Done That! splash screen.

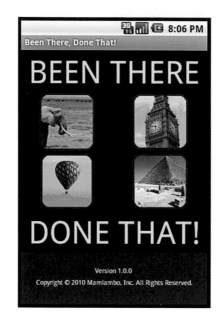

Defining Main Menu Screen Features

The main menu screen serves as the main navigational screen in the game. This screen displays after the splash screen and requires the user to choose where to go next. Its functionality should be encapsulated within the `QuizMenuActivity` class. This screen should do the following:

- Automatically display after the splash screen
- Allow the user to choose Play Game, Settings, Scores, or Help

Figure 6.3 shows a mockup of the main menu screen.

Defining Help Screen Features

The help screen tells the user how to play the game. Its functionality should be encapsulated within the `QuizHelpActivity` class. This screen should do the following:

- Display help text to the user and enable the user to scroll through text
- Provide a method for the user to suggest new questions

FIGURE 6.3
The Been There,
Done That!
main menu
screen.

Figure 6.4 shows a mockup of the help screen.

FIGURE 6.4
The Been There,
Done That! help
screen.

Defining Scores Screen Features

The scores screen allows the user to view game scores. Its functionality should be encapsulated within the QuizScoresActivity class. This screen should do the following:

▶ Display top score statistics

▶ Show the latest score if the user is coming from the game screen

Figure 6.5 shows a mockup of the scores screen.

FIGURE 6.5
The Been There,
Done That!
scores screen.

Defining Settings Screen Features

The settings screen allows users to edit and save game settings, including username and other important features. Its functionality should be encapsulated within the QuizSettingsActivity class. This screen should do the following:

▶ Allow the user to input game settings

▶ Allow the user to invite friends to play

Figure 6.6 shows a mockup of the basic settings screen.

FIGURE 6.6
The Been There, Done That! settings screen.

Defining Game Screen Features

The game screen displays the trivia quiz. Its functionality should be encapsulated within the `QuizGameActivity` class. This screen should do the following:

▶ Display a series of yes/no questions

▶ Handle input and keep score and state of the quiz

▶ Transition to the scores screen when the user is finished playing

Figure 6.7 shows a mockup of the game screen.

Implementing an Application Prototype

Now that you have a rough idea what the Been There, Done That! application will do and how it will look, it's time to start coding. This involves the following steps:

1. Creating a new Android project in Eclipse

2. Adding some project resources, including strings and graphics

3. Creating a layout for each screen

4. Implementing an activity for each screen

5. Creating a set of application-wide preferences

The code for this project is available on the book website,
http://www.informit.com/title/9780321673350.

Creating a New Android Project

You can begin creating a new Android project for your application by using the Eclipse Android project wizard.

The project has the following settings:

- ▶ Project name: TriviaQuiz

- ▶ Build target: Android 2.1 + Google APIs

- ▶ Application name: Been There, Done That!

- ▶ Package name: com.androidbook.triviaquiz

- ▶ Create activity: QuizSplashActivity

Using these settings, you can create the basic Android project. However, you need to make a few adjustments.

Did you Know?

> In the code provided with this book (available at http://www.informit.com/title/9780321673350), the package names contain the hour number of the project they represent. For example, the package name for this hour is com.android-book.triviaquiz6. This allows the projects to coexist on the handset and makes it easier to load all of them at once.

Adding Project Resources

The Been There, Done That! project requires some additional resources. Specifically, you need to add a Layout file for each activity and a text string for each activity name, and you need to change the application icon to something more appropriate.

Adding String Resources

First, you modify the strings.xml resource file. You delete the hello string and create six new string resources—one for each screen. For example, you should create a string called help with a value of "Help Screen". When you are done, the strings.xml file should look like this:

```xml
<?xml version="1.0" encoding="utf-8"?>
<resources>
    <string
        name="app_name">Been There, Done That!</string>
    <string
        name="help">Help Screen</string>
    <string
        name="menu">Main Menu Screen</string>
    <string
```

```
        name="splash">Splash Screen</string>
    <string
        name="settings">Settings Screen</string>
    <string
        name="game">Game Screen</string>
    <string
        name="scores">Scores Screen</string>
</resources>
```

Adding Layout Resources

Next, you need layout files to match each activity you will be creating. First, you rename the main.xml layout splash.xml. Then you copy the splash.xml file five more times, resulting in one layout for each activity: game.xml, help.xml, menu.xml, scores.xml, and settings.xml.

You may notice that there is an error in each Layout file. This is because the TextView control in the layout refers to the @string/hello string, which no longer exists. For each layout file, you need to use the Eclipse layout editor to change the String resource loaded by the TextView control. For example, game.xml needs to replace the reference to @string/hello with the new string you created called @string/game. Now when each layout loads, it displays the screen it is supposed to represent.

Adding Drawable Resources

While you are adding resources, you should change the icon for your application to something more appropriate. Starting with a nice public domain image of Earth from NASA, you can create a 48×48 pixel PNG file called quizicon.png and add this resource file to the /drawable resource directory. Then you can delete the icon.png file used by default.

Did you Know?

> In the project code for this chapter, and future chapters, you will see that there is only a single drawable resource directory named /drawable. Whenever the Android system goes about picking a drawable resource, it only looks in this directory instead of the three default directories, /drawable-ldpi, /drawable-mdpi, and /drawable-hdpi. For this book, the icon quizicon.png file contains the hour number to differentiate each project visually.

Implementing Application Activities

To implement a base Activity class, you simply copy the source file called QuizSplashActivity.java. Then you create a new class file called QuizActivity. This class should look very simple for now:

```
package com.androidbook.triviaquiz6;
import android.app.Activity;
public class QuizActivity extends Activity {
    public static final String GAME_PREFERENCES = "GamePrefs";
}
```

You will add to this class later. Next, you update the QuizSplashActivity class to extend from the QuizActivity class instead of directly from the Activity class.

Creating the Rest of the Application Activities

You can copy the QuizSplashActivity five more times, once for each activity you need: QuizMenuActivity, QuizHelpActivity, QuizScoresActivity, QuizSettingsActivity, and QuizGameActivity.

Note the handy way that Eclipse updates the class name when you copy a class file. You can also create class files by right-clicking the package name com.android-book.triviaquiz and choosing New Class. Eclipse presents a dialog where you can fill in class file settings.

> For more tips on working with Eclipse, check out Appendix B, "Eclipse IDE Tips and Tricks."

By the Way

Note that there is an error in each Java file. This is because each activity is trying to load the main.xml layout file, which no longer exists. You need to modify each class to load the specific layout associated with the activity. For example, in the QuizHelpActivity class, you modify the setContentView() method to load the layout file you created for the help screen as follows:

```
setContentView(R.layout.help);
```

You make similar changes to the other activity files, such that each call to setContentView() loads the corresponding layout file.

Updating the Android Manifest File

You now need to make some changes to the Android manifest file. First, you modify the application icon resource to point at the @drawable/quizicon icon you created. Second, you need to register all your new activities in the manifest file so they will run properly. Finally, you set the Debuggable application attribute to true and verify that you have QuizSplashActivity set as the default activity to launch.

For the book code, we've only created a single icon. However, even if you've created three differently sized icons and placed them in the three default directories (/drawable-ldpi, /drawable-mpi, and /drawable-hdpi), only a single reference to the icon is required. Just make sure all of the icons are named exactly the same. This allows the Android system to choose the most appropriate one for the hardware the application is running on.

Creating Application Preferences

The Been There, Done That! trivia game needs a simple way to store some basic state information and user data. You can use Android's shared preferences (android.content.SharedPreferences) to add this functionality.

You can access shared preferences, by name, from any activity within the application. Therefore, declare the name of your set of preferences in the base class QuizActivity so that they are easily accessible to all subclasses:

```
public static final String GAME_PREFERENCES = "GamePrefs";
```

There is no limit to the number of sets of shared preferences you can create. You can use the preference name string to divide preferences into categories, such as game preferences and user preferences. How you organize shared preferences is up to you.

To add shared preferences to the application, take the following steps:

1. Use the getSharedPreferences() method to retrieve an instance of a SharedPreferences object.

2. Create a SharedPreferences.Editor object to modify preferences.

3. Make changes to the preferences by using the editor.

4. Commit the changes by using the commit() method in the editor.

Saving Specific Shared Preferences

Each preference is stored as a key/value pair. Preference values can be the following types:

▶ Boolean

▶ Float

▶ Integer

- ► Long

- ► String

After you have decided what preferences you want to save, you need to get an instance of the SharedPreferences object and use the Editor object to make the changes and commit them. In the following example, you save two preferences—the user's name and age:

```
import android.content.SharedPreferences;
// ...
SharedPreferences settings =
    getSharedPreferences(GAME_PREFERENCES, MODE_PRIVATE);
SharedPreferences.Editor prefEditor = settings.edit();
prefEditor.putString("UserName", "JaneDoe");
prefEditor.putInt("UserAge", 22);
prefEditor.commit();
```

You can also use the shared preferences editor to clear all preferences, using the clear() method, and to remove specific preferences by name, using the remove() method.

Retrieving Shared Preferences

Retrieving shared preference values is even simpler than creating them because you don't need an editor. The following example shows how to retrieve shared preference values:

```
SharedPreferences settings =
    getSharedPreferences(GAME_PREFERENCES, MODE_PRIVATE);
if (settings.contains("UserName") == true) {
    // We have a user name
    String user = Settings.getString("UserName", "Default");
}
```

You can use the SharedPreferences object to check for a preference by name, retrieve strongly typed preferences, or retrieve all the preferences and store them in a map.

Although you have no immediate needs for shared preferences yet in Been There, Done That! you now have the infrastructure set up to use them as you need them within all the application activities. This will be handy when you begin to implement each activity later in the book.

Running the Game Prototype

You are almost ready to run and test your application. But first, you need to create a debug configuration for your new project within Eclipse.

Creating a Debug Configuration   *Page 17*

You need to create a debug configuration for each project within Eclipse. Be sure to set the preferred AVD for the project to one that is compatible with the Google APIs (API Level 7). If you do not have one configured (or are unsure), simply click the Android SDK and AVD Manager button in Eclipse. From here, you can determine which AVDs are appropriate for the application and create new ones, as necessary.

Launching the Prototype in the Emulator

It's time to launch the Been There, Done That! application in the Android emulator. You can do this by using the little bug icon in Eclipse or by clicking the Run button on the debug configuration you just created.

As you can see in Figure 6.8, the application does very little so far. It has a pretty icon, which a user can click to launch the default activity, QuizSplashActivity. This activity displays its TextView control, informing you that you have reached the splash screen. There is no real user interface yet for the application, and you still need to wire up the transitions between the different activities. However, you now have a framework to build on. In the next few hours, you will flesh out the different screens and begin to implement game functionality.

FIGURE 6.8
The prototype for Been There, Done That! in the application drawer.

Exploring the Prototype Installation

The Been There, Done That! application does very little so far, but you can use tools on the Android emulator to peek at all you've done so far:

▶ **Application Manager**—This is helpful for determining interesting information about an application. In the emulator, navigate to the home screen, click the Menu button and choose Settings, Applications, Manage Applications and then choose the Been There, Done That! item from the list of applications. Here you can see some basic information about the application, including storage and permissions used, as well as information about the cache and so on.

▶ **Dev Tools**—This tool helps you inspect the application in more detail. In the emulator, pull up the application drawer, launch the Dev Tools application, and choose Package Browser. Navigate to the package name `com.androidbook.triviaquiz`. This tool reads information out of the manifest and allows you to inspect the settings of each activity registered.

Of course, you can also begin to investigate the application by using the DDMS perspective of Eclipse. For example, you could check out the application directory for the `com.androidbook.triviaquiz` package on the Android file system. You could also step through the code of `QuizSplashActivity`.

Summary

In this hour, you built a basic prototype on which you can build in subsequent chapters. You designed a prototype and defined its requirements in some detail. Then you created a new Android project, configured it, and created an activity for each screen. You also added custom layouts and implemented shared preferences for the application.

Q&A

Q. *What class might you inherit from to provide an application with consistent shared components?*

A. By creating your own shared `Activity` base class, you can implement behavior that will exist within each screen.

Q. *Can an activity have its own preferences?*

A. Yes, preferences can be shared among activities, and an activity can have its own preferences. To access shared preferences, use the `getSharedPreferences()` method. To access activity-level preferences, use the `getPreferences()` method.

Q. *What two things need to be configured before you can run and debug an Android application in Eclipse?*

A. You need to have configured both an AVD and the debug configuration. Then you can easily launch your application straight from Eclipse for debugging and testing.

Workshop

Quiz

1. True or False: The Been There, Done That! application has three activities.

2. What data types are supported within application shared preferences?

   A. Boolean, Float, Integer, Long, and String

   B. Boolean, Integer, and String

   C. All types that are available in Java

3. True or False: You only need to put your base activity class (for example, `QuizActivity`) in the Android manifest file.

Answers

1. False. The Been There, Done That! application has an activity for each screen. It also has a base class activity, from which all other activities are derived. The design has seven total activity classes.

2. A. Boolean, Float, Integer, Long, and String preferences are possible.

3. False. Each activity needs its own entry in the Android manifest file.

Exercises

1. Add a preference to the application preferences called lastLaunch. Have the QuizSplashActivity read and save the current time each time the onCreate() method is called. When this preference is read, log it using the Log.i() method.

2. Create a set of activity-level preferences for QuizSettingsActivity, using the getPreferences() method instead of the getSharedPreferences() method.

HOUR 7

Implementing an Animated Splash Screen

What You'll Learn in This Hour:

▶ Designing a splash screen
▶ Updating the splash screen layout
▶ Working with animation

In this hour, we focus on implementing the splash screen of the Been There, Done That! application. After roughly sketching the screen design, you can determine exactly what Android View controls you need to implement the splash.xml layout file. When you are satisfied with the screen layout, you can add some tweened animations to give the splash screen some pizzazz. Finally, you need to make sure to transition from the splash screen to the main menu screen smoothly after your animations have completed.

Designing the Splash Screen

You'll implement the Been There, Done That! application from the ground up, beginning with the screen users see first: the splash screen. Recall from Hour 6, "Designing an Application Framework," that you had several requirements for this screen. Specifically, the screen should display some information about the application (title and version information) in a visually appealing way and then, after some short period of time, automatically move on to the main menu screen. Figure 7.1 provides a rough design for the splash screen.

FIGURE 7.1
Rough design
for the Been
There, Done
That! splash
screen.

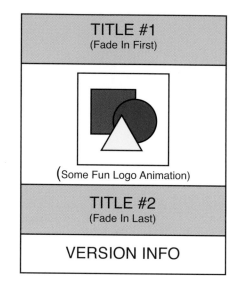

For the time being, you will focus on designing the splash screen in portrait mode, but you will try to avoid making the porting effort difficult for landscape or square orientations. With the simple design of the splash screen, you can be confident that the elements can scale reasonably well to other orientations, provided that you tweak font and graphic sizes later. Porting issues is discussed in a future chapter.

Implementing the Splash Screen Layout

Now that you know how your splash screen should look, you need to translate the rough design into the appropriate layout design. Recall that the /res/layout/ splash.xml layout file is used by QuizSplashActivity. You need to update the default layout, which simply displays a single TextView control (informing us it is the splash screen) to contain controls for each of the elements in the rough design.

Screen layout controls come in many forms. Each control is a rectangle that can control a specific part of the screen. You are using two common screen controls on your splash screen:

► A TextView control displays a text string onscreen.

► An ImageView control displays a graphic onscreen.

You also need some way to organize various View controls on the screen in an orderly fashion. For this, you use Layout controls. For example, LinearLayout allows placement of child views in a vertical or horizontal stack.

In addition to LinearLayout, there are a number of other Layout controls. Layouts may be nested and control only part of the screen, or they may control the entire screen. It is quite common for a screen to be encapsulated in one large parent layout—often a LinearLayout control. Table 7.1 lists the available Layout controls.

TABLE 7.1   Common Layout Controls

Layout Control Name	Description	Key Attributes/Elements
LinearLayout	Each child view is placed after the previous one, in a single row or column.	Orientation (vertical or horizontal).
RelativeLayout	Each child view is placed in relation to the other views in the layout, or relative to the edges of the parent layout.	Many alignment attributes to control where a child view is positioned relative to other child View controls.
FrameLayout	Each child view is stacked within the frame, relative to the top-left corner. View controls may overlap.	The order of placement of child View controls is important, when used with appropriate gravity settings.
TableLayout	Each child view is a cell in a grid of rows and columns.	Each row requires a TableRow element.

> As of Android 1.5 SDK, the AbsoluteLayout control, which requires specific X/Y values, was deprecated yet has remained available for use. Although this control is not recommended for use, occasionally having exact X/Y sizing control can be useful for specific kinds of layouts that require pixel-perfect precision. The SDK's own WebView control uses this layout.

By the Way

Layouts and their child View controls have certain attributes that help control their behavior. For example, all layouts share the attributes android:layout_width and android:layout_height, which control how wide and high an item is. These attribute values can be dimensions, such as a number of pixels, or use a more flexible approach: fill_parent or wrap_content. Using fill_parent instructs a layout to scale to the size of the parent layout, and using wrap_content "shrink wraps" the child View control within the parent, giving it only the space of the child View control's dimensions. A number of other interesting properties can be used to control specific layout behavior, including margin settings and type-specific layout attributes.

Let's use a `TableLayout` control to display some `ImageView` controls as part of the splash screen.

In the splash screen design, you can use a vertical `LinearLayout` control to organize the screen elements, which are, in order, a `TextView` control, a `TableLayout` control with some `TableRow` control elements of `ImageView` controls, and then two more `TextView` controls. Figure 7.2 shows the layout design of the splash screen.

FIGURE 7.2
Layout design for the Been There, Done That! splash screen.

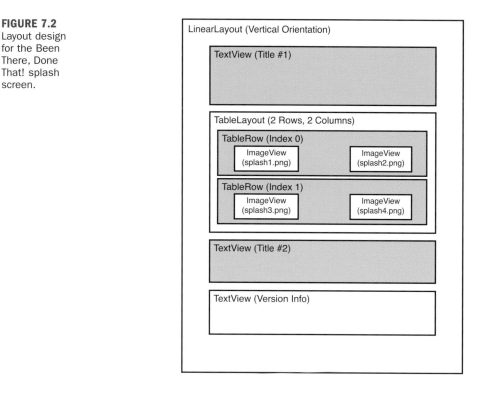

LinearLayout (Vertical Orientation)

TextView (Title #1)

TableLayout (2 Rows, 2 Columns)

TableRow (Index 0)

ImageView (splash1.png) ImageView (splash2.png)

TableRow (Index 1)

ImageView (splash3.png) ImageView (splash4.png)

TextView (Title #2)

TextView (Version Info)

Adding New Project Resources

Now that you have your layout design for the splash screen, you need to create the string, color, and dimension resources to use within the layout.

You begin by adding four new graphic resources to the `/res/drawable` directory (creating the directory, if necessary): `splash1.png`, `splash2.png`, `splash3.png`, and `splash4.png`. These graphics will be displayed in the `TableLayout` control in the center of the splash screen.

The code for this project is available on the book website, http://www.informit.com/title/9780321673350.

Then you can add three new strings to the /res/values/strings.xml resource file: one for the top title (Been There), one for the bottom title (Done That!), and one for some version information (multiple lines). Technically, you can now remove the splash string because you will no longer be using it.

Next, you create a new resource file called /res/values/colors.xml to contain the three color resources you need: one for the title text color (a golden yellow), one for the version text color (grayish white), and one for the version text background color (deep blue).

Because you will be setting the overall background color of the splash screen to black, you do not need to create a special resource. Instead, you just use the built-in Android resource @android:color/black.

Did you Know?

Finally, you need to create some dimension resources in a new resource file called /res/values/dimens.xml. You create three new dimension values: one to control the title font size (24pt), one to control the version text font size (5pt), and one to allow for nice line spacing between the lines of the version text (3pt).

After you have saved the resource files, you can begin to use your new resources in the splash.xml layout resource file.

Updating the Splash Screen Layout

You could modify the existing splash.xml layout, but it is sometimes easier to start from scratch by using the Eclipse layout resource editor to remove all existing controls. You then take the following steps to generate the layout you want, based on your intended layout design:

1. Begin by adding a new LinearLayout control and setting its background attribute to @android:color/black and its orientation to vertical. All subsequent controls will be added inside the LinearLayout control. It's often easiest to use the Outline view of Eclipse to add View controls within one another or move them around.

2. Add a TextView control called TextViewTopTitle. Set layout_width to fill_parent and layout_height to wrap_content. Set the control's text attribute to the string resource, its textColor attribute to the yellow color resource, and its textSize to the dimension resource you created.

3. Add a TableLayout control called TableLayout01. Set layout_width to fill_parent and layout_height to wrap_content. Also, set the stretchColumns attribute to *, to stretch any column, as necessary, to fit the screen.

4. Within the `TableLayout` control add a `TableRow` control. Within the `TableRow` control add two `ImageView` controls. For the first `ImageView` control, set the `src` attribute to the `splash1.png` drawable resource `@drawable/splash1`. Add a second `ImageView` control and set its `src` attribute to the `splash2.png` resource file.

5. Repeat step 4, creating a second `TableRow` control. Again, add `ImageView` controls for `splash3.png` and `splash4.png`.

6. Much as in step 2, add another `TextView` control called `TextViewBottomTitle` within the parent `LinearLayout`. Set its `layout_width` attribute to `fill_parent` and `layout_height` to `wrap_content`. Set its `text` attribute to the appropriate string, its `textColor` attribute to the yellow color, and its `textSize` attribute to the dimension resource you created.

7. For the version information, create one last `TextView` control, called `TextViewBottomVersion`. Set its `layout_width` attribute to `fill_parent` and `layout_height` to `fill_parent`. Set its `text` attribute to the appropriate string, its `textColor` attribute to the grayish color, and its `textSize` attribute to the dimension resource you created earlier. Also, set its `background` attribute to the color resource (dark blue) and `lineSpacingExtra` to the spacing dimension resource value you created.

8. Tweak the `layout_gravity` and `gravity` settings on the various controls until you think the layout looks reasonable in the Eclipse resource editor preview.

At this point, save the `splash.xml` layout file and run the Been There, Done That! application in the Android emulator. The Splash screen should look as shown in Figure 7.3.

You could stop here, except that your splash screen still lacks pizzazz. Also, you need some way to transition from the splash screen to the main menu screen.

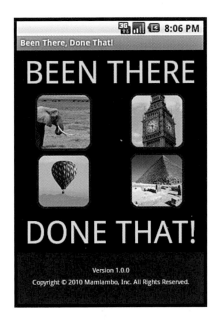

FIGURE 7.3
The Been There,
Done That!
splash screen.

Working with Animation

One great way to add zing to your splash screen would be to add some animation. The Android platform supports four types of graphics animation:

▶ **Animated GIF images**—Animated GIFs are self-contained graphics files with multiple frames.

▶ **Frame-by-frame animation**—The Android SDK provides a similar mechanism for frame-by-frame animation in which the developer supplies the individual graphic frames and transitions between them (see the AnimationDrawable class).

▶ **Tweened animation**—Tweened animation is a simple and flexible method of defining specific animation operations that can then be applied to any view or layout.

▶ **OpenGL ES**—Android's OpenGL ES API provides advanced three-dimensional drawing, animation, lighting, and texturing capabilities.

For your application, the tweened animation makes the most sense. Android provides tweening support for alpha (transparency), rotation, scaling, and translating (moving) animations. You can create sets of animation operations do be done simultaneously, in a timed sequence, and after a delay. Thus, tweened animation is a perfect choice for your splash screen.

With tweened animation, you create an animation sequence, either programmatically or by creating animation resources in the /res/anim directory. Each animation sequence needs its own XML file, but the animation may be applied to any number of View controls.

> You can use the built-in animations provided in the android.R.anim class.

Adding Animation Resources

For your splash screen, you need to create three custom animations in XML and save them to the /res/anim resource directory: fade_in.xml, fade_in2.xml, and custom_anim.xml.

The first animation, fade_in.xml, simply fades its target from an alpha value of 0 (transparent) to an alpha value of 1 (opaque) over the course of 2500 milliseconds, or 2.5 seconds. There is no built-in animation editor in Eclipse. The XML for the fade_in.xml animation looks like this:

```xml
<?xml version="1.0" encoding="utf-8" ?>
<set
    xmlns:android="http://schemas.android.com/apk/res/android"
    android:shareInterpolator="false">
    <alpha
        android:fromAlpha="0.0"
        android:toAlpha="1.0"
        android:duration="2500">
    </alpha>
</set>
```

You can apply this animation to the top TextView control with your title text.

Next, you create the fade_in2.xml animation. This animation does exactly the same thing as the fade_in animation, except that you set the startOffset attribute to 2500 milliseconds. This means that this animation will actually take 5 seconds total: It waits 2.5 seconds and then fades in for 2.5 seconds. Because 5 seconds is long enough to display the splash screen, you should plan to listen for fade_in2 to complete and then transition to the main menu screen.

Finally, you need some fun animation sequence for the TableLayout graphics. In this case, your animation set contains multiple, simultaneous operations: a rotation, some scaling, and an alpha transition. As a result, the target View spins into existence. The custom_anim.xml file looks like this:

```xml
<?xml version="1.0" encoding="utf-8" ?>
<set
    xmlns:android="http://schemas.android.com/apk/res/android"
    android:shareInterpolator="false">
    <rotate
        android:fromDegrees="0"
        android:toDegrees="360"
        android:pivotX="50%"
        android:pivotY="50%"
        android:duration="2000" />
    <alpha
        android:fromAlpha="0.0"
        android:toAlpha="1.0"
        android:duration="2000">
    </alpha>
    <scale
        android:pivotX="50%"
        android:pivotY="50%"
        android:fromXScale=".1"
        android:fromYScale=".1"
        android:toXScale="1.0"
        android:toYScale="1.0"
        android:duration="2000" />
</set>
```

As you can see, the rotation operation takes 2 seconds to rotate from 0 to 360 degrees, pivoting around the center of the view. The alpha operation should look familiar; it simply fades in over the same 2-second period. Finally, the scale operation scales from 10% to 100% over the same 2-second period. This entire animation takes 2 seconds to complete.

After you have saved all three of your animation files, you can begin to apply the animations to specific views.

Animating Specific Views

Animations must be applied and managed programmatically. Remember, costly operations, such as animations, should be stopped if the application is paused for some reason. The animation can resume when the application comes back into the foreground.

Let's start with a simplest case: applying the fade_in animation to your title TextView control, called TextViewTopTitle. All you need to do is retrieve an instance of your TextView control in the onCreate() method of the QuizSplashActivity class, load the animation resource into an Animation object, and call the startAnimation() method of the TextView control:

```java
TextView logo1 = (TextView) findViewById(R.id.TextViewTopTitle);
Animation fade1 = AnimationUtils.loadAnimation(this, R.anim.fade_in);
logo1.startAnimation(fade1);
```

When an animation must be stopped—for instance, in the `onPause()` method of the activity—you simply call the `clearAnimation()` method. For instance, the following onPause() method demonstrates this for the corner logos:

```
@Override
protected void onPause() {
    super.onPause();
    // Stop the animation
    TextView logo1 = (TextView) findViewById(R.id.TextViewTopTitle);
    logo1.clearAnimation();

    TextView logo2 = (TextView) findViewById(R.id.TextViewBottomTitle);
    logo2.clearAnimation();

    // ... stop other animations
}
```

Animating All Views in a Layout

In addition to applying animations to individual `View` controls, you can also apply them to each child `View` control within a Layout (such as `TableLayout` and each `TableRow`), using `LayoutAnimationController`.

To animate `View` controls in this fashion, you must load the animation, create `LayoutAnimationController`, configure it as necessary, and then call the layout's `setLayoutAnimation()` method. For example, the following code loads the cus - tom_anim animation, creates a `LayoutAnimationController`, and then applies it to each `TableRow` in the `TableLayout` control:

```
Animation spinin = AnimationUtils.loadAnimation(this, R.anim.custom_anim);
LayoutAnimationController controller =
    new LayoutAnimationController(spinin);
TableLayout table = (TableLayout) findViewById(R.id.TableLayout01);
for (int i = 0; i < table.getChildCount(); i++) {
    TableRow row = (TableRow) table.getChildAt(i);
    row.setLayoutAnimation(controller);
}
```

There is no need to call any `startAnimation()` method in this case because `LayoutAnimationController` handles that for you. Using this method, the animation is applied to each child view, but each starts at a different time. (The default is 50% of the duration of the animation—which, in this case, would be 1 second.) This gives you the nice effect of each `ImageView` spinning into existence in a cascading fashion.

Stopping `LayoutAnimationController` animations is no different from stopping individual animations: You simply use the `clearAnimation()` method. The additional lines to do this in the existing onPause() method are shown here:

```
TableLayout table = (TableLayout) findViewById(R.id.TableLayout01);
for (int i = 0; i < table.getChildCount(); i++) {
    TableRow row = (TableRow) table.getChildAt(i);
    row.clearAnimation();
}
```

Handling Animation Life Cycle Events

Now that you are happy with your animations, you just need to make
QuizSplashActivity transition to QuizMenuActivity when the animations
are complete. To do this, you create a new Intent control to launch the
QuizMenuActivity class and call the startActivity() method. You should also
call the finish() method of QuizSplashActivity because you do not want to keep
this activity on the stack (that is, you do not want the Back button to return to this
screen).

Of your animations, the fade_in2 animation takes the longest, at 5 seconds total.
This animation is therefore the one you want to trigger your transition upon. You do
so by creating an AnimationListener object, which has callbacks for the animation
life cycle events: start, end, and repeat. In this case, only the onAnimationEnd()
method has an interesting implementation. Here is the code to create the
AnimationListener and implement the onAnimationEnd() callback:

```
Animation fade2 = AnimationUtils.loadAnimation(this, R.anim.fade_in2);
fade2.setAnimationListener(new AnimationListener() {
    public void onAnimationEnd(Animation animation) {
        startActivity(new Intent(QuizSplashActivity.this,
            QuizMenuActivity.class));
        QuizSplashActivity.this.finish();
    }
});
```

Now if you run the Been There, Done That! application again, either on the emulator or on the handset, you see some nice animation on the splash screen. The user
then transitions smoothly to the main menu screen, which is the next screen on
your to-do list.

Summary

Congratulations! You've now implemented the first screen of the Been There, Done
That! trivia quiz. In this hour, you designed a screen and then identified the appropriate layout and View components needed to implement your design. After you
included the appropriate resources, you were able to configure the splash.xml layout file. Finally, you added some tweened animations to the screen and then handled the transition between QuizSplashActivity and QuizMenuActivity.

Q&A

Q. *How well does the Android platform perform with regard to animation?*

A. The Android platform has reasonable performance with animations. However, it is very easy to overload a screen with animations and other controls. For example, if you were to place a `VideoView` control in the middle of the screen with all the animations, you might see distinct performance issues. Always test operations, such as animations, on a handset to be sure your implementation is feasible.

Q. *Why did you iterate through each child view of the* `TableLayout` *control instead of accessing each* `TableRow` *control (*`R.id.TableRow01` *and* `R.id.TableRow02`*) by name?*

A. It would be perfectly acceptable to access each `TableRow` element by name if each one is guaranteed to exist in all cases. You will be able to take advantage of this iterative approach later, when you port your project to different screen orientations. For now, the Splash screen draws well only in portrait mode.

Q. *What would happen if you applied* `LayoutAnimationController` *to* `TableLayout` *instead of each* `TableRow`*?*

A. If you applied `LayoutAnimationController` to `TableLayout`, each `TableRow` control—instead of each `ImageView` control—would spin into existence. It would be a different, less visually appealing, effect.

Workshop

Quiz

1. True or False: There is no way to stop an animation once it has started.

2. What types of operations are supported with tweened animation?

   A. Transparency, motion, and 3D rotation

   B. Alpha, scale, rotate, and translate

   C. Dance, sing, and be merry

3. True or False: `LinearLayout` can be used to allow all child `View` objects to draw above and below each other (vertical).

4. Which of these is not a built-in layout in the Android SDK?

   A. FrameLayout

   B. CircleLayout

   C. HorizontalLayout

   D. RelativeLayout

Answers

1. False. Use the clearAnimation() method to clear all pending and executing animations on a given view.

2. B. Tweened animation can include any combination of alpha transitions (transparency), scaling (growth or shrinking), two-dimensional rotation, and translation (moving) from one point to another.

3. True. In addition, LinearLayout can be used for all child View objects to draw to the left and right of each other (horizontal).

4. B and C. FrameLayout and RelativeLayout are both included in the Android SDK.

Exercises

1. Modify LayoutAnimationController to apply animations of each child view within a TableRow control in random order by using the setOrder() method with a value of 2 (random).

2. Modify LayoutAnimationController to apply animations to each child view within a TableLayout control instead of each TableRow control. View the resulting animation.

3. Modify the splash screen layout to play a short video instead of animating the ImageView controls. First replace the TableLayout control with a VideoView control. Then set the URI of VideoView to the URL of a web video in the appropriate format, using the Uri.parse() method and the VideoView control's setVideoURI() method. Finally, remove AnimationListener and use a VideoView control's OnCompletionListener instead to transition to the main menu screen when the video completes.

HOUR 8

Implementing the Main Menu Screen

What You'll Learn in This Hour:

▶ Designing the main menu screen

▶ Implementing the main menu screen layout

▶ Working with `ListView` controls

▶ Working with other menu types

In this hour, you learn about some of the different menu mechanisms available in Android. You begin by implementing the main menu screen of the Been There, Done That! application, using new controls, such as `ListView` and `RelativeLayout`. You then learn about other screens that can benefit from special types of menus, such as the options menu.

Designing the Main Menu Screen

To design the main menu screen, you begin by roughly sketching what you want it to look like. If you review the screen requirements, you see that this screen provides essential navigation for the rest of the application. Users can choose from four different options: play the game, review the help, configure the settings, or view the high scores. Figure 8.1 shows a rough design of the main menu screen.

FIGURE 8.1
Rough design
for the Been
There, Done
That! main
menu screen.

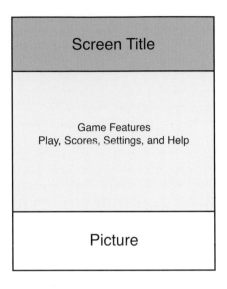

There are a number of different ways you could implement the main menu screen. For example, you could create a button for each option, listen for clicks, and funnel the user to the appropriate screen. However, if the number of options grows, this method would not scale well. Therefore, a list of the options, in the form of a `ListView` control, is more appropriate. This way, if the list becomes longer than the screen, you have built-in scrolling capability.

In addition to the screen layout, you want the main menu screen to have some bells and whistles. You begin with the default behavior of each layout control and then add some custom flair to those controls. For example, you could add a nice background image behind the entire screen and add a custom selection graphic to the `ListView` control.

Finally, you wire up the `ListView` control to ensure that when a user clicks on a specific list option, he or she is taken to the appropriate screen. This will allow users to easily access the rest of the screens you need to implement within the Been There, Done That! application.

Determining Main Menu Screen Layout Requirements

Now that you know how you want your main menu screen to look, you need to translate your rough design into the appropriate layout design. In this case, you need to update the /res/layout/menu.xml layout file that is used by QuizMenuActivity. In the case of the main menu layout, you want some sort of header, followed by a ListView control and then an ImageView control.

Building the Screen Header with RelativeLayout

You know you want to display a TextView control for the screen title in the header. Wouldn't it be nice if you also included graphics on each side of the TextView control? This is a perfect time to try out RelativeLayout, which allows each child view to be placed in relation to the parent layout or other child view controls. Therefore, you can easily describe the header as a RelativeLayout control with three child layouts:

- An ImageView control aligned to the top left of the parent control
- A TextView control aligned to the top center of the parent control
- An ImageView control aligned to the top right of the parent control

Adding the ListView Control

Next in your layout, you include the ListView control. A ListView control is simply a container that holds a list of View objects. The default is for a ListView control to contain TextView controls, but ListView controls may contain many different View controls.

A ListView control of TextView controls works fine for this example. To override the default behavior of each child TextView, you need to make a layout resource to act as the template for each TextView control in the ListView control. Also, you can make the menu more interesting by adding a custom divider and selector to the ListView control.

Finishing Touches for the Main Menu Layout

You finish off the layout by adding the `ImageView` control after the `ListView` control. As before, you need to wrap your screen in a vertically oriented `LinearLayout` control so that the `RelativeLayout`, `ListView`, and `ImageView` controls are shown in a top-down fashion. Figure 8.2 shows the layout design of the main menu screen.

FIGURE 8.2
Layout design for the Been There, Done That! main menu screen.

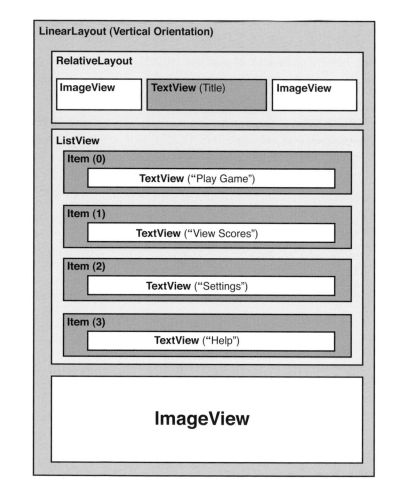

Implementing the Main Menu Screen Layout

To implement the main menu screen, you begin by adding new resources to the project. Then you must update the `menu.xml` layout resource to reflect the main menu screen design.

Adding New Project Resources

Now that you have your layout designed, you need to create the drawable, string, color, and dimension resources you will use in the layouts used by the main menu screen.

You begin by adding four new graphic resources to the `/res/drawable` directory: `bkgrnd.jpg`, `divider.png`, `half.png`, and `textured.png`. LinearLayout will use the `bkgrnd.jpg` graphic file as the background image. The ListView control will use the `divider.png` and `textured.png` graphics for the custom divider and selector, respectively. The ImageView control will use the `half.png` graphic at the bottom of the screen.

You continue by adding and modifying several new strings in the `/res/values/strings.xml` resource file so that you have a string for each menu option, as well as one for the title TextView control.

Finally, update the color resources in `/res/menu/colors.xml` to include colors for the screen title TextView attributes as well as the TextView items displayed within the ListView. You should also update the resources in `/res/values/dimens.xml` to include dimensions for the title text and the ListView item text.

For specific resource configurations, you can use the values provided in the book source code as a guide, or configure your own custom values.

After you have saved the resource files, you can begin to use them in the layout resource files used by the main menu screen.

Updating the Main Menu Screen Layouts

Perhaps you have noticed by now that the main menu screen relies on layout resource files—plural. The master layout file, `menu.xml`, defines the layout of the overall screen. You must also create a new layout file template for each item in your ListView control.

Updating the Master Layout

Again, you open the Eclipse layout resource editor and remove all existing controls from the menu.xml layout file. You then follow these steps to generate the layout you want, based on your intended layout design:

1. Add a new LinearLayout control and set its background attribute to @drawable/bkgrnd. All subsequent controls will be added inside this LinearLayout control.

2. Add a RelativeLayout control. Set its layout_width attribute to wrap_content and its layout_height attribute to wrap_content.

3. Within the RelativeLayout control, add an ImageView control. Set the ImageView control's layout_alignParentLeft and layout_alignParentTop attributes to true. Set the image's src attribute to the @drawable/quizicon graphic.

4. Still within the RelativeLayout control, add a TextView control for the title text. Set the TextView control's text, textSize, and textColor attributes to the resources you just created. Then set the layout_centerHorizontal and layout_alignParentTop attributes to true.

Did you Know?

> You can make TextView text "glow" by setting the shadow attributes, including shadowColor, shadowDx, shadowDy, and shadowRadius.

5. Finish the RelativeLayout control by adding one more ImageView control. Set the control's layout_alignParentRight and layout_alignParentTop attributes to true. Set the image's src attribute to the @drawable/quizicon graphic.

6. Next, we must add a second RelativeLayout to hold the ListView and ImageView controls. Start by adding a new RelativeLayout outside of the one we were just working in, but still inside the LinearLayout.

7. Now add the last ImageView control inside this new RelativeLayout. Set its src attribute to the @drawable/half graphic, its layout_width attribute to fill_parent, and its layout_height attribute to fill_parent to ensure that the control fills any space at the bottom of the screen. Additionally, set its layout_alignParentBottom attribute to true and scaleType attribute to fitEnd, so that after it scales it'll still be at the bottom.

8. Now add a `ListView` control called `ListView_Menu` just below the `ImageView`. Set its `layout_width` attribute to `fill_parent` and `layout_height` attribute to `wrap_content`. Additionally, set its `layout_alignParentTop` attribute to `true`. We add this second attribute so the control will draw over the top of the image.

At this point, save the `menu.xml` layout file.

> The Eclipse layout resource editor does not display `ListView` controls in design mode. You must view a `ListView` control by using the Android emulator. In this case, the layout designer does not reflect actual application look and feel.

Watch Out!

Adding the `ListView` Template Layout

You now need to create a new layout called `/res/layout/menu_item.xml` that will serve as a template for your `ListView` items. In this case, the `menu_item.xml` layout file will contain a `TextView` control.

The `TextView` control has all the typical attributes assigned except for one: the text itself. The `text` attribute will be supplied by the `ListView` control. At this point, you can tweak the `TextView` attributes for `textColor` and `textSize`, which you created as color and dimension resources earlier.

The `menu_item.xml` file looks like this:

```
<TextView
    xmlns:android="http://schemas.android.com/apk/res/android"
    android:layout_width="fill_parent"
    android:textSize="@dimen/menu_item_size"
    android:text="test string"
    android:layout_gravity="center_horizontal"
    android:layout_height="wrap_content"
    android:shadowRadius="5"
    android:gravity="center"
    android:textColor="@color/menu_color"
    android:shadowColor="@color/menu_glow"
    android:shadowDy="3"
    android:shadowDx="3" />
```

> It can be helpful to set the `text` attribute to a test string so you can see how the TextView control's attributes look in the Eclipse resource designer. This string will be programmatically overwritten by the `ListView` control.

Did you Know?

At this point, save the `menu_item.xml` layout file.

Working with the `ListView` Control

Now you should switch your focus to the `QuizMenuActivity.java` file. Here you need to flesh out the `ListView` control. First, you need to fill the `ListView` control with content, and then you need to listen for user clicks on specific items in the `ListView` control and send the user to the appropriate screen.

Filling a `ListView` Control

Your `ListView` control needs content. `ListView` controls can be populated from a variety of data sources, including arrays and databases, using data adapters. In this case, you have a fixed list of four items, so a simple `String` array is a reasonable choice for your `ListView` data.

Begin by retrieving an instance of the `ListView` control just after the `setContentView()` method call in the `onCreate()` method of your activity. To populate your `ListView` control, you must first retrieve it by using the `findViewById()` method, as follows:

```
ListView menuList = (ListView) findViewById(R.id.ListView_Menu);
```

Next, you need to define the `String` values you will use to populate the `TextView` items within the `ListView` control. In this case, you will load the four resource strings representing the choices:

```
String[] items = { getResources().getString(R.string.menu_item_play),
        getResources().getString(R.string.menu_item_scores),
        getResources().getString(R.string.menu_item_settings),
        getResources().getString(R.string.menu_item_help) };
```

Now that you have retrieved the `ListView` control and have the data you want to stuff into it, you need to use a data adapter to map the data to the layout template you created (`menu_item.xml`). The choice of adapter depends on the type of data being used. In this case, you use `ArrayAdapter`:

```
ArrayAdapter<String> adapt = new ArrayAdapter<String>(this,
    R.layout.menu_item, items);
```

Next, you need to tell the `ListView` control to use the adapter:

```
menuList.setAdapter(adapt);
```

At this point, you can save the `QuizMenuActivity.java` file and run the Been There, Done That! application in the Android emulator. After the splash screen finishes, the main menu screen should look much like the screen shown in Figure 8.3.

FIGURE 8.3
The Been There,
Done That!
splash screen.

> If you get tired of watching the splash screen appear when you launch the application, simply modify the `AndroidManifest.xml` file to launch `QuizMenuActivity` by default until you are done testing.

Did you Know?

As you can see, the main menu screen is beginning to take shape. However, clicking the menu items doesn't yet have the desired response.

Listening for `ListView` Events

You need to listen for and respond to specific events within the `ListView` control. Although there are a number of events to choose from, you are most interested in the event that occurs when a user clicks an item in the `ListView` control.

To listen for item clicks, you use the `setOnItemClickListener()` method of the `ListView`. Specifically, you implement the `onItemClick()` method of the `AdapterView.OnItemClickListener` class, like this:

```
menuList.setOnItemClickListener(new AdapterView.OnItemClickListener() {
    public void onItemClick(AdapterView<?> parent, View itemClicked,
        int position, long id) {
        TextView textView = (TextView) itemClicked;
        String strText = textView.getText().toString();
        if (strText.equalsIgnoreCase(getResources().getString(
            R.string.menu_item_play))) {
            // Launch the Game Activity
            startActivity(new Intent(QuizMenuActivity.this,
                QuizGameActivity.class));
```

```
        } else if (strText.equalsIgnoreCase(getResources().getString(
                R.string.menu_item_help))) {
            // Launch the Help Activity
            startActivity(new Intent(QuizMenuActivity.this,
                    QuizHelpActivity.class));
        } else if (strText.equalsIgnoreCase(getResources().getString(
                R.string.menu_item_settings))) {
            // Launch the Settings Activity
            startActivity(new Intent(QuizMenuActivity.this,
                    QuizSettingsActivity.class));
        } else if (strText.equalsIgnoreCase(getResources().getString(
                R.string.menu_item_scores))) {
            // Launch the Scores Activity
            startActivity(new Intent(QuizMenuActivity.this,
                    QuizScoresActivity.class));
        }
    }
});
```

The onItemClick() method passes in all the information needed to determine
which item was clicked. In this case, one of the simplest ways is to cast the view
clicked to a TextView control (because you know all items are TextView controls,
although you might want to verify this by using instanceof) and just extract the
specific Text control and map it to the appropriate screen. Another way to determine which item was clicked would be to check the View control's id attribute.

Now if you implement the OnItemClickListener() method and rerun the application in the emulator, you can use the main menu to transition between the screens
in the Been There, Done That! application.

Customizing ListView Control Characteristics

Now you're ready to customize the rather bland (especially for a game menu)
default ListView control with a custom divider and selection graphics. A ListView
control has several parts— a header, the list of items, and a footer. By default, the
ListView control displays no header or footer.

Did you Know?

> If you have a screen with only a ListView control, consider using the
> ListActivity class, which simplifies ListView management.

Adding a Custom Divider

A ListView divider is displayed between each ListView item. The divider attribute
can be either a color or a drawable graphic resource. If a color is specified, then a
horizontal line (whose thickness is configurable) will be displayed between items in
the list. If a drawable graphic resource is used, the graphic will appear between
items. By default, no divider is displayed above the first list item nor below the last.

Adding a Custom Selector

A `ListView` selector indicates which list item is currently selected within the list. The `ListView` selector is controlled by the `listSelector` attribute. The default selector of a `ListView` control is a bright orange band.

Try It Yourself ▼

To add a divider to the `ListView` control, simply open the `menu.xml` layout file and change the `ListView` control's `divider` attribute to the `@drawable/divider` graphic resource (a squiggly yellow line) you added earlier.

Now, add a custom selector to the `ListView` control. To do this, simply open the `menu.xml` layout file and change the `ListView` control's `listSelector` attribute to the `@drawable/textured` graphic resource (a textured orange halo) you added earlier.

▲

If you make the changes to the `ListView` divider and selector and re-launch the Been There, Done That! application in the emulator, the main menu screen should look as shown in Figure 8.4.

FIGURE 8.4
The Been There, Done That! main menu screen with a customized `ListView` control.

Working with Other Menu Types

The Android platform has two other types of useful menu mechanisms:

▶ **Context menus**—A context menu pops up when a user performs a long-click on any `View` object. This type of menu is often used in conjunction with `ListView` controls filled with similar items, such as songs in a playlist. The user can then long-click on a specific song to access a context menu with options such as Play, Delete, and Add to Playlist for that specific song.

▶ **Options menus**—An options menu pops up whenever a user clicks the Menu button on the handset. This type of menu is often used to help the user handle application settings and such.

Because we've been focusing on application screen navigation in this hour, let's consider where these different menus are appropriate in the Been There, Done That! application. This application design lends itself well to an options menu for the game screen, which would enable the user to pause while answering trivia questions to access the settings and help screens easily and then return to the game screen.

Adding an Options Menu to the Game Screen

To add an options menu to the game screen, you need to add a special type of resource called a menu resource. You can then change `QuizGameActivity` class to enable an options menu and handle menu selections.

Adding Menu Resources

For your options menu, you create a menu definition resource in XML and save it to the `/res/menu` resource directory as `gameoptions.xml`.

A menu resource contains a `<menu>` tag followed by a number of `<item>` child elements. Each `<item>` element represents a menu option and has a number of attributes. The following are some commonly used attributes:

▶ `id`—This attribute allows you to easily identify the specific menu item.

▶ `title`—This attribute is the string shown for the options menu item.

▶ `icon`—This is a drawable resource representing the icon for the menu item.

Your options menu will contain only two options: Settings and Help. Therefore, your `gameoptions.xml` menu resource is fairly straightforward:

```xml
<menu
    xmlns:android="http://schemas.android.com/apk/res/android">
    <item
        android:id="@+id/settings_menu_item"
        android:title="@string/menu_item_settings"
        android:icon="@android:drawable/ic_menu_preferences"></item>
    <item
        android:id="@+id/help_menu_item"
        android:title="@string/menu_item_help"
        android:icon="@android:drawable/ic_menu_help"></item>
</menu>
```

built-in drawable resource

You set the `title` attribute of each menu option by using the same `String` resources you used on the main menu screen. Note that instead of adding new drawable resources for the options menu icons, you use built-in drawable resources from the Android SDK to have a common look and feel across applications.

> **Did you Know?**
>
> You can use the built-in drawable resources provided in the `android.R.drawable` class just as you would use resources you include in your application package. If you want to see what each of these shared resources looks like, check the Android SDK installed on your machine. Specifically, browse the `/platforms` directory, choose the appropriate target platform, and check its `/data/res/drawable` directory.

Adding an Options Menu to an Activity

For an options menu to show when the user presses the Menu button on the game screen, you must provide an implementation of the `onCreateOptionsMenu()` method in the `QuizGameActivity` class. Specifically, you need to inflate (load) the menu resource into the options menu and set the appropriate `Intent` information for each menu item. Here is a sample implementation of the `onCreateOptionsMenu()` method for `QuizGameActivity`:

```java
@Override
public boolean onCreateOptionsMenu(Menu menu) {
    super.onCreateOptionsMenu(menu);
    getMenuInflater().inflate(R.menu.gameoptions, menu);
    menu.findItem(R.id.help_menu_item).setIntent(
        new Intent(this, QuizHelpActivity.class));
    menu.findItem(R.id.settings_menu_item).setIntent(
        new Intent(this, QuizSettingsActivity.class));
    return true;
}
```

Handling Options Menu Selections

To listen for when the user launches the options menu and selections a menu option, you implement the onOptionsItemSelected() method of the activity. For example, you start the appropriate activity by extracting the intent from the menu item selected as follows:

```
@Override
public boolean onOptionsItemSelected(MenuItem item) {
    super.onOptionsItemSelected(item);
    startActivity(item.getIntent());
    return true;
}
```

Did you Know?

> The method given here for handling onOptionsItemSelected() works as designed. It's not technically required if the only thing your menu will do is launch the Intent set via the setIntent() method. However, to add any other functionality to each MenuItem requires the implementation of this method.

There you have it: You have created an options menu on the game screen. If you save the class and run the application once more, you will see that you can navigate to the game screen, press the Menu button, and use a fully functional options menu (see Figure 8.5).

FIGURE 8.5
The Been There, Done That! game screen with an options menu.

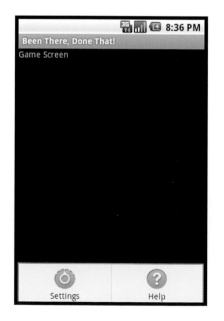

Summary

You've made excellent progress. The main menu screen is now fully functional, and you've learned key skills for developing Android applications, including how to use new layouts such as RelativeLayout, as well as how to use the powerful ListView control. You've also learned about the other types of navigation mechanisms available in Android and implemented an options menu on the game screen.

Q&A

Q. *What is the difference between a* ListView *control's* setOnClickListener() *method and the* setOnItemClickListener() *method?*

A. The setOnClickListener() method listens for a click anywhere in the entire ListView control. The setOnItemClickListener() method listens for a click in a specific View item within the ListView control.

Q. *There is no default item selected in the* ListView *control I created. How can I have it default to a specific item?*

A. To have a ListView control highlight a specific list item by default, use the setSelection() method.

Workshop

Quiz

1. True or False: Context menus are launched using the Menu button.

2. What mechanism acts as the "glue" between a data source and a ListView control?

   A. A database

   B. An interpolator

   C. A data adapter

3. What type of layout is most appropriate for aligning child `View` controls in relation to the parent control?

    A. `RelativeLayout`

    B. `AbsoluteLayout`

    C. `LinearLayout`

4. True or False: Using `ListActivity` is a convenient way to build screens that are just `ListView` objects.

Answers

1. False. Options menus are launched using the Menu button. Context menus are launched using a long-click on a `View` control.

2. C. A data adapter, such as `ArrayAdapter`, is used to match a data source to the layout template used by a `ListView` control to display each list item.

3. A. `RelativeLayout` is especially handy when its child `View` controls need to be aligned to the top, bottom, left, right, and center of the parent layout. `RelativeLayout` can also be used to position child `View` controls relative to one another inside the parent layout.

4. True. `ListActivity` simplifies the handling of `ListView` controls.

Exercises

1. Review some of the other data adapters available for use with the `ListView` control. Update the `ListView` control so that each list item contains an `ImageView` icon and the `TextView` control. (Hint: Implement a custom data adapter.)

2. Add a third option to the game screen's options menu to allow the user to access the scores screen.

3. Modify the `LinearLayout` control of `menu.xml` to include an animation that fades in so that the entire main menu screen fades in.

HOUR 9

Developing the Help and Scores Screens

What You'll Learn in This Hour:

▶ Designing and implementing the help screen
▶ Working with files
▶ Designing and implementing the scores screen
▶ Designing screens with tabs
▶ Working with XML

In this hour, you implement two more screens of the Been There, Done That! application: the help and scores screens. You begin with the help screen, using a TextView control with text supplied from a text file, which allows you to explore some of the file support classes of the Android SDK. Next, you design and implement the scores screen. With its more complicated requirements, the scores screen is ideal for trying out the tab set control called TabHost. Finally, you test the scores screen by parsing mock XML score data and displaying the appropriate information on each tab.

Designing the Help Screen

The help screen requirements are straightforward: This screen must display a large quantity of text and have scrolling capability. Figure 9.1 shows a rough design of the help screen.

FIGURE 9.1
Rough design for the Been There, Done That! help screen.

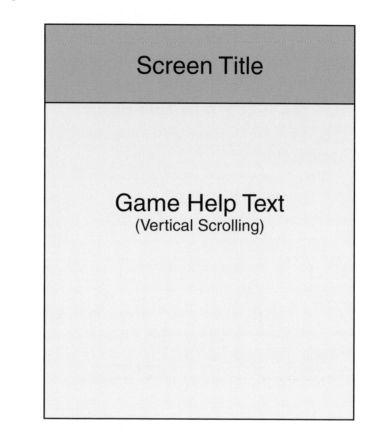

You want the application screens to share some common features. Therefore, you can have the help screen mimic some of the menu screen features such as a header. To translate your rough design into the appropriate layout design, you need to update the `/res/layout/help.xml` layout file and the `QuizHelpActivity` class.

You want the same sort of title header you used in the menu screen (using a `RelativeLayout`), followed by a `TextView` control with scrolling capability. Figure 9.2 shows the layout design for the help screen.

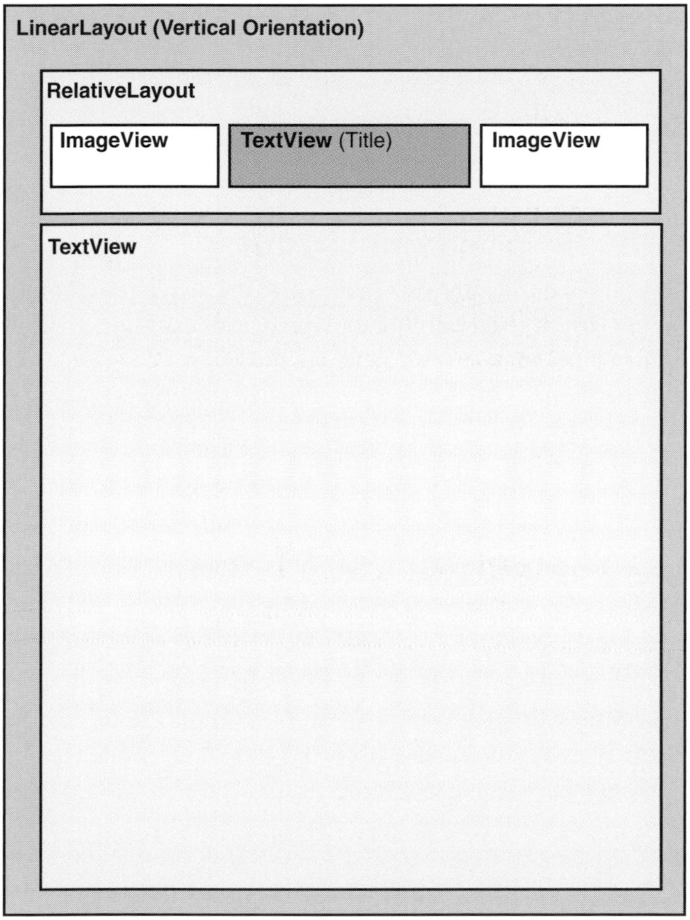

FIGURE 9.2
Layout design
for the Been
There, Done
That! help
screen.

Implementing the Help Screen Layout

To implement the help screen, you begin by adding new resources to the project. Then you must update the help.xml layout resource to reflect the help screen design.

Adding New Project Resources

In addition to any new string, color, and dimension resources you use within the layout for the help screen, you also need to add a new type of resource: a raw file resource file. In this instance, you include a text file called /res/raw/quizhelp.txt that includes a number of paragraphs of help text, which you will display in the main TextView control of the help screen.

Updating the Help Screen Layout

The help.xml layout file dictates the user interface of the help screen. At this point, you open the Eclipse layout resource editor and remove all existing controls from the layout. You then follow these steps to generate the layout you want, based on the screen design:

1. Add a new LinearLayout control and set its background attribute to @drawable/bkgrnd. All subsequent controls will be added inside the LinearLayout control.

2. Add the same header you created in the menu.xml layout. It should contain a RelativeLayout control with two ImageView controls and a TextView control. Set the TextView control's text attribute to the string resource called @string/help to reflect the appropriate screen title.

3. Outside the RelativeLayout control but still within the LinearLayout control, add a TextView control called TextView_HelpText. Set its layout_width attribute to fill_parent and its layout_height attribute to fill_parent.

Did you Know?

You can automatically link phone numbers, web addresses, email addresses, and postal addresses that show in the TextView control to the Android Phone Dialer, Web Browser, Email, and Map applications by setting the linksClickable attribute to true and the autoLink attribute to all for the TextView control.

At this point, save the help.xml layout file.

Did you Know?

You can make TextView control text bold or italic by using the textStyle attribute.

Working with Files

Now that the `help.xml` layout file is complete, you need to update the `QuizHelpActivity` class to read the `quizhelp.txt` file and save the resulting text into the `TextView` control called `TextView_HelpText`.

Adding Raw Resource Files

Raw resource files, such as the `quizhelp.txt` text file, can be added to the project by simply including them in the `/raw` resources project directory. This can be done by either creating them as a new file, dragging them in from a file management tool, or any other way you're accustomed to adding files to Android projects in Eclipse.

> Each Android application has its own private directory on the Android file system for storing application files. In addition to all the familiar `File` and `Stream` classes available, you can access private application files and directories by using the following `Context` class methods: `fileList()`, `getFilesDir()`, `getDir()`, `openFileInput()`, `openFileOutput()`, `deleteFile()`, and `getFileStreamPath()`.

Did you Know?

Accessing Raw File Resources

The Android platform includes many of the typical Java file I/O classes, including stream operations. To read string data from a file, use the `openRawResource()` method, as in the following example:

```
InputStream iFile = getResources().openRawResource(R.raw.quizhelp);
```

Now that you have an `InputStream` object, you can read the file, line-by-line or byte-by-byte, and create a string. There are a number of ways to do this. When you have a proper string with the help text, you simply retrieve the `TextView` control using the `findViewById()` method and set the text using the `TextView` control's `setText()` method, as follows:

```
TextView helpText = (TextView) findViewById(R.id.TextView_HelpText);
String strFile = inputStreamToString(iFile);
helpText.setText(strFile);
```

> The previous text references a helper method called `inputStreamToString()` which is available with the `QuizHelpActivity` class implementation provided with this book. The method simply reads in an `InputStream` and returns a `String` of the contents.

By the Way

At this point, save the `QuizHelpActivity.java` file and run the Been There, Done That! application in the Android emulator. After the splash screen finishes, choose the help screen option from the main menu. The help screen should look much like Figure 9.3.

FIGURE 9.3
The Been There, Done That! help screen.

> 3G 📶 📧 8:19 PM
> Been There, Done That!
>
> 🔍 **Help Screen** 🔍
>
> *Have you been there?*
> *Have you done that?*
>
> *BEEN THERE, DONE THAT! is a trivia*
> *quiz dedicated to those who love*
> *travel and adventure. By answering a*
> *series of Yes or No questions, you gain*
> *points toward being the most well-*
> *traveled and field-tested person on the*
> *planet. Share your experiences and*
> *compete with your friends.*
>
> *GAME SETTINGS*
>
> *<TBD>*
>
> *SUPPORT INFORMATION*

▼   ## Try It Yourself

Now that you have the help screen displaying the appropriate information, you might want to improve the look of it to more closely match Figure 9.3. Start by changing the font size of the help text in the `TextView` control. Then consider changing other attributes, such as padding, font, text colors, and so on. For more information, see the attributes configured in the `TextView` implementation provided
▲   with the book code.

Designing the Scores Screen

Now that you've created the help screen, you can turn your attention to another screen with somewhat similar features: the scores screen. The requirements for this screen include showing several different scores to the user. There are two types of scores: the all-time-high scores and the user's friends' scores. You want to show both on the same screen. Each screen shown will include the user's name, score, and overall ranking.

There are a number of ways you could implement the scores screen. For example, you could use a `TextView` control or `ListView` control to display the score information. However, you are working with a small screen, and you don't want to overwhelm the user with too much information. Because you have two different sets of data to display, two tabs would be ideal for this screen. Figure 9.4 shows a rough design of the scores screen.

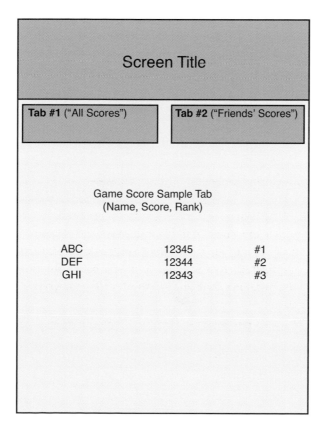

FIGURE 9.4
Rough design for the Been There, Done That! scores screen.

Determining Scores Screen Layout Requirements

Now that you know how you want your scores screen to look, you need to translate your rough design into the appropriate layout design. In this case, you need to update the /res/layout/scores.xml layout file that is used by the QuizScoresActivity class. In the case of the scores layout, you can again take advantage of the RelativeLayout control to add a familiar title bar to the top of the scores screen. In this case, the header will be followed by a TabHost control with two tabs, each of which will be a TableLayout control of scores—one tab for all scores and one for friends' scores.

Adding the TabHost Control

To add tabbing support to the scores screen, you include a TabHost control, which is a container with child tabs, each of which may contain some layout content. TabHost is a somewhat complex control. In order to configure it within an XML layout file, you need to follow a set of guidelines:

- Include a TabHost control
- Ensure that there is a LinearLayout within the TabHost control
- Ensure that there is a specially named TabWidget control and FrameLayout control within the LinearLayout control
- Define the contents of each tab in the FrameLayout control

Figure 9.5 shows the layout design for the scores screen.

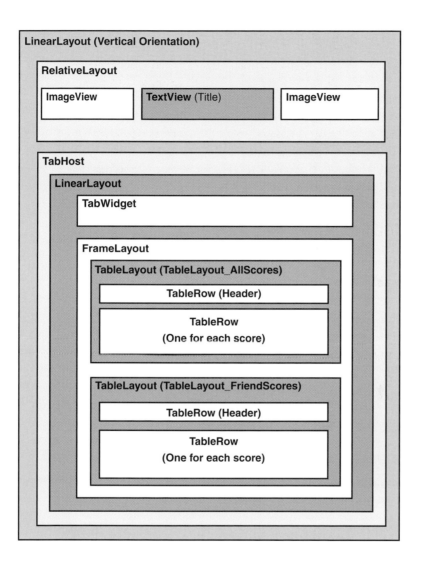

FIGURE 9.5
Layout design
for the Been
There, Done
That! scores
screen.

Implementing the Scores Screen Layout

To implement the scores screen, you begin by adding new resources to the project. Then you need to update the scores.xml layout resource to reflect the scores screen design.

Adding New Project Resources

In addition to the new string, color, and dimension resources you use in the scores screen layout, you must also add a new type of resource: an XML file resource file.

The scores for the Been There, Done That! application will eventually be sourced from a remote server, but for now, you can build the screen and use some mock score data. This mock score data will be provided in XML, so you can mimic the structure you will use when the real scores are available.

In this instance, you include in the `/res/xml/` resource directory two XML files—`allscores.xml` and `friendscores.xml`—that represent the mock score data:

```xml
<?xml version="1.0" encoding="utf-8"?>
    <!— This is a mock score XML chunk —>
<scores>
    <score
        username="LED"
        score="12345"
        rank="1" />
    <score
        username="SAC"
        score="12344"
        rank="2" />
    <score
        username="NAD"
        score="12339"
        rank="3" />
</scores>
```

The score data uses a very simple schema. A single <scores> element has a number of child <score> elements. Each <score> element has three attributes: username, score, and rank. For this example, you can assume that the score data will be sorted and limited to the top 20 or so scores.

Updating the Scores Screen Layout

The scores screen user interface is defined in the `scores.xml` layout file. To update this layout to your intended layout design, you follow these steps:

> The Eclipse layout resource editor does not display TabHost controls properly in design mode. To design this kind of layout, you should stick to the XML layout mode. You must use the Android emulator or an Android device to view the tabs.

1. Remove all the old controls, as you have done for other layouts in this book.

2. Add a new LinearLayout control, setting its android:background attribute to @drawable/bkgrnd. All subsequent controls will be added inside this LinearLayout control.

3. Add the same header you created in other layouts. It should contain of a RelativeLayout control with two ImageView controls and a TextView control. Set the TextView control's text attribute to the string resource @string/scores to reflect the appropriate screen title.

4. Outside the `RelativeLayout` control but still within the `LinearLayout`, add a TabHost control called TabHost1. Set its `layout_width` and `layout_height` attributes to `fill_parent`. *(edit on the XML screen*

5. Inside the `TabHost` control, add another `LinearLayout` control, with its orientation attribute set to `vertical`. Set its `layout_width` and `layout_height` attributes to `fill_parent`.

6. Inside the inner `LinearLayout` control, add a `TabWidget` control. Set the control's id attribute to `@android:id/tabs`.

7. Within the inner `LinearLayout` control at the same level as the `TabWidget` control, add a `FrameLayout` control. Set the `FrameLayout` control's id attribute to `@android:id/tabcontent` and its `layout_width` and `layout_height` attributes to `fill_parent`.

8. Define the content of your tabs. Within the `FrameLayout` control, add two `TableLayout` controls, one for each tab. You will use these `TableLayout` controls to display the scores. Name the first `TableLayout` control `TableLayout_AllScores` and the second `TableLayout_FriendScores`. Set the `layout_width` and `layout_height` attributes to `fill_parent`. Set the `stretchColumns` attribute to `*` to allow columns to resize based on the content.

> When creating a tabbed view in this way, you must name the identifier as listed above: `@android:id/tabcontent`; otherwise, exceptions will be thrown at runtime. This references a special Android package resource. It is not the same as using `@+id/tabcontent`. That would create a new identifier for a layout object in your own application package.

Watch Out!

You can make many controls scrollable by wrapping them within a `ScrollView` control. For example, to give a `TableLayout` control a vertical scrollbar, wrap it in a `ScrollView` control and set the `scrollbars` attribute to `vertical`. You also need to set its `layout_width` and `layout_height` attributes.

The `TabHost` section of the scores screen layout file (with optional scrolling `TableLayout` tabs) should look something like this:

```
<TabHost
    android:id="@+id/TabHost1"
    android:layout_width="fill_parent"
    android:layout_height="fill_parent">
    <LinearLayout
        android:orientation="vertical"
        android:layout_width="fill_parent"
        android:layout_height="fill_parent">
        <TabWidget
            android:id="@android:id/tabs"
```

```
            android:layout_width="fill_parent"
            android:layout_height="wrap_content" />
        <FrameLayout
            android:id="@android:id/tabcontent"
            android:layout_width="fill_parent"
            android:layout_height="fill_parent">
            <ScrollView
                android:id="@+id/ScrollViewAllScores"
                android:layout_width="fill_parent"
                android:layout_height="fill_parent"
                android:scrollbars="vertical">
                <TableLayout
                    android:id="@+id/TableLayout_AllScores"
                    android:layout_width="fill_parent"
                    android:layout_height="fill_parent"
                    android:stretchColumns="*">
                </TableLayout>
            </ScrollView>
            <ScrollView
                android:id="@+id/ScrollViewFriendScores"
                android:layout_width="fill_parent"
                android:layout_height="fill_parent"
                android:scrollbars="vertical">
                <TableLayout
                    android:id="@+id/TableLayout_FriendScores"
                    android:layout_width="fill_parent"
                    android:layout_height="fill_parent"
                    android:stretchColumns="*"></TableLayout>
            </ScrollView>
        </FrameLayout>
    </LinearLayout>
</TabHost>
```

At this point, save the `scores.xml` layout file.

Watch Out!

> At this point, if you switch to the Layout view, Eclipse may display a "NullPointerException: null" error. The Layout designer doesn't support TabHost controls as of Android 2.1. The layout will draw just fine in the emulator and on devices.

Designing a Screen with Tabs

Now you need to switch your focus to the `QuizScoresActivity.java` file and wire up the controls needed by the `TabHost` control. First, you need to initialize the `TabHost` control and then you need to fill it with two tabs, making the default tab the All Scores tab. Finally, you use mock score data to populate the `TableLayout` control in each tab.

Configuring the `TabHost` Control

The `TabHost` control must be initialized before it will function properly. Therefore, you first retrieve it by using the `findViewById()` method. Next, you must call the `TabHost` control's `setup()` method, which initializes the `TabHost` and "glues" the specially named `TabWidget` and `FrameLayout` controls together to form a tab set, as follows:

```
TabHost host = (TabHost) findViewById(R.id.TabHost1);
host.setup();
```

Adding Tabs to the `TabHost` Control

Now that you have retrieved your `TabHost` control and initialized it, you need to configure each tab using the `addTab()` method. This method takes a `TabSpec` parameter, which describes the tab contents. For example, the following code creates the All Scores tab:

```
TabSpec allScoresTab = host.newTabSpec("allTab");
allScoresTab.setIndicator(getResources().getString(R.string.all_scores),
    getResources().getDrawable(android.R.drawable.star_on));
allScoresTab.sctContent(R.id.ScrollViewAllScores);
host.addTab(allScoresTab);
```

The `TabSpec` control called `allScoresTab` has the tag reference `"allTab"`. The actual tab label contains a `TextView` control and an icon (a star). Finally, you set the contents of the tab to `ScrollViewAllScores`, which wraps the `TableLayout` control called `TableLayout_AllScores`, defined in the `scores.xml` layout resource. Next, you add a second tab called `friendsTab` to the `TabHost` control. The second tab is implemented much like the first, only with different content (friend scores only, not all scores).

Setting the Default Tab

At this point, you need to identify which tab to show by default. To do this, you call the `setCurrentTabByTag()` method and pass in the tag name of the tab:

```
host.setCurrentTabByTag("allTab");
```

Save the `QuizScoresActivity.java` file and run the application in the Android emulator. If you navigate to the scores screen, you see the two tabs, but you still have no score data to display.

> If you have a screen that only displays a `TabHost` control, consider using the `TabActivity` class to simplify management of the `TabHost` control.

Watch Out!

Working with XML

The Android platform has a number of mechanisms for working with XML data, including support for the following:

- ▶ SAX (Simple API for XML)
- ▶ XML Pull Parser
- ▶ Limited DOM Level 2 core support

The XML technology you use depends on your specific project. For this example, you simply want to read through a simple XML file and extract the mock score data.

Retrieving XML Resources

First, you need to access the mock XML data you saved in the project resources. Specifically, you want to parse the /res/xml/allscores.xml file.

You can initialize an instance of an XmlResourceParser by using the getXML() method, as follows:

```
XmlResourceParser mockAllScores = getResources().getXml(R.xml.allscores);
```

Parsing XML Files with XmlResourceParser

The mock score files have a very simple schema with only two tags: <scores> and <score>. You want to find each <score> tag and extract its username, rank, and score attributes. Because you can assume a small amount of data, you can implement your parsing routing by using a simple while() loop to iterate through the events by using the next() method, as follows:

```
int eventType = -1;
boolean bFoundScores = false;
// Find Score records from XML
while (eventType != XmlResourceParser.END_DOCUMENT) {
    if (eventType == XmlResourceParser.START_TAG) {
        // Get the name of the tag (eg scores or score)
        String strName = scores.getName();
        if (strName.equals("score")) {
            bFoundScores = true;
            String scoreValue = scores.getAttributeValue(null, "score");
            String scoreRank = scores.getAttributeValue(null, "rank");
            String scoreUserName =
                scores.getAttributeValue(null, "username");
            insertScoreRow(scoreTable, scoreValue, scoreRank,
                scoreUserName);
        }
```

```
    }
    eventType = scores.next();
}
```

Within the loop, you watch for the START_TAG event. When the tag name matches the <score> tag, you know you have a piece of score data. You then extract the data by using the getAttributeValue() method. For each score you find, you add a new TableRow control to the appropriate TableLayout control (in the appropriate tab).

Applying Finishing Touches to the Scores Screen

After you have written the code to parse the two mock XML files and populate the two TableLayout controls in the TabHost control, you need only make a few minor additions to QuizScoresActivity. You should add a header TableRow to each TableLayout control, with nicely styled column headers, as well as handling for the case where no score data is available.

When you're done applying these finishing touches, you save the class and run the application in the emulator or on the device. When you navigate to the scores screen, you see that both tabs are populated with data (see Figure 9.6).

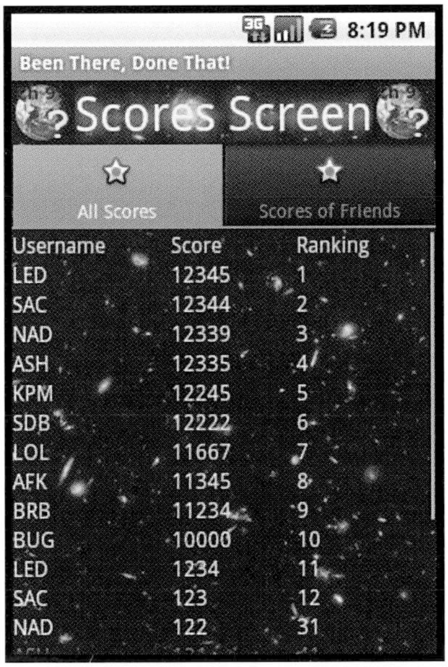

FIGURE 9.6
The Been There, Done That! scores screen.

Summary

In this hour, you added two new screens to the Been There, Done That! trivia application. As you implemented the help screen, you learned how to display large amounts of data by using a scrolling `TextView` control. You also learned how to access a file resource and change layout characteristics programmatically. With the scores screen, you learned about the `TabHost` control as well as how to parse XML to display some mock score data.

Q&A

Q. *Why do I need to name certain controls within the* `TabHost` *control with specific Android* `id` *attributes?*

A. Occasionally, you will find situations in which you need to name layout controls with specific names in order for the controls to work properly. The more complex a control, the more likely it requires a bit of "glue" (or "magic") for the Android system to load the right templates and resources to display the control in a familiar way. Usually, these kinds of naming requirements are documented in the Android SDK.

Q. *There is a bit of a delay when loading the scores screen. Why?*

A. There are a number of reasons this screen appears less responsive than other screens. First, you are parsing XML, which can be a costly operation. Second, you create a large number of `View` controls to display the score data. You must always be careful to offload intense processing from the main UI thread to make the application more responsive and avoid unnecessary shutdown by the Android system. You could easily add a worker thread to handle the XML, and you might also consider other, more efficient, controls for displaying the score data. Finally, with Eclipse, when the debugger is attached, performance of an application greatly degrades.

Workshop

Quiz

1. True or False: A `TextView` control can display a large amount of text.

2. What class can be used to simplify tab screens?

   A. `Tabify`

   B. `TabActivity`

   C. `TabController`

3. True or False: XML files are handled by the XML Resource Manager, so no parsing is necessary.

4. What type of control can be used to enable scrolling?

   A. `ScrollLayout`

   B. `Scroller`

   C. `ScrollView`

Answers

1. True. The `TextView` control can display large quantities of text, with optional horizontal and vertical scrollbars.

2. B. A screen that requires only a tab set can use the `TabActivity` class to handle tabbing setup and tasks efficiently.

3. False. XML files can be included but still need to be parsed. Three parsers are available, with the default resource parser being XML Pull Parser.

4. C. The `ScrollView` control can be used to wrap child `View` controls within a scrolling area.

Exercises

1. Launch the application and click each of the links in the help screen text. Note how easy it can be to integrate Android applications into the Android platform. Try launching some other kinds of intents and seeing what happens. For a good list of intents, check out the Intents Registry at http://www.openintents.org/en/intentstable.

2. Add a third tab to the scores screen to display the user's current score. Make the content of this new tab different from the other two tabs by including a TextView control instead of a TableLayout control. The user's current score will be be stored as an application preference.

HOUR 10

Building Forms to Collect User Input

What You'll Learn in This Hour:

▶ Designing and implementing the settings screen
▶ Working with `EditText` controls
▶ Working with `Button` controls
▶ Working with `Spinner` controls
▶ Saving form data with `SharedPreferences`

In this hour, you begin to implement the settings screen of the Been There, Done That! application. The settings screen displays a form for entering application configuration information, including the user's login and profile settings. Different settings necessitate the use of different input controls, including `EditText`, `Spinner`, and `Button` controls. Finally, you need to ensure that each setting is saved and stored in a persistent manner as part of the application's preferences.

Designing the Settings Screen

The settings screen must allow the user to configure a number of game settings and save them. Game settings may be text input fields, drop-down lists, or other, more complex, controls. (You eventually want to handle social gaming with friends, but you will deal with that requirement later.) For now, you begin by implementing a simple settings screen with five basic game settings:

▶ **Nickname**—The name to be displayed on score listings. This text field should be no more than 20 characters long—an arbitrary but reasonable length for your purposes.

▶ **Email**—The unique identifier for each user. This is a text field.

▶ **Password**—A mechanism to handle user verification. This is a password text field. When setting the password, the user should input the password twice for verification. The password text may be stored as plaintext.

▶ **Date of Birth**—To verify minimum age, when necessary. This is a date field but often displayed in a friendly way users understand and can easily interact with.

▶ **Gender**—A piece of demographic information, which could be used for special score listings or to target ads to the user. This can be set to three different settings: Male (1), Female (2), or Prefer Not to Say (0).

Figure 10.1 shows a rough design for the settings screen.

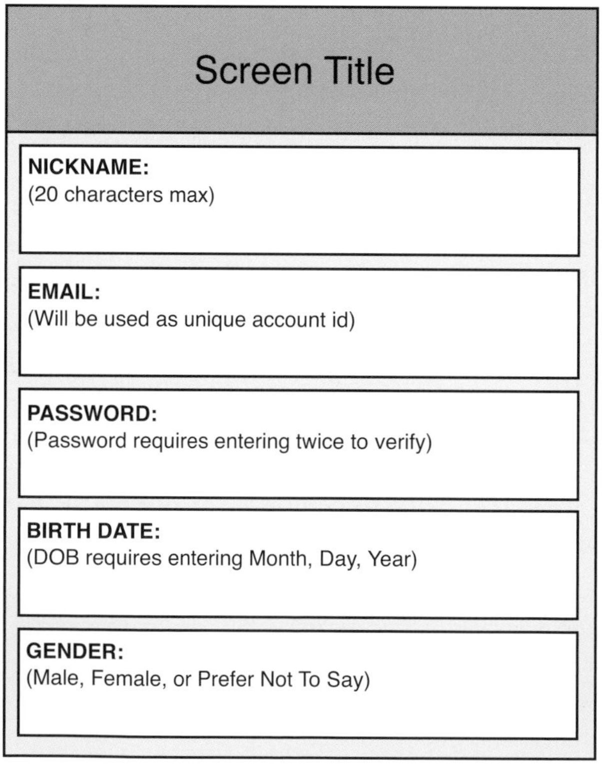

FIGURE 10.1
Rough design for the Been There, Done That! settings screen.

Screen Title

NICKNAME:
(20 characters max)

EMAIL:
(Will be used as unique account id)

PASSWORD:
(Password requires entering twice to verify)

BIRTH DATE:
(DOB requires entering Month, Day, Year)

GENDER:
(Male, Female, or Prefer Not To Say)

The application settings screen will contain quite a few different controls, so you need to be careful with screen real estate. You begin here, as you have on other screens, with the customary title bar.

Below the title, you add a region for each setting. Because you may add new settings in the future, you should encapsulate the settings area of the screen within a ScrollView control. This way, if all the settings fields do not fit on a screen, the user can scroll. The ScrollView control can have only a single child control, so you can encapsulate the bulk of your settings in another vertical LinearLayout control.

Each setting requires two "rows" in the LinearLayout control: a TextView row that displays the setting name label and a row for the input control to capture its value. For example, the Nickname setting would require a row with a TextView control to display the label string ("Nickname:") and a row for an EditText control to allow the user to input a string of text.

Now you need to determine which control is most appropriate for each setting:

- ▶ The Nickname and Email fields are simply different types of single-line text input, so they can be EditText controls.

- ▶ The Password setting requires two EditText controls. However, the Password text need not be displayed on the settings screen directly. Instead, you create a Button control to launch a Dialog window to allow the user to change the password (using the two EditText controls). The main settings screen can just display whether a password has been set in a TextView control.

- ▶ The Date of Birth setting requires a DatePicker control. Because the DatePicker control is actually three separate controls—a month picker, a day picker, and a year picker—it takes up a lot of space on the screen. Therefore, instead of including it directly on the screen, you can add a Button control to launch a DatePickerDialog control. The user selects the appropriate date and closes the dialog, and the resulting date is displayed (but not editable) on the main settings screen within a TextView control.

- ▶ The Gender setting is simply a choice between three values, so a Spinner (drop-down) control is most appropriate.

Figure 10.2 shows the layout design of the basic settings screen.

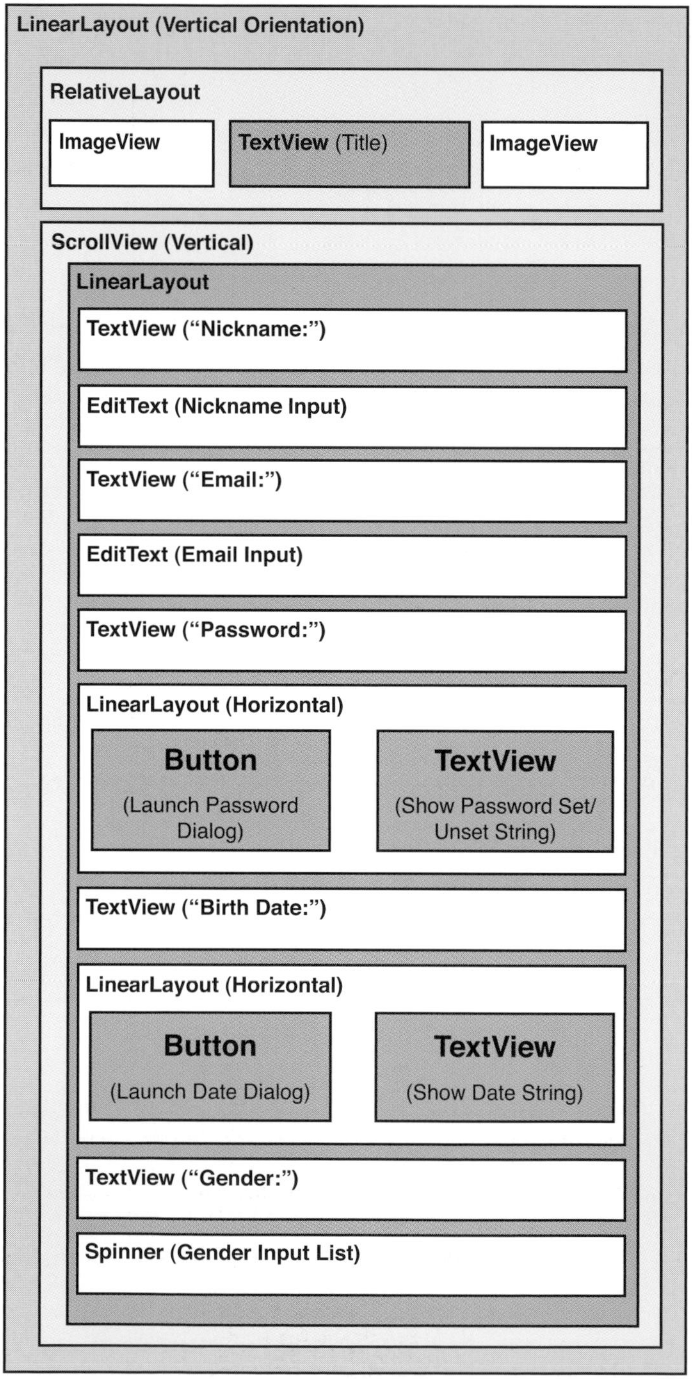

FIGURE 10.2
Layout design
for the Been
There, Done
That! settings
screen.

LinearLayout (Vertical Orientation)

RelativeLayout

| ImageView | TextView (Title) | ImageView |

ScrollView (Vertical)

LinearLayout

TextView ("Nickname:")

EditText (Nickname Input)

TextView ("Email:")

EditText (Email Input)

TextView ("Password:")

LinearLayout (Horizontal)

| **Button** (Launch Password Dialog) | **TextView** (Show Password Set/ Unset String) |

TextView ("Birth Date:")

LinearLayout (Horizontal)

| **Button** (Launch Date Dialog) | **TextView** (Show Date String) |

TextView ("Gender:")

Spinner (Gender Input List)

Implementing the Settings Screen Layout

To implement the settings screen, you begin by adding new resources to the project. You then update the `settings.xml` layout resource to reflect the settings screen design.

Adding New Project Resources

Screens with form fields seem to rely on more resources than most other screen types. You need to add a number of new resources to support the settings screen. In addition to the string, dimension, and color resources, you also need to add a new type of resource: a string array.

Adding New String Resources

The settings screen relies on numerous new string resources. You add the following text resources to the `strings.xml` resource file:

- Text for each setting's `TextView` label (for example, `"Nickname:"`)
- Text for each `Button` control (for example, `"Set Password"`)
- Text to display in a `TextView` control when the password is set or not set
- Text to display in a `TextView` control when the Date of Birth field is not set
- Text to display in a `TextView` control when the two Password fields match or don't match
- Text for each Gender option in the `Spinner` control (for example, `"Male"`)

After you have added these strings, save the `strings.xml` resource file.

Adding New String Array Resources

`Spinner` controls, like `ListView` controls, use data adapters. You have your gender string resources defined, but you still need to group them into some sort of dataset.

The simplest dataset is an array (and the corresponding `ArrayAdapter` control). To group the gender string resources (`"Male"`, `"Female"`, `"Prefer Not To Say"`) together into an array, you create a new resource type called a `String` array.

To create a `String` array resource, you must add a new resource file called `/res/values/arrays.xml`. Within this file, you create a new `string-array` element called genders. Within this `string-array` element, you add three `Item` elements, one for each string resource.

Assume that you added to the `strings.xml` resource file the following three gender resource strings defined earlier:

```
<string
    name="gender_male">Male</string>
<string
    name="gender_female">Female</string>
<string
    name="gender_neutral">Prefer Not To Say</string>
```

Within the `arrays.xml` resource file, you set each item in the genders string array to the appropriate string resource. For example, the first `Item` element in the array (with an index of 0) would have the value @string/gender_neutral. The resulting `arrays.xml` resource file follows:

```
<?xml version="1.0" encoding="utf-8"?>
<resources>
    <string-array
        name="genders">
        <item>@string/gender_neutral</item>
        <item>@string/gender_male</item>
        <item>@string/gender_female</item>
    </string-array>
</resources>
```

Save the `arrays.xml` resource file. Now when you want to load the genders string array resource into memory, you can access it programmatically by using the `R.array.genders` resource identifier.

Updating the Settings Screen Layout

The `settings.xml` layout file dictates the user interface of the settings screen. Again, you open the Eclipse layout resource editor and remove all existing controls from the layout. You then follow these steps to generate the layout you want, based on your earlier design:

1. Add the customary `LinearLayout` control, with its background attribute set to @drawable/bkgrnd. All subsequent controls will be added inside the `LinearLayout` control.

2. Add the same title bar controls you've added to other screens.

3. Below the title bar, add a `ScrollView` control to encapsulate your settings. Set its `isScrollContainer` attribute to `true` and its `scrollbars` attribute to vertical. Set its `layout_width` and `layout_height` attributes to `fill_parent`.

4. Within the `ScrollView` control, add a `LinearLayout` control to encapsulate your settings. Set its `orientation` attribute to vertical. Set its `layout_width`

and layout_height attributes to fill_parent. All subsequent controls will be added within this LinearLayout control.

5. Within the LinearLayout control, add a TextView control to display the Nickname label text. Below the TextView control for the label, add an EditText control. Set its id attribute to EditText_Nickname, its maxLength attribute to 20, its maxLines attribute to 1, and its inputType attribute to textPersonName.

6. Add a TextView control to display the Email label text. Then add another EditText control below it, setting its id attribute to EditText_Email, its maxLines attribute to 1, and its inputType attribute to textEmailAddress.

7. Add the Password settings region of the form by adding another TextView control to display the Password label text. Below it, add a horizontal LinearLayout control with two controls: a Button control and a TextView control. Configure the Button control with the id attribute Button_Password and the text attribute set to the Password button text string resource. Configure the TextView control to display the Password setting state string ("Password not set", for now).

8. At the same level as the Password setting region, add a region for the Date of Birth setting. Start by adding another TextView control to display the Date of Birth label text. Next, add another horizontal LinearLayout control with two controls: a Button control and a TextView control. Configure the Button control with the id attribute Button_DOB and the text attribute set to the Date of Birth button text string resource. Configure the TextView control to display the Date of Birth setting state string ("Date not set", for now).

9. Add one last settings region for the Gender drop-down by adding a TextView control to display the Gender label text. Then add a Spinner control and set its id attribute to Spinner_Gender.

10. Before saving, adjust any text sizes, fonts, colors, height, or width settings until the screen draws as desired.

At this point, save the settings.xml layout file.

Using Common Form Controls

Now that the settings.xml layout file is complete, you need to update the QuizSettingsActivity class to populate the controls and allow editing and saving of form data. This section shows you how to save and restore data to the form.

Working with `EditText` Controls

The `EditText` control, which is derived from the `TextView` control, is used to collect textual input from the user. Figure 10.3 shows a simple `EditText` control.

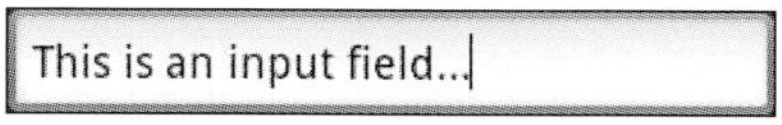

FIGURE 10.3
An `EditText`
control for text
input.

This is an input field...

Configuring `EditText` Controls

All the typical attributes of a `TextView` control (for example, `textColor`, `textSize`) are available to `EditText` controls. The following are some `EditText` attributes that are commonly used for the settings screen:

▶ `inputType`—Instructs the Android system about how to help the user fill in the text. For example, you set the `inputType` attribute of the `EditText` control for the Email field to `textEmailAddress`, which instructs the Android system to use the email-oriented soft keyboard (with the @ sign). The `inputType` value called `textPassword` automatically masks the user's password as it is typed.

▶ `minLines` and `maxLines`—Restrict the number of lines of text allowed in the control.

▶ `maxLength`—Restricts the number of characters of text allowed in the control. For example, you can limit the number of characters allowed in the Nickname setting by setting the `maxLength` attribute of the Nickname setting's `EditText` control to `20`.

Handling Text Input

As with a `TextView` control, you can access the text stored in an `EditText` control by using the `getText()` and `setText()` methods. For example, to extract the string typed into the `EditText` control called `EditText_Nickname`, you use the `getText()` method as follows:

```
EditText nicknameText = (EditText) findViewById(R.id.EditText_Nickname);
String strNicknameToSave = nicknameText.getText().toString();
```

The `getText()` method returns an `Editable` object, but in this case, you simply want its `String` value equivalent.

Committing `EditText` **Input**

To handle `EditText` input to a form, you need to determine when new text has
been entered. To do this, you can listen for `EditText` key events and commit the
text entered when certain keys are pressed. For example, to listen for the Enter key
during input of the Nickname setting, you would register `View.OnKeyListener` by
using the `setOnKeyListener()` method of the `EditText` control, as follows:

```
final EditText nicknameText =
    (EditText) findViewById(R.id.EditText_Nickname);
nicknameText.setOnKeyListener(new View.OnKeyListener() {
    public boolean onKey(View v, int keyCode, KeyEvent event) {
        if ((event.getAction() == KeyEvent.ACTION_DOWN) &&
            (keyCode == KeyEvent.KEYCODE_ENTER)) {
            String strNicknameToSave = nicknameText.getText().toString();
            // TODO: Save Nickname setting (strNicknameToSave)
            return true;
        }
        return false;
    }
});
```

Listening for `EditText` **Keystrokes**

Eventually, you will design a Password dialog. Say that you want to match the text
strings within two `EditText` password fields, called `EditText_Pwd1` and
`EditText_Pwd2`, while the user is typing. A third `TextView` control, called
`TextView_PwdProblem`, provides feedback about whether the passwords match.

First, you need to retrieve each of the controls:

```
final EditText p1 = (EditText) findViewById(R.id.EditText_Pwd1);
final EditText p2 = (EditText) findViewById(R.id.EditText_Pwd2);
final TextView error = (TextView) findViewById(R.id.TextView_PwdProblem);
```

Next, you add `TextWatcher` to the second `EditText` control, using the
`addTextChangedListener()` method, like this:

```
p2.addTextChangedListener(new TextWatcher() {
    @Override
    public void afterTextChanged(Editable s) {
        String strPass1 = p1.getText().toString();
        String strPass2 = p2.getText().toString();
        if (strPass1.equals(strPass2)) {
            error.setText(R.string.settings_pwd_equal);
        } else {
            error.setText(R.string.settings_pwd_not_equal);
        }
    }

    // Other required overrides do nothing
});
```

The user can type the password into the `EditText_Pwd1` EditText control normally. However, each time the user types a character into the `EditText_Pwd2` control, you compare the text in both `EditText` controls and set the text of the `TextView` control called `TextView_PwdProblem` to reflect whether the text matches (see Figure 10.4).

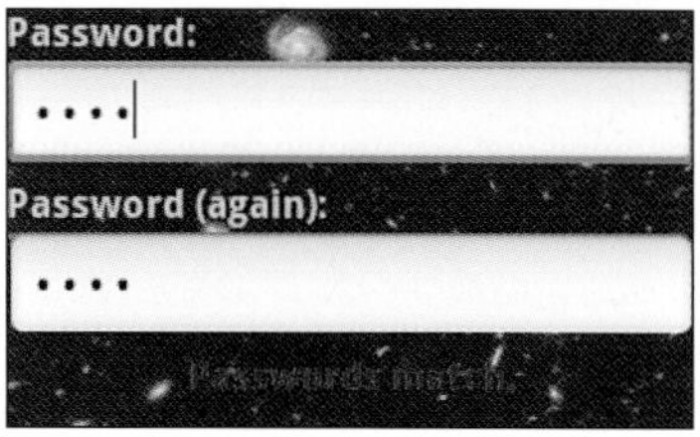

FIGURE 10.4
A Password dialog with two EditText controls and a TextView control.

Working with Button Controls

The `Button` control on the Android platform is relatively straightforward, as form controls go. Generally speaking, a `Button` control is simply a clickable area with a text string label. Figure 10.5 shows a `Button` control.

FIGURE 10.5
A Button control.

Configuring Button Controls

Many of the typical attributes of `TextView` controls, such as `textColor` and `textSize`, are available for the `Button` text label. You need two simple `Button` controls for the settings screen: one for launching the Password `Dialog` window and one for launching the `DatePickerDialog`. You configure these `Button` controls by giving each a unique identifier and setting the `text` attribute labels of each. You also set each `Button` control's `layout_width` and `layout_height` attributes to `wrap_content` so that each button scales appropriately, based on the text label.

The Android platform actually supports two kinds of Button controls: the basic Button control and the `ImageButton` control. An ImageButton control behaves much like a regular Button control, only instead of displaying a text label, it displays a Drawable image resource.

You can use attributes to modify the look of a `Button` control. For example, you can change the shape of the button (by default, a white rectangle with rounded corners) by setting the `background`, `drawableTop`, `drawableBottom`, `drawableLeft`, and `drawableRight` attributes of the `Button` to a Drawable resources.

Try It Yourself

Try changing the look of the Button control called Button_DOB by taking the following steps in the settings.xml layout file:

1. Change the background property of the Button control to the Drawable graphic resource called @drawable/textured.

2. Change the drawableTop property of the Button control to the Drawable graphic resource called @drawable/divider.

3. Change the drawableBottom property of the Button control to the Drawable graphic resource called @drawable/divider. Note that the Button control is now an ugly orange menace on the screen. You've created a monster.

4. Change the Button control back to the default Button control look and feel by removing the background, drawableTop, and drawableBottom properties from Button_DOB.

Handling Button Clicks

Handling the click event of a Button control is achieved by using the setOnClickListener() method. Specifically, you need to implement the onClick() method of View.OnClickListener. This is where any event handling for clicks should take place.

For example, to handle when a user clicks the Button control called Button_DOB, you add the following code to the onCreate() method of the QuizSettingsActivity class to handle the event:

```
Button pickDate = (Button) findViewById(R.id.Button_DOB);
pickDate.setOnClickListener(new View.OnClickListener() {
    public void onClick(View v) {
        // Handle date picking dialog
    }
});
```

You retrieve the Button control by using the findViewById() method, and then you set View.OnClickListener for the control by using the setOnClickListener() method. It is within the onClick() method that you want to trigger DatePickerDialog to be launched. However, you are not quite ready to implement this Dialog window yet. Instead, you can drop in a useful little helper pop-up message called a toast.

A toast is a view that pops up in the foreground to display a message for a few seconds and then disappears.

For example, you could add a Toast message to the onClick() method of the Button_DOB, like this:

```
Toast.makeText(QuizSettingsActivity.this,
    "TODO: Launch DatePickerDialog",
    Toast.LENGTH_LONG).show();
```

Figure 10.6 shows the resulting Toast message.

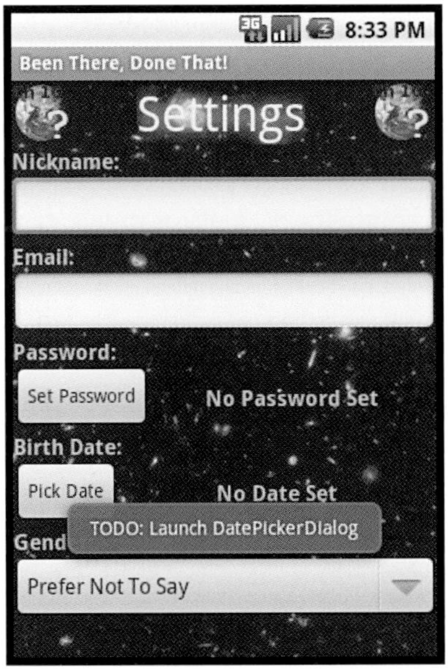

FIGURE 10.6
A Toast mes-
sage triggered
by a button
click.

Working with Spinner Controls

The Spinner control is basically the Android platform's version of a drop-down list. The control looks much like a drop-down when closed (see Figure 10.7, left), but when the Spinner control is activated, it displays a chooser window (see Figure 10.7, right) instead of drawing the drop-down on the main screen.

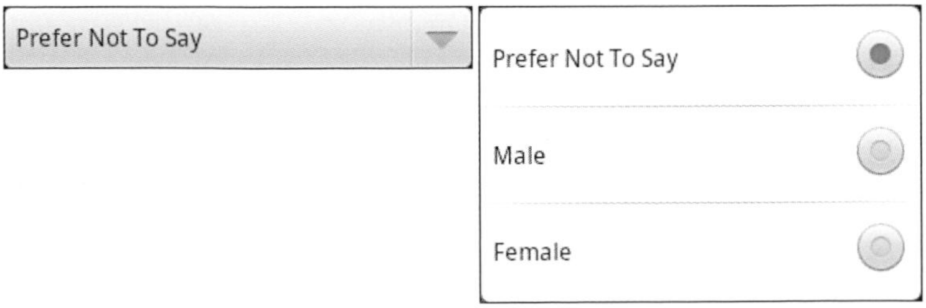

FIGURE 10.7
A Spinner con-
trol closed (left)
and open
(right).

Configuring Spinner **Controls**

Most of the configuration for a Spinner control must be handled programmatically. As with a ListView control, a Spinner control uses a data adapter to map its contents from a dataset to each view displayed in the control. To load a Spinner control with data, you follow these steps:

1. Retrieve the Spinner control from the layout.

2. Configure a data adapter to map the data to the control.

3. Call the setAdapter() method of the Spinner control.

To load the Spinner control from the layout, you use the familiar findViewById() method:

```
final Spinner spinner = (Spinner) findViewById(R.id.Spinner_Gender);
```

Next, you configure your data adapter. A Spinner control displays its data differently when it's closed than when it's open. Therefore, you need to provide layout templates for both display states. Fortunately, the Android platform includes several special layout resources to help create Spinner controls that contain text. Specifically, you can use the layout resource named android.R.layout.simple_spinner_item to create the appropriate view for each item in a default Spinner control. You can use the android.R.layout.simple_spinner_dropdown_item layout resource as the drop-down view resource template.

Using these handy built-in layout templates, you can load your String Array resource called genders into an ArrayAdapter control by using the createFromResource() method:

```
ArrayAdapter<?> adapter = ArrayAdapter.createFromResource(this,
        R.array.genders, android.R.layout.simple_spinner_item);
adapter.setDropDownViewResource(
    android.R.layout.simple_spinner_dropdown_item);
```

Finally, you call the setAdapter() method of the Spinner control to bind the data to the control:

```
spinner.setAdapter(adapter);
```

Handling Spinner Selections

After the Spinner control has been filled with data, you can control which item is selected by using the setSelection() method. For example, you know that the option for female gender is stored in the string array at index 2 (because you use a

0-based string array). Because you conveniently decide to map the indexes directly to the gender values, you can set the Spinner control to the Female option by using the setSelection() method, as follows:

```
spinner.setSelection(2);
```

The Spinner class also includes a number of methods for retrieving the current item selected.

Listening for Selection Events

You want to save the Spinner control option chosen as soon as the user selects one. To do this, you use the setOnItemSelectedListener() method of the Spinner control to listen for selection events. Specifically, you need to implement the onItemSelected() method of AdapterView.OnItemSelectedListener, like this:

```
spinner.setOnItemSelectedListener(
    new AdapterView.OnItemSelectedListener() {
        @Override
        public void onItemSelected(AdapterView<?> parent, View itemSelected,
            int selectedItemPosition, long selectedId) {
            // TODO: Save item index (selectedItemPosition) as Gender setting
        }

        // … Other required overrides
    });
```

> With certain versions of the Android SDK, you might also need to provide the appropriate stub implementations for other required methods of the AdapterView.OnItemSelectedListener class.

At this point, save the QuizSettingsActivity.java file and run the Been There, Done That! application in the Android emulator. After the splash screen finishes, choose the settings screen option. The screen should look as shown in Figure 10.8.

FIGURE 10.8
The Been There,
Done That! set-
tings screen.

Saving Form Data with SharedPreferences

You can use the persistent storage mechanism called SharedPreferences to store
the application game settings. Using these preferences, you can save all the form
values on the settings screen.

Defining SharedPreferences Entries

Earlier you added a string to the QuizActivity base class for your game preferences:

```
public static final String GAME_PREFERENCES = "GamePrefs";
```

Now you need to add a preference String name for each of the values you want to
store to the QuizActivity class:

```
public static final String GAME_PREFERENCES_NICKNAME = "Nickname"; // String
public static final String GAME_PREFERENCES_EMAIL = "Email"; // String
public static final String GAME_PREFERENCES_PASSWORD = "Password"; // String
public static final String GAME_PREFERENCES_DOB = "DOB"; // Long
public static final String GAME_PREFERENCES_GENDER = "Gender"; // Int
```

Saving Settings to SharedPreferences

Now that you have defined the preference settings, you can save any committed form field to the game preferences. Within the QuizSettingsActivity class, you begin by defining a SharedPreferences member variable:

```
SharedPreferences mGameSettings;
```

Within the onCreate() method of the activity, you initialize this member variable as follows:

```
mGameSettings =
    getSharedPreferences(GAME_PREFERENCES, Context.MODE_PRIVATE);
```

You pass in the name of your SharedPreferences (the String called GAME_PREF-ERENCES you created in the QuizActivity class). The mode called MODE_PRIVATE is the default permission used for private application files.

Now anyplace you need to save a preference, you simply open SharedPreferences.Editor, assign a specific preference setting, and commit the change. For example, to save the Nickname EditText information, you retrieve the text by using the EditText control's getText() method:

```
final EditText nicknameText =
    (EditText) findViewById(R.id.EditText_Nickname);
String strNickname = nicknameText.getText().toString();
```

After you have extracted the String value from the EditText input field, you can save it to SharedPreferences.Editor, using the putString() method:

```
Editor editor = mGameSettings.edit();
editor.putString(GAME_PREFERENCES_NICKNAME, strNickname);
editor.commit();
```

The Nickname, Email, and Password settings can be saved as String values, but the Date of Birth and Gender settings are of long and integer types, respectively. To save these settings, you must extract the value from the appropriate control, convert it if necessary, and save it using the SharedPreferences.Editor methods putLong() and putInt().

For now, you can commit the input from the Nickname, Email, and Gender fields. You will work further with the Date of Birth and Password fields in the next hour, when you implement the DatePickerDialog and Password Dialog window. If you go back through the QuizSettingsActivity class and look for the places where you have TODO comments, you can see exactly where you need to commit the data.

Reading Settings from SharedPreferences

When you begin saving settings in a persistent fashion, you are going to need to be able to read them back out and load them into the form (for editing). To do this, you need to access the game preferences and check whether specific settings exist. For example, you might want to check and see if the Nickname setting is set, and if so, load its value into the EditText input field called EditText_Nickname. You can do this by using the contains() and getString() methods of SharedPreferences:

```
final EditText nicknameText =
    (EditText) findViewById(R.id.EditText_Nickname);
if (mGameSettings.contains(GAME_PREFERENCES_NICKNAME)) {
    nicknameText.setText(mGameSettings.getString(
        GAME_PREFERENCES_NICKNAME, ""));
}
```

Here, you check for the existence of a specific setting name defined as GAME_PREFER-ENCES_NICKNAME in SharedPreferences by using the contains() method. If the contains() method returns true, you extract the value of that setting (a String setting) from SharedPreferences by using the getString() method.

The Nickname, Email, and Password settings are strings and can be extracted using the getString() method. However, the Date of Birth setting must be extracted using the getLong() method, and the Gender setting requires the getInt() method.

> Application preferences are stored on the Android file system as XML files. Preferences files can be accessed using the File Explorer of the Eclipse DDMS perspective. SharedPreferences files are found in the following directory:
>
>   /data/data/<package name>/shared_prefs/<preferences filename>.xml

Did you Know?

Finally, for testing purposes, you override the onDestroy() method of QuizSettingsActivity to log all current settings whenever the settings screen is destroyed:

```
@Override
protected void onDestroy() {
    Log.d(DEBUG_TAG, "SHARED PREFERENCES");
    Log.d(DEBUG_TAG, "Nickname is: "
        + mGameSettings.getString(GAME_PREFERENCES_NICKNAME, "Not set"));
    Log.d(DEBUG_TAG, "Email is: "
        + mGameSettings.getString(GAME_PREFERENCES_EMAIL, "Not set"));
    Log.d(DEBUG_TAG, "Gender (M=1, F=2, U=0) is: "
        + mGameSettings.getInt(GAME_PREFERENCES_GENDER, 0));
    // We are not saving the password yet
    Log.d(DEBUG_TAG, "Password is: "
        + mGameSettings.getString(GAME_PREFERENCES_PASSWORD, "Not set"));
    // We are not saving the date of birth yet
    Log.d(DEBUG_TAG, "DOB is: "
        + DateFormat.format("MMMM dd, yyyy", mGameSettings.getLong(
```

```
            GAME_PREFERENCES_DOB, 0)));
    super.onDestroy();
}
```

Now whenever `QuizSettingsActivity` is destroyed (for example, when a user presses the Back button), the preferences that have been committed are displayed in the LogCat console.

Summary

In this hour, you added a form to the settings screen of the Been There, Done That! trivia application. The form handles various fields, including text input of various kinds, using `EditText` controls, and a drop-down list, using a `Spinner` control. You also conserved screen space by implementing two `Button` controls, which can be wired up in the future to launch `Dialog` windows. Finally, you implemented a simple `SharedPreferences` mechanism to load and save game settings for use in the application.

Q&A

Q. *Why not use the typical Save and Cancel buttons that you'd see on a web form?*

A. Mobile input forms may certainly be designed using this traditional approach, but consider the overhead in terms of state management. (`Activity` life cycle events, such as suspend and resume, would need to save and restore pending input.) A common approach for mobile input forms is to commit form fields as they are completed.

Q. *Does a* `Spinner` *control have to be populated from an array?*

A. No, the underlying data of a Spinner control can be populated from numerous data sources using a data adapter. For example, the contents of a Spinner control might instead come from a database.

Workshop

Quiz

1. True or False: EditText controls are derived from TextView controls.

2. What types of button controls are available on the Android platform?

   A. Button

   B. TextButton

   C. ImageButton

3. True or False: You can store Calendar data in SharedPreferences.

Answers

1. True. The TextView class, with its familiar attributes and methods, such as getText() and setText(), is the base class of the EditText class.

2. A and C. There are two button controls in Android: Button is a simple button with a text label. ImageButton is a button with a Drawable graphic label.

3. False. The only types supported by SharedPreferences are Boolean, float, int, long, and String. To save dates or times, consider storing them as long values (milliseconds from epoch).

Exercises

1. Add a Toast to the Password Dialog Button click handler. Make it display the message "Clicked!" when the Button is clicked.

2. Modify each EditText control to save its contents when the user presses the up key (KEYCODE_DPAD_UP) or down key (KEYCODE_DPAD_DOWN) on the directional keypad in addition to the Enter key (KEYCODE_ENTER).

3. Implement a Clear button that deletes all game preferences, using the clear() method of SharedPreferences.Editor. Don't forget to call the commit() method.

HOUR 11

Using Dialogs to Collect User Input

What You'll Learn in This Hour:

- ▶ Working with activity dialogs
- ▶ Using `DatePickerDialog`
- ▶ Handling and formatting date information
- ▶ Building custom dialogs

In this hour, you complete the Been There, Done That! settings screen by adding several `Dialog` windows to `QuizSettingsActivity`. Each `Dialog` window is specially designed to collect a specific type of input from the user. First, you add a `Dialog` window called `DatePickerDialog` to collect date input, allowing the user to supply his or her date of birth, and then you build a custom `Dialog` window to facilitate changing the user's password.

Working with Activity Dialogs

An activity can use `Dialog` windows to organize information and react to user-driven events. For example, an activity might display a dialog informing the user of an error or asking to confirm an action such as deleting a piece of information. Using the `Dialog` mechanism for simple tasks helps keep the number of `Activity` classes in an application manageable.

Exploring the Different Types of Dialog Windows

There are a number of different Dialog window types available in the Android SDK, including the following:

▶ Dialog—The basic class for all Dialog types (see Figure 11.1a).

▶ AlertDialog—A dialog with one, two, or three Button controls (see Figure 11.1b).

▶ CharacterPickerDialog—A dialog for choosing an accented character associated with a base character (see Figure 11.1c).

▶ DatePickerDialog—A dialog with a DatePicker control (see Figure 11.1d).

▶ ProgressDialog—A dialog with a determinate or indeterminate ProgressBar control (see Figure 11.1e).

▶ TimePickerDialog—A dialog with a TimePicker control (see Figure 11.1f).

FIGURE 11.1
The different Dialog window types available in Android.

If none of the existing Dialog window types is adequate, you can create custom Dialog windows that meet your specific layout requirements. We will discuss custom Dialog windows later in this hour.

Tracing the Life Cycle of an Activity Dialog

Each Dialog window must be defined within the activity in which it will be used. A Dialog window may be launched once or used repeatedly. Understanding how an activity manages the `Dialog` window life cycle is important to implementing a `Dialog` window correctly. Let's look at the key methods that an activity must use to manage a `Dialog` window:

▶ The `showDialog()` method is used to display a `Dialog` window.

▶ The `dismissDialog()` method is used to stop showing a `Dialog` window. The `Dialog` window is kept around in the activity's `Dialog` window pool. If the `Dialog` window is shown again, using `showDialog()`, the cached version is displayed once more.

▶ The `removeDialog()` method is used to remove a `Dialog` window from the `Activity` object's `Dialog` window pool. The `Dialog` window will no longer be kept around for future use. If you call `showDialog()` again, the `Dialog` window must be re-created.

Defining a Dialog

A dialog used by an activity must be defined in advance. Each dialog has a special `Dialog` identifier (an integer). When the `showDialog()` method is called, you pass in this `Dialog` identifier as a parameter. At that point, the `onCreateDialog()` method is called and must return a dialog of the appropriate type.

You must override the `onCreateDialog()` method of an activity and return the appropriate dialog for a given identifier. If an activity has multiple `Dialog` windows, the `onCreateDialog()` method can use a `switch` statement to return the appropriate `Dialog` window, based on the incoming parameter—the `Dialog` identifier.

Initializing a Dialog

Because a `Dialog` window may be kept around by an activity, it may be important to re-initialize a dialog each time it is shown instead of just when it is created the first time. For this purpose, you can override the `onPrepareDialog()` method of the activity.

While the `onCreateDialog()` method may be called only once for initial dialog creation, the `onPrepareDialog()` method is called each time the `showDialog()` method is called, giving the activity a chance to initialize the dialog each time it is shown to the user.

Launching a Dialog

You can display any dialog defined within an activity by calling its `showDialog()` method and passing it a valid `Dialog` identifier—one that will be recognized by the `onCreateDialog()` method.

Dismissing a Dialog

Most Dialog types have automatic dismissal circumstances. However, if you want to force a dialog to be dismissed, you can simply call the dismissDialog() method and pass in the Dialog identifier.

Removing a Dialog from Use

Dismissing a Dialog window does not destroy it. If the dialog is shown again, its cached contents will be redisplayed. If you want to force an activity to remove a dialog and not reuse it, you call the removeDialog() method and pass in the valid Dialog identifier.

Using DatePickerDialog

Now you should add a Dialog window to the QuizSettingsActivity class. Specifically, you should add DatePickerDialog to handle input of the user's date of birth. Adding DatePickerDialog to QuizSettingsActivity involves several steps:

1. Define a unique identifier for the dialog within the activity.

2. Implement the onCreateDialog() method of the activity to return DatePickerDialog when supplied the unique identifier.

3. Implement the onPrepareDialog() method of the activity to initialize DatePickerDialog with the date of birth preference or the current date.

4. Launch the DatePickerDialog using the showDialog() method, with the unique Dialog identifier.

Adding the DatePickerDialog to the QuizSettingsActivity Class

To create DatePickerDialog, you must first declare a unique identifier to represent the dialog, as follows:

```
static final int DATE_DIALOG_ID = 0;
```

Next, you need to implement the onCreateDialog() method of QuizSettingsActivity and include a case statement for the new Dialog identifier:

```
@Override
protected Dialog onCreateDialog(int id) {
    switch (id) {
    case DATE_DIALOG_ID:
        // TODO: Return a DatePickerDialog here
```

```
    }
    return null;
}
```

Now let's look at how to construct a DatePickerDialog in detail. Within the switch
statement for DATE_DIALOG_ID, you must return a valid DatePickerDialog for display. The constructor for DatePickerDialog includes a
DatePickerDialog.OnDateSetListener parameter, where you can provide an
implementation of the onDateSet() method to handle when the user chooses a specific date of birth and save it to the SharedPreferences:

```
DatePickerDialog dateDialog =
    new DatePickerDialog(this,
        new DatePickerDialog.OnDateSetListener() {
            public void onDateSet(DatePicker view, int year,
                int monthOfYear, int dayOfMonth) {
                Time dateOfBirth = new Time();
                dateOfBirth.set(dayOfMonth, monthOfYear, year);
                long dtDob = dateOfBirth.toMillis(true);
                dob.setText(DateFormat
                    .format("MMMM dd, yyyy", dtDob));
                Editor editor = mGameSettings.edit();
                editor.putLong(GAME_PREFERENCES_DOB, dtDob);
                editor.commit();
            }
        }, 0, 0, 0);
```

A DatePicker control has three different input controls: month, day, and year.
Therefore, to create DatePickerDialog, you must set these date fields individually.
Because DatePickerDialog can be launched any number of times, you do not initialize its date within the onCreateDialog() method but instead pass in default values (three zeros). Finally, you return the new DatePickerDialog you created in the
onCreateDialog() method switch statement:

```
return dateDialog;
```

Initializing DatePickerDialog

You want to initialize DatePickerDialog each and every time it is displayed, so you
override the onPrepareDialog() method to set DatePicker to either today's date or
the birth date saved in the game preferences.

Did you Know?

You can use the Calendar class to get the current date on the device. The
Calendar class has fields for each of the "parts" of the date: day, month, and
year. You can use this feature of the Calendar class to configure
DatePickerDialog with a specific date.

The onPrepareDialog() method passes in both the Dialog identifier and the instance of the Dialog window, so you can modify it as needed. For example, in this case, you want to update the date of DatePickerDialog, so you use the updateDate() method:

```
@Override
protected void onPrepareDialog(int id, Dialog dialog) {
    super.onPrepareDialog(id, dialog);
    switch (id) {
    case DATE_DIALOG_ID:
        // Handle any DatePickerDialog initialization here
        DatePickerDialog dateDialog = (DatePickerDialog) dialog;
        int iDay, iMonth, iYear;
        // Check for date of birth preference
        if (mGameSettings.contains(GAME_PREFERENCES_DOB)) {
            // Retrieve Birth date setting from preferences
            long msBirthDate = mGameSettings.getLong(GAME_PREFERENCES_DOB, 0);
            Time dateOfBirth = new Time();
            dateOfBirth.set(msBirthDate);
            iDay = dateOfBirth.monthDay;
            iMonth = dateOfBirth.month;
            iYear = dateOfBirth.year;
        } else {
            Calendar cal = Calendar.getInstance();
            // Today's date fields
            iDay = cal.get(Calendar.DAY_OF_MONTH);
            iMonth = cal.get(Calendar.MONTH);
            iYear = cal.get(Calendar.YEAR);
        }
        // Set the date in the DatePicker to the date of birth OR to the
        // current date
        dateDialog.updateDate(iYear, iMonth, iDay);
        return;
    }
}
```

Launching DatePickerDialog

You have configured DatePickerDialog, but it doesn't display unless the user clicks the appropriate Button control on the main settings screen. The user triggers DatePickerDialog by pressing the Button control called Button_DOB.

You registered for click events on the Button_DOB control and currently make a Toast call. Now you can change this to call the showDialog() method, which launches DatePickerDialog, as shown in Figure 11.2:

```
Button pickDate = (Button) findViewById(R.id.Button_DOB);
pickDate.setOnClickListener(new View.OnClickListener() {
    public void onClick(View v) {
        showDialog(DATE_DIALOG_ID);
    }
});
```

FIGURE 11.2
DatePicker-
Dialog used for
date of birth
input.

You can use the `DateFormat` class to format a date string. The `DateFormat` class works well with `Calendar` dates as well as `long` format dates (milliseconds since epoch). For example, to format a `long` date in the form January 1, 2010, you could use the `format()` method of the `DateFormat` method as follows:

```
String strDate = DateFormat.format("MMMM dd, yyyy", dtDob);
```

Did you Know?

Working with Custom Dialogs

When the basic `Dialog` types do not suit your purpose, you can create a custom dialog. One easy way to create a custom dialog is to begin with `AlertDialog` and use an `AlertDialog.Builder` class to override its default layout. To create a custom dialog this way, follow these steps:

1. Design a custom layout resource to display in `AlertDialog`.

2. Define the custom `Dialog` identifier in the activity.

3. Update the activity's `onCreateDialog()` method to build and return the appropriate custom `AlertDialog`.

4. Launch the dialog using the `showDialog()` method.

Adding a Custom Dialog to the Settings Screen

In the Been There, Done That! application, you want to include a custom dialog to handle entering and verifying a new password. Figure 11.3 shows the password dialog states (matching and not matching passwords).

The custom password dialog you want to create requires two text input fields for entering password data. When the two passwords match, the password will be set. Figure 11.4 shows a rough design of the settings screen in this case.

FIGURE 11.4
Rough design
for the Been
There, Done
That! password
dialog.

The password dialog is simply a subform of the settings screen that has two
`EditText` input fields. You also need a `TextView` control below the input fields to
tell the user whether the passwords match.

Figure 11.5 shows the layout design of the password dialog.

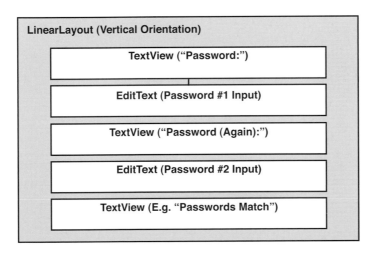

FIGURE 11.5
Layout design
for the Been
There, Done
That! settings
screen.

You can take advantage of the built-in `Button` controls that can be configured for
use with `AlertDialog`. The three buttons need not be included in your layout
design.

Implementing the Password Dialog Layout

Now it's time to implement the new layout that will be used by the password dialog. You begin by creating a new layout resource file called `password_dialog.xml`. This layout file dictates the user interface of the dialog. To create this file, you follow these steps:

1. Open the Eclipse layout resource editor and add a new file called `/res/layout/password_dialog.xml` to the project.

2. Add a `LinearLayout` control. Set its `id` attribute to `root` and set its `orientation` attribute to `vertical`. Set its `layout_width` and `layout_height` attributes to `fill_parent`. All subsequent controls will be added inside this `LinearLayout` control.

3. Add a `TextView` control to display the Password label text. Then add an `EditText` control and set its `id` attribute to `EditText_Pwd1`, its `maxLines` attribute to 1, and its `inputType` attribute to `textPassword`.

4. Add another `TextView` control to display the Password label text again. Then add another `EditText` control and set its `id` attribute to `EditText_Pwd2`, its `maxLines` attribute to 1, and its `inputType` attribute to `textPassword`.

5. Finally, add a `TextView` control with the `id` attribute `TextView_PwdProblem` to display the password status label text. This `TextView` control will display whether the two password fields match.

At this point, save the `password_dialog.xml` layout file.

Adding the Password Dialog to the `QuizSettingsActivity` Class

To create a custom `AlertDialog`, you must first declare a unique identifier to represent the dialog, as follows:

```
static final int PASSWORD_DIALOG_ID = 1;
```
put at the beginning

Next, you need to update the `onCreateDialog()` method of `QuizSettingsActivity` to include a `case` statement for the new `Dialog` identifier:

```
case PASSWORD_DIALOG_ID:
    // Build Dialog
    // Return Dialog
```

Now let's look at how to build the password dialog from the ground up. You begin by inflating (loading) the layout you created into a `View` control:

```
LayoutInflater inflater =
    (LayoutInflater) getSystemService(Context.LAYOUT_INFLATER_SERVICE);
final View layout =
    inflater.inflate(R.layout.password_dialog,
        (ViewGroup) findViewById(R.id.root));
```

To load the password_dialog.xml layout file into a view, you must retrieve LayoutInflater and then call the inflate() method, passing in the layout resource identifier as well as the root layout control's identifier (in this case, the LinearLayout encapsulating the Dialog controls, called root).

Once a layout has been inflated into a View, it can be modified programmatically much like a regular layout. At this point, controls can be populated with data, and event listeners can be registered.

For example, to retrieve the EditText_Pwd1 control from the layout view, you call the findViewById() method, as follows:

```
final EditText p1 =
    (EditText) layout.findViewById(R.id.EditText_Pwd1);
final EditText p2 =
    (EditText) layout.findViewById(R.id.EditText_Pwd2);
```

At this point, you register any event listeners on the EditText fields, such as those discussed earlier to watch EditText input and match the strings as the user types.

For example, you can register to listen for text change events in the second EditText password field using a TextWatcher and match the contents of the field to that in the first EditText field. You can then display the password matching status in the third TextView control we created called TextView_PwdProblem:

```
final TextView error =
    (TextView) layout.findViewById(R.id.TextView_PwdProblem);
p2.addTextChangedListener(new TextWatcher() {
    @Override
    public void afterTextChanged(Editable s) {
        String strPass1 = p1.getText().toString();
        String strPass2 = p2.getText().toString();
        if (strPass1.equals(strPass2)) {
            error.setText(R.string.settings_pwd_equal);
        } else {
            error.setText(R.string.settings_pwd_not_equal);
        }
    }

    // ... other required  overrides do nothing
});
```

The TextWatcher has a number of methods which require implementation. However, the one we're must interested in is the afterTextChanged() method.

Now that you have inflated the view and configured it for use, you can to attach it to AlertDialog. To do this, you use the AlertDialog.Builder class:

```
AlertDialog.Builder builder = new AlertDialog.Builder(this);
builder.setView(layout);
builder.setTitle(R.string.settings_button_pwd);
```

First, you set the view of AlertDialog.Builder to the layout you inflated. Then you set the title of the Dialog window with the setTitle() method.

Your dialog will have two Button controls: a positive button (OK) and a negative button (Cancel). Because you do not want this dialog cached for reuse by the activity, both Button handlers need to call the removeDialog() method, which destroys the dialog:

```
QuizSettingsActivity.this
    .removeDialog(PASSWORD_DIALOG_ID);
```

The positive button (OK) requires some handling. When the user clicks the positive button, you need to extract the password text from the EditText controls, compare it, and, if two strings match, store the new password:

```
builder.setPositiveButton(android.R.string.ok,
    new DialogInterface.OnClickListener() {
        public void onClick(DialogInterface dialog, int which) {
            TextView passwordInfo =
                (TextView) findViewById(R.id.TextView_Password_Info);
            String strPassword1 = p1.getText().toString();
            String strPassword2 = p2.getText().toString();
            if (strPassword1.equals(strPassword2)) {
                Editor editor = mGameSettings.edit();
                editor.putString(GAME_PREFERENCES_PASSWORD,
                    strPassword1);
                editor.commit();
                passwordInfo.setText(R.string.settings_pwd_set);
            } else {
                Log.d(DEBUG_TAG, "Passwords do not match. "
                    + "Not saving. Keeping old password (if set).");
            }
            QuizSettingsActivity.this
                .removeDialog(PASSWORD_DIALOG_ID);
        }
    });
```

The negative button, Cancel, simply returns the user to the main screen. You configure the negative button using the setNegativeButton() method of the builder:

```
builder.setNegativeButton(android.R.string.cancel,
    new DialogInterface.OnClickListener() {
        public void onClick(DialogInterface dialog, int whichButton) {
            QuizSettingsActivity.this
                .removeDialog(PASSWORD_DIALOG_ID);
        }
    });
```

When your dialog is fully configured using the builder, you call the `create()` method to generate the custom `AlertDialog` and return it:

```
AlertDialog passwordDialog = builder.create();
return passwordDialog;
```

Launching the Custom Password Dialog

A custom dialog, such as your password dialog, is launched the same way as a regular dialog: using the `showDialog()` method of the activity. On the settings screen of the Been There, Done That! application, the user triggers the custom password dialog to launch by pressing the `Button` control called `Button_Password`. Therefore, you can register for click events on this `Button` control and launch the password dialog accordingly:

```
Button setPassword = (Button) findViewById(R.id.Button_Password);
setPassword.setOnClickListener(new View.OnClickListener() {
    public void onClick(View v) {
        showDialog(PASSWORD_DIALOG_ID);
    }
});
```

Figure 11.6 shows the resulting settings screen, with `Dialog` controls.

FIGURE 11.6
The complete Been There, Done That! settings screen.

Summary

In this hour, you learned how an activity can use `Dialog` controls to simplify screen functionality and layout—specifically on the settings screen of the Been There, Done That! application. A dialog can be used to display appropriate information to the user in the form of a pop-up window. There are `Dialog` types for inputting dates, times, and special characters as well as helper `Dialog` types for showing progress or displaying alert messages. You can also create custom `Dialog` controls.

Q&A

Q. *How is dialog information saved within an activity?*

A. Each activity keeps a pool of `Dialog` controls around for use and will reuse a `Dialog` control when asked to be shown again. Basically, a dialog is shown using the `showDialog()` method and added to the pool. Each dialog is dismissed but sticks around in the pool until either the activity is destroyed or the `removeDialog()` method is called explicitly.

Q. *How can I determine which activity launched a* `Dialog` *control?*

A. You can use the `getOwnerActivity()` method of the `Dialog` class to determine the parent activity of a specific `Dialog` control.

Workshop

Quiz

1. What class can be used to create pop-up windows within an activity?

   A. `Popup`

   B. `ActivityWindow`

   C. `Dialog`

2. True or False: You can use the same dialog for multiple uses if the layout is the same.

3. True or False: Only certain layouts can be used with a dialog, such as `Alert` and `ContinueOrCancel`.

Answers

1. C. The `Dialog` class and its subclasses are used to create pop-up windows within an activity, using the `onCreateDialog()` and `showDialog()` methods.

2. True. But if you want the data shown to be different, you need to override `onPrepareDialog()` in the activity.

3. False. You can use any layout you want for a dialog.

Exercises

1. Update the `DatePickerDialog onDateSet()` method to save the date of birth to a `TextView` to display on the main settings screen.

2. Update the password dialog to display the status of the password (set or unset) in a `TextView` on the main settings screen.

HOUR 12

Adding Application Logic

What You'll Learn in This Hour:

▶ Designing the game screen
▶ Working with `ViewSwitcher` **Controls**
▶ Data structures and parsing XML
▶ Wiring up the game logic and keeping game state

In this hour, you wire up the screen at the heart of the Been There, Done That! application—the game play screen. This screen prompts the user to answer a series of trivia questions and stores the resulting score information. Because the screen must display a dynamic series of images and text strings, you can use several new `View` controls, including `ImageSwitcher` and `TextSwitcher`, to help transition between questions in the quiz. You can also update `QuizGameActivity` with game logic and game state information, including the retrieval of batches of new questions, as a user progresses through the quiz.

Designing the Game Screen

The game screen must lead the user through a series of trivia questions and log the number of positive responses (the score). Each trivia question has a corresponding graphic to display. For example, the game might show the user a picture of a mountain and ask if the user has ever climbed a mountain.

Unlike previous screens you have developed, the game screen does not need the customary title bar. Instead, you want to use the entire screen to display the game components. Figure 12.1 shows a rough design of the game screen.

FIGURE 12.1
Rough design for the Been There, Done That! game screen.

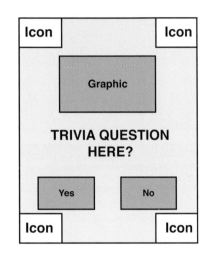

You want the game screen to share some common features with the rest of the application: It should use the same background graphic, font, and color scheme as the other screens. To translate the rough design into the appropriate layout design, you need to update the /res/layout/game.xml layout file and the QuizGameActivity class.

RelativeLayout works especially well for displaying icon graphics in each of the four corners of the screen. You can also use another RelativeLayout to display each question to the user, using one ImageView control and one TextView control, as well as two Button controls to handle responses.

Figure 12.2 shows the basic layout design of the game screen.

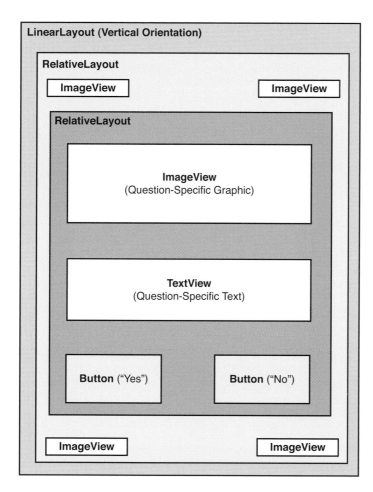

FIGURE 12.2
Layout design
for the Been
There, Done
That! game
screen.

Each time the user clicks a `Button` control, the game screen will update the `ImageView` and `TextView` controls to display the next question. To smoothly transition (and animate) from one question to the next, you can use the special controls `ImageSwitcher` and `TextSwitcher`, which are subclasses of the `ViewSwitcher` class.

A `ViewSwitcher` control can animate between two child `View` controls: the current `View` control and the next `View` control to display. Only one `View` control is displayed at any time, but animations, such as fades or rotates, can be used during the transition between `View` controls. These child `View` controls are generated using `ViewFactory`. For example, `ImageSwitcher` and its corresponding `ViewFactory` can be used to generate the current question `ImageView` and switch in the next question's `ImageView` when the user clicks a `Button` control. Similarly, a `TextSwitcher` control has two child `TextView` controls, with transitional animation applying to the text.

Figure 12.3 shows the updated layout design of the game screen, which uses an ImageSwitcher control and a TextSwitcher control.

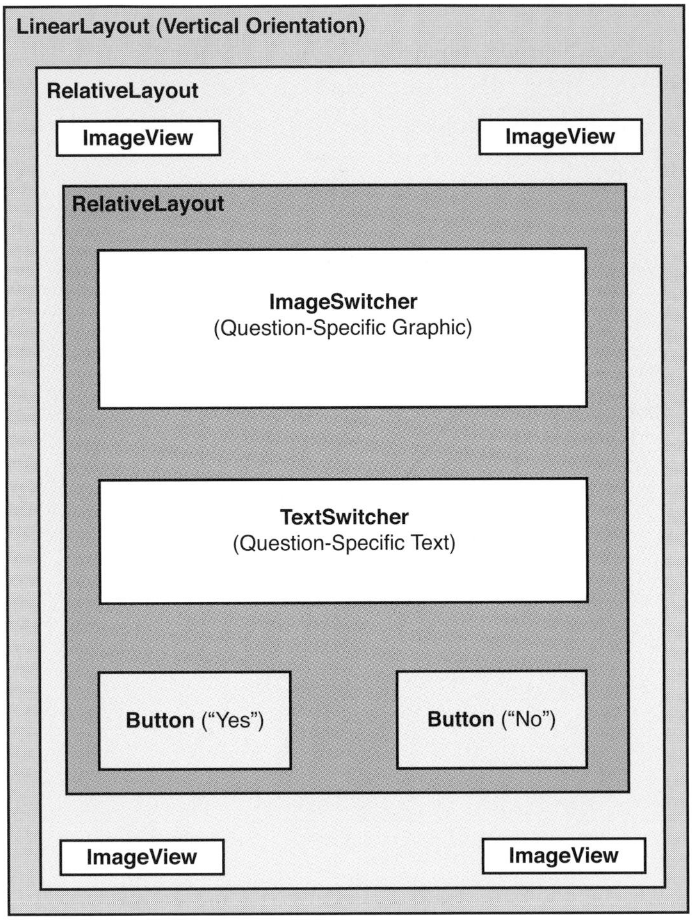

FIGURE 12.3
Revised layout
design for the
Been There,
Done That! game
screen with
ImageSwitcher
and
TextSwitcher
controls.

Implementing the Game Screen Layout

To implement the game screen, you begin by adding new resources to the project. Then you need to update the game.xml layout resource to reflect the game screen design.

Adding New Project Resources

For the game screen, you need to add some new resources:

▶ String resources for the text on the Button controls as well as the text to display when no questions are available

▶ Miscellaneous `Dimension` and `Color` resources needed to design the game screen controls

▶ Two XML resources with mock question batches

You should now be comfortable creating any `String`, `Dimension`, and `Color` resources you need for the screen layout, so let's talk for a moment about the mock question batches.

Eventually, the questions used by the Been There, Done That! application will be retrieved from a server on the Internet. However, for now, you can create two batches of mock questions that can be accessed locally as XML: `/res/xml/samplequestions.xml` and `/res/xml/samplequestions2.xml`. Later, when you add network support to the application, you will retrieve this same XML from a server. By including mock batches of questions now, you can iron out the game logic without worrying about network connectivity.

Regardless of whether the batch of questions is sourced locally or from a remote server, the XML block looks the same. Here is what it looks like:

```
<?xml version-"1.0" encoding="utf-8"?>
    <!— This is a mock question XML chunk —>
<questions>
    <question
        number="1"
        text=
          "Have you ever been on an African safari?"
        imageUrl=
          "http://www.perlgurl.org/Android/BeenThereDoneThat/Questions/q1.png"
    />
    <question
        number="2"
        text=
          "Have you ever climbed a mountain?"
        imageUrl=
          "http://www.perlgurl.org/Android/BeenThereDoneThat/Questions/q2.png"
    />
    <question
        number="3"
        text=
          "Have you ever milked a cow?"
        imageUrl=
          "http://www.perlgurl.org/Android/BeenThereDoneThat/Questions/q3.png"
    />
</questions>
```

As you can see, the XML is very simple. It has one tag called <questions>, which can contain a number of <question> tags. Each <question> tag has three attributes: the question identifier (number), the question itself (text), and the URL to the image associated with the question (imageUrl). Note that you use remote graphics sourced from the Internet instead of adding each and every question graphic to the resources of the application.

Updating the Game Screen Layout

The game.xml layout file dictates the user interface of the game screen. Again, you open the Eclipse layout resource editor and remove all existing controls from the layout. You then follow these steps to generate the layout you want, based on your design:

1. Add a new LinearLayout control and set its background attribute to @drawable/bkgrnd. All subsequent controls will be added inside the LinearLayout control.

2. Add a RelativeLayout control and set layout_width to wrap_content and layout_height to wrap_content. *(fill_parent)*

3. Within the RelativeLayout control, add four ImageView controls—one for each corner of the screen. Set each control's image src attribute to the @drawable/quizicon graphic. Give each ImageView control a specific id attribute: @+id/ImageView_Header, @+id/ImageView_Header2, @+id/ImageView_Header3, and @+id/ImageView_Header4.

4. Find the ImageView control with the id attribute set to ImageView_Header and set its layout_alignParentLeft and layout_alignParentTop attributes to true.

5. Find the ImageView control with the id attribute set to ImageView_Header2 and set its layout_alignParentRight and layout_alignParentTop attributes to true.

6. Find the ImageView control with the id attribute set to ImageView_Header3 and set its layout_alignParentLeft and layout_alignParentBottom attributes to true.

7. Find the ImageView control with the id attribute set to ImageView_Header4 and set its layout_alignParentRight and layout_alignParentBottom attributes to true.

8. Still within the RelativeLayout control, add another RelativeLayout control for the trivia question region after the ImageView control; name it ImageView_Header2. Set its id attribute to the value @+id/RelativeLayout_Content. Set layout_width to wrap_content and layout_height to wrap_content. Also, set its gravity attribute to center and its layout_margin to 45px.

9. Within the new RelativeLayout control, add an ImageSwitcher control with an id of @+id/ImageSwitcher_QuestionImage. Set layout_width to wrap_content and layout_height to wrap_content. Also, set its layout_alignParentTop and layout_centerInParent attributes to true.

10. Below the ImageSwitcher control, add a TextSwitcher control with an id of @+id/TextSwitcher_QuestionText. Set layout_width to wrap_content and layout_height to wrap_content. Also, set its layout_centerInParent attribute to true and its layout_below attribute to @+id/ImageSwitcher_QuestionImage.

11. Below the TextSwitcher control, add a Button control with an id of @+id/Button_Yes. Set layout_width to wrap_content and layout_height to wrap_content. Also, set its layout_alignParentBottom and layout_alignParentLeft attributes to true. Set its text attribute to a resource string ("Yes") and tweak any other attributes to make the Button control look nice.

12. Add another Button control below the previous Button control, with an id of @+id/Button_No. Set the layout_width to wrap_content and the layout_height to wrap_content. Also, set its layout_alignParentBottom and layout_alignParentRight attributes to true. Set its text attribute to a resource string ("No") and tweak any other attributes to make the Button control look nice.

At this point, save the game.xml layout file.

The Eclipse layout resource editor does not display TextSwitcher or ImageSwitcher controls in design mode. You must view the resulting TextView and ImageView controls generated by the switchers by using the Android emulator. In this case, the layout designer does not reflect actual application look and feel.

Watch Out!

Working with ViewSwitcher **Controls**

For situations in which an activity is going to be updating the content of a View control repeatedly, the Android SDK provides a mechanism called a ViewSwitcher control. Using a ViewSwitcher is an efficient way to update content on a screen. A ViewSwitcher control has two children and handles transition from the currently visible child view to the next view to be displayed. The child View controls of a ViewSwitcher control can be generated programmatically using ViewFactory.

There are two subclasses of the ViewSwitcher class:

▶ TextSwitcher—A ViewSwitcher control that allows swapping between two TextView controls.

▶ ImageSwitcher—A ViewSwitcher control that allows swapping between two ImageView controls.

Although a ViewSwitcher control only ever has two children, it can display any number of View controls in succession. ViewFactory generates the content of the next view, such as the ImageSwitcher and TextSwitcher controls for iterating through the question images and text.

> You can create a custom switcher by implementing your own subclass of the ViewSwitcher class.

Using ViewFactory **to Generate** ViewSwitcher **Views**

When you create a ViewSwitcher control, you can configure ViewFactory using the setFactory() method. ViewFactory has one required method, the makeView() method. This method must return a View of the appropriate type. For example, ViewFactory for TextSwitcher should return a properly configured TextView, whereas ViewFactory for ImageSwitcher would return ImageView.

Here is an implementation of a ViewFactory control for an ImageSwitcher control that you could use to generate each question graphic on the game play screen:

```
private class MyImageSwitcherFactory implements ViewSwitcher.ViewFactory {
    public View makeView() {
        ImageView imageView = new ImageView(QuizGameActivity.this);
        imageView.setScaleType(ImageView.ScaleType.FIT_CENTER);
        imageView .setLayoutParams(new ImageSwitcher.LayoutParams(
            LayoutParams.FILL_PARENT, LayoutParams.FILL_PARENT));
        return imageView ;
    }
}
```

Note that the source, or contents, of the view have not been configured in the makeView() method. Instead, you can consider this a template that the ViewSwitcher control will use to display each child view.

When you create a ViewSwitcher control, you can configure its ViewFactory using the setFactory() method. For example, to set ViewFactory of the ImageSwitcher control you created for MyImageSwitcherFactory, you do the following:

```
ImageSwitcher questionImageSwitcher =
    (ImageSwitcher) findViewById(R.id.ImageSwitcher_QuestionImage);
questionImageSwitcher.setFactory(new MyImageSwitcherFactory());
```

Similarly, you must create a ViewFactory to generate the TextView controls for each question on the game screen. Here is an implementation of a ViewFactory called MyTextSwitcherFactory that does just that:

```
private class MyTextSwitcherFactory implements ViewSwitcher.ViewFactory {
    public View makeView() {
        TextView textView = new TextView(QuizGameActivity.this);
        textView.setGravity(Gravity.CENTER);
        Resources res = getResources();
        float dimension = res.getDimension(R.dimen.game_question_size);
        int titleColor = res.getColor(R.color.title_color);
        int shadowColor = res.getColor(R.color.title_glow);
        textView.setTextSize(dimension);
        textView.setTextColor(titleColor);
        textView.setShadowLayer(10, 5, 5, shadowColor);
        return textView;
    }
}
```

Note that, much like the MyImageSwitcherFactory implementation, the MyTextSwitcherFactory also implements the makeView() method—this time generating the appropriate TextView control with some text size, color, and gravity attributes.

Working with TextSwitcher

The TextSwitcher control enables an activity to animate between two TextView controls. You need to include a TextSwitcher control called TextSwitcher_ QuestionText in the layout of the game screen to display each trivia question to the user.

Initializing a TextSwitcher Control

To initialize a TextSwitcher control, you simply set its ViewFactory and then use the setCurrentText() method, like so:

```
TextSwitcher questionTextSwitcher = (TextSwitcher)
    findViewById(R.id.TextSwitcher_QuestionText);
questionTextSwitcher.setFactory(new MyTextSwitcherFactory());
questionTextSwitcher.setCurrentText("First Text String");
```

Updating a TextSwitcher Control

When you want to update a TextSwitcher control with a new TextView control, you can call the setText() method:

```
TextSwitcher questionTextSwitcher = (TextSwitcher)
    findViewById(R.id.TextSwitcher_QuestionText);
questionTextSwitcher.setText("Next Text String");
```

Calling the setText() method causes MyTextSwitcherFactory to generate a new
TextView control with the String contents supplied in the setText() parameter.

Working with ImageSwitcher

The ImageSwitcher control enables an activity to animate between two ImageView
controls. You have included an ImageSwitcher control called ImageSwitcher_
QuestionImage in the layout of the game screen to display each trivia question
image to the user.   *see Android developer web.*

Initializing an ImageSwitcher Control

To initialize an ImageSwitcher control, you simply set its ViewFactory and then
use one of the three methods to set the image. In this case, you use the
setImageDrawable() method, like so:

```
ImageSwitcher questionImageSwitcher = (ImageSwitcher)
    findViewById(R.id.ImageSwitcher_QuestionImage);
questionImageSwitcher.setFactory(new MyImageSwitcherFactory());
Drawable image = getQuestionImageDrawable(startingQuestionNumber);
questionImageSwitcher.setImageDrawable(image);
```

By the Way

Unfortunately, you cannot use the setImageURI() method with a remote (online)
URL with ImageSwitcher at this time. Instead, you need to perform a bit of extra
work to download the image from the supplied URL and save it into an image
Drawable object. The implementation of the getQuestionImageDrawable()
method does just that:

```
private Drawable getQuestionImageDrawable(int questionNumber) {
    Drawable image;
    URL imageUrl;

    try {
        // Create a Drawable by decoding a stream from a remote URL
        imageUrl = new URL(getQuestionImageUrl(questionNumber));
        Bitmap bitmap = BitmapFactory.decodeStream(imageUrl.openStream());
        image = new BitmapDrawable(bitmap);
    } catch (Exception e) {
        Log.e(DEBUG_TAG, "Decoding Bitmap stream failed.");
        image = getResources().getDrawable(R.drawable.noquestion);
    }
    return image;
}
```

> The getQuestionImageUrl() method is a simple helper method that retrieves
> the appropriate graphic web address for a given question. This information is
> stored in the Hashtable of questions. (We'll talk more about how we handle ques-
> tions in a moment.) For the full implementation of the getQuestionImageUrl()
> method, see the code provided with this book.
>
> You use the URL class to encapsulate the remote address to the PNG image file
> you want to load into ImageSwitcher. You then dump the data into
> BitmapDrawable. Finally, using the stream methods requires the android.per-
> mission.INTERNET permission, which needs to be added to the Android manifest
> file for the project.

Updating ImageSwitcher

When you want to update ImageSwitcher with a new ImageView control, you call
the setImageDrawable() method:

```
ImageSwitcher questionImageSwitcher =
    (ImageSwitcher) findViewById(R.id.ImageSwitcher_QuestionImage);
Drawable image = getQuestionImageDrawable(nextQuestionNumber);
questionImageSwitcher.setImageDrawable(image);
```

Calling the setImageDrawable() method causes MyImageSwitcherFactory to generate a new ImageView control with the Drawable object supplied in the
setImageDrawable() parameter.

Animating ViewSwitcher

To animate the transition between the child View controls of ViewSwitcher, you use
the setInAnimation() and setOutAnimation() methods. For example, to add
fade-in and fade-out animations to the TextSwitcher control, you could load and
set the built-in Android fade animations as follows:

```
Animation in = AnimationUtils.loadAnimation(this, android.R.anim.fade_in);
Animation out = AnimationUtils.loadAnimation(this, android.R.anim.fade_out);
TextSwitcher questionTextSwitcher =
    (TextSwitcher) findViewById(R.id.TextSwitcher_QuestionText);
questionTextSwitcher.setInAnimation(in);
questionTextSwitcher.setOutAnimation(out);
```

Now each time the setText() method or setCurrentText() method of
TextSwitcher is called, this fade animation will run. You can now improve the
question transition further by adding the same animations to the ImageSwitcher
displaying the question images.

Wiring Up Game Logic

The Been There, Done That! application has an open-ended set of trivia questions. Therefore, you cannot save all the questions as resources but instead need to develop a simple way to get new questions on-the-fly. Also, by storing the complete set of trivia questions in a remote location, you streamline the application on the handset, saving disk space.

In the final version of the application, you will be retrieving new batches of questions from the Internet. For now, though, you can retrieve several batches of questions from local XML files. The application can keep a working set of questions in memory, and new batches of questions can be loaded as required. To implement the game logic for the game screen, follow these steps:

1. Update `SharedPreferences` with game state settings.

2. Handle the retrieval and parsing batches of trivia questions (XML) into a relevant data structure.

3. Implement `Button` click handling to drive the `ImageSwitcher` and `TextSwitcher` updates as well as the game logic.

4. Handle edge cases, such as when no more questions are available.

The following sections describe these steps in more detail.

Updating `SharedPreferences` to Include Game State Settings

To keep track of game state, you need to add two more `Integer` settings to the application `SharedPreferences`: the game score and the current question number. To add these preferences, you first declare the preference name `String` values to the `QuizActivity.java` class:

```
public static final String GAME_PREFERENCES_SCORE = "Score";
public static final String GAME_PREFERENCES_CURRENT_QUESTION = "CurQuestion";
```

Next, you define the `SharedPreferences` object as a member variable of the `QuizGameActivity` class:

```
SharedPreferences mGameSettings;
```

You initialize the `mGameSettings` member variable in the `onCreate()` method of the `QuizGameActivity` class:

```
mGameSettings = getSharedPreferences(GAME_PREFERENCES, Context.MODE_PRIVATE);
```

Now you can use `SharedPreferences` throughout the class, as needed, to read and write game settings such as the current question and the game score. For example, you could get the current question by using the `getInt()` method of `SharedPreferences` as follows:

```
int startingQuestionNumber =
    mGameSettings.getInt(GAME_PREFERENCES_CURRENT_QUESTION, 0);
```

Retrieving, Parsing, and Storing Trivia Question Data

When the Been There, Done That! application runs out of questions to display to the user, it attempts to retrieve a new batch of questions. This architecture makes enabling networking for the application more straightforward in future hours because the parsing of the XML remains the same.

Each batch of questions arrives as a simple XML file, which needs to be parsed. You can store the current batch of questions in memory by using a simple but powerful data structure—in this case, a `Hashtable` member variable.

Declaring Helpful String Literals for Question Parsing

Take a moment to review the XML format used by the question batches, discussed earlier. To parse the question batches, you need to add several `String` literals to represent the XML tags and attributes to the `QuizActivity.java` class:

```java
public static final String XML_TAG_QUESTION_BLOCK = "questions";
public static final String XML_TAG_QUESTION = "question";
public static final String XML_TAG_QUESTION_ATTRIBUTE_NUMBER = "number";
public static final String XML_TAG_QUESTION_ATTRIBUTE_TEXT = "text";
public static final String XML_TAG_QUESTION_ATTRIBUTE_IMAGEURL = "imageUrl";
```

While you are at it, you can also define the default batch size, to simplify allocation of storage for questions while parsing the XML:

```java
public static final int QUESTION_BATCH_SIZE = 15;
```

Storing the Current Batch of Questions in a Hashtable

Now within the `QuizGameActivity` class, you can implement a simple helper class called `Question` to encapsulate each trivia question:

```java
private class Question {
    int mNumber;
    String mText;
    String mImageUrl;

    public Question(int questionNum, String questionText, String
        questionImageUrl) {
        mNumber = questionNum;
        mText = questionText;
```

```
        mImageUrl = questionImageUrl;
    }
}
```

You will not be storing all the questions locally. Instead, you fetch a batch of questions at a time (for now, from local mock XML files, later from the web). You need a place to store these questions, so declare a `Hashtable` member variable within the `QuizGameActivity` class to hold a batch `Question` objects in memory after you have parsed a batch of XML:

```
Hashtable<Integer, Question> mQuestions;
```

> The Android SDK includes many commonly used Java classes. For example, you'll find many familiar data structures (such as `Hashtable`) and utility classes in the `java.util` package, as well as additional specialized classes in the `android.util` package.

You can instantiate the `Hashtable` member variable in the `onCreate()` method of the `QuizGameActivity` class as follows:

```
mQuestions = new Hashtable<Integer, Question>(QUESTION_BATCH_SIZE);
```

Now, assuming we have some XML representing a new batch of questions, we can create an `XmlResourceParser` object called `questionBatch`. The `XmlResourceParser` can be used it to extract the data for each question and save into a `Hashtable` member variable of type `Question`, using the `put()` method, like this:

```
String questionNumber =
    questionBatch.getAttributeValue(null, XML_TAG_QUESTION_ATTRIBUTE_NUMBER);
Integer questionNum =
    new Integer(questionNumber);
String questionText =
    questionBatch.getAttributeValue(null, XML_TAG_QUESTION_ATTRIBUTE_TEXT);
String questionImageUrl =
    questionBatch.getAttributeValue(null, XML_TAG_QUESTION_ATTRIBUTE_IMAGEURL);

// Save data to our hashtable
mQuestions.put(questionNum,
    new Question(questionNum, questionText, questionImageUrl));
```

You can check for the existence of a specific question in the `Hashtable` member variable by question number, using the `containsKey()` method. You can also retrieve a specific `Question` object by its question number by using the `get()` method:

```
Question curQuestion = (Question) mQuestions.get(questionNumber);
```

Handling Button Presses

The Button controls on the game screen are used to drive the ImageSwitcher and
TextSwitcher controls. Each time the user clicks a Button control, any score
changes are logged, and the ViewSwitcher controls are updated to display the next
question. In this way, the Button controls drive the activity forward, and the user
progresses through the trivia quiz questions.

There is little difference between the handling of the Yes and No Button controls.
Let's take a closer look at the OnClickListener.OnClick() method of the Yes
Button control:

```
Button yesButton = (Button) findViewById(R.id.Button_Yes);
yesButton.setOnClickListener(new View.OnClickListener() {
    public void onClick(View v) {
        handleAnswerAndShowNextQuestion(true);
    }
});
```

The View.onClickListener() method for the corresponding No Button is almost
identical to the Yes Button control handler shown here. The only difference is that
you pass a false value into the handleAnswerAndShowNextQuestion() method.
This is a custom method you will implement to log the score change and handle
any ViewSwitcher logic.

Now let's look in more detail at the handleAnswerAndShowNextQuestion() method,
which takes one parameter, boolean bAnswer. First, examine the following pseudo-
code showing what this Button handler will do:

```
private void handleAnswerAndShowNextQuestion(boolean bAnswer) {
    // Load game settings like score and current question
    // Update score if answer is "yes"
    // Load the next question, handling if there are no more questions
}
```

Now let's work through the pseudo-code and implement this method. First, you must
retrieve the current game settings, including the game score and the next question
number, from SharedPreferences:

```
int curScore =
    mGameSettings.getInt(GAME_PREFERENCES_SCORE, 0);
int nextQuestionNumber =
    mGameSettings.getInt(GAME_PREFERENCES_CURRENT_QUESTION, 1) + 1;
```

Next, you need to increment the value of the next question in SharedPreferences:

```
Editor editor = mGameSettings.edit();
editor.putInt(GAME_PREFERENCES_CURRENT_QUESTION, nextQuestionNumber);
```

If the user clicked the Yes button, you also need to update the score and save it to
SharedPreferences:

```
if (bAnswer == true) {
    editor.putInt(GAME_PREFERENCES_SCORE, curScore + 1);
}
```

After you have changed all the SharedPreferences values necessary, you save the
changes with the commit() method of the editor:

```
editor.commit();
```

Next, you check whether the next question is available in the hashtable. If you need
to retrieve a new batch of questions, do so now:

```
if (mQuestions.containsKey(nextQuestionNumber) == false) {
    // Load next batch
    try {
        loadQuestionBatch(nextQuestionNumber);
    } catch (Exception e) {
        Log.e(DEBUG_TAG, "Loading updated question batch failed", e);
    }
}
```

Finally, you update the TextSwitcher and the ImageSwitcher controls with the text
and image for the next question:

```
if (mQuestions.containsKey(nextQuestionNumber) == true) {
    // Update question text
    TextSwitcher questionTextSwitcher =
        (TextSwitcher) findViewById(R.id.TextSwitcher_QuestionText);
    questionTextSwitcher.setText(getQuestionText(nextQuestionNumber));

    // Update question image
    ImageSwitcher questionImageSwitcher =
        (ImageSwitcher) findViewById(R.id.ImageSwitcher_QuestionImage);
    Drawable image = getQuestionImageDrawable(nextQuestionNumber);
    questionImageSwitcher.setImageDrawable(image);
} else {
    handleNoQuestions();
}
```

When you run the application and launch the game screen, it should look something like Figure 12.4.

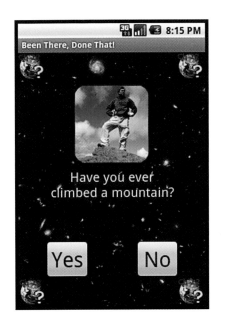

FIGURE 12.4
The Been There,
Done That!
game screen.

There are two easy ways to "reset" the quiz for testing purposes. The first method is to delete the application's SharedPreferences file from the Android file system and restart the emulator. You use the Eclipse DDMS perspective to navigate to the data directory of the application and delete the associated SharedPreferences file. You can also uninstall and reinstall the application by using the Settings Menu item from the Android Home screen. Adding a reset mechanism to the Been There, Done That! application is left as an exercise to the reader at the end of this hour.

Addressing Edge Cases

If there are no more questions available, you must inform the user. This case is handled by the handleNoQuestions() method. First, you set the text and image to appropriate values, as follows:

```
TextSwitcher questionTextSwitcher =
    (TextSwitcher) findViewById(R.id.TextSwitcher_QuestionText);
questionTextSwitcher.setText(getResources().getText(R.string.no_questions));
ImageSwitcher questionImageSwitcher =
    (ImageSwitcher) findViewById(R.id.ImageSwitcher_QuestionImage);
questionImageSwitcher.setImageResource(R.drawable.noquestion);
```

You should also take this opportunity to disable the `Button` controls:

```
Button yesButton =
    (Button) findViewById(R.id.Button_Yes);
yesButton.setEnabled(false);

Button noButton =
    (Button) findViewById(R.id.Button_No);
noButton.setEnabled(false);
```

When the application runs out of questions, the game screen looks as shown in Figure 12.5. The user is informed that there are no more questions available and is not allowed to press any of the `Button` controls. Instead, the user must press the Back button and return to the main menu.

FIGURE 12.5
The Been There, Done That! game screen when no questions are available.

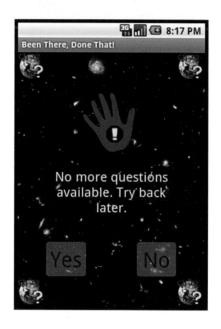

Summary

In this hour, you implemented the most important screen of the Been There, Done That! application—the game screen. You learned how to animate between `View` controls by using `ImageSwitcher` and `TextSwitcher`. You also got your first look at the various data structures available in the Android SDK and used a `Hashtable` member variable to store a batch of questions parsed from XML. Finally, you used the application's `SharedPreferences` to keep track of settings and game state information.

Q&A

Q. *If I'm storing images locally, can I use the* `ImageSwitcher setImageURI()` *method instead of the* `setImageDrawable()` *method?*

A. Of course. In fact, we recommend it. If the graphic is locally available, use the `setImageURI()` method to greatly simplify the code for loading a graphic into an `ImageSwitcher` (or `ImageView`) control. There is no need for streams or `Drawable` objects in memory.

Q. *When using a* `ViewSwitcher` *control, can I set my own animations?*

A. Yes, you can create any animation you want between the old `View` control and the new `View` control. However, keep in mind that once a `View` control has been switched out, the only way to bring it back is by setting it as the next `View` control. There is no notion of a previous `View` control with the `ViewSwitcher` control.

Workshop

Quiz

1. What subclasses are available for the `ViewSwitcher` class?

   A. `TextSwitcher`

   B. `VideoSwitcher`

   C. `ImageSwitcher`

   D. `AudioSwitcher`

2. True or False: The `TextView` controls used by a `TextSwitcher` control must be defined before the `TextSwitcher` control can be used.

3. True or False: Standard packages such as `java.io`, `java.math`, `java.net`, and `java.util` are available within the Android SDK.

Answers

1. A and C. The ViewSwitcher class has two subclasses: TextSwitcher (for animating between two TextView controls) and ImageSwitcher (for animating between two ImageView controls).

2. False. The TextView controls displayed by a TextSwitcher control can be created on-the-fly by using ViewFactory.

3. True. Many standard Java packages are available within the Android SDK. There are also a number of packages specially designed for Android under the android.* package tree. See the Android SDK documentation for a complete list of available packages.

Exercises

1. Add a new option to the options menu of the game screen to reset the trivia quiz. Make sure you clear only the appropriate game settings, not all of the preferences, in SharedPreferences.

2. Modify the application to use a different data structure, like a linked list, instead of a Hashtable.

Working with Images and the Camera

What You'll Learn in This Hour:

▶ Designing the avatar feature
▶ Working with `ImageButton` controls
▶ Launching activities and handling results
▶ Working with the camera and the gallery
▶ Working with bitmaps

In this hour, you add a new feature to the Been There, Done That! application—the ability for the user to add a custom avatar or small graphic from the settings screen. The user will be able to set the avatar in two ways: by using the camera that is built in to the handset or by choosing an image that is already stored on the handset.

Designing the Avatar Feature

Many mobile applications today are networked and have some social component. One way for users to differentiate themselves from others is by setting custom icons to represent who they are. To give users this ability, you can implement the avatar feature on the settings screen. Avatars come in many forms; an avatar may be a close-up photograph of the user's face, or it might be a funky graphic that speaks to the user's personality.

To incorporate of the avatar feature into the Been There, Done That! Settings screen, you need to modify the screen design slightly to include the graphic as well as some mechanism by which the user can change the graphic. Figure 13.1 shows a rough design of how the avatar feature will be incorporated into the settings screen.

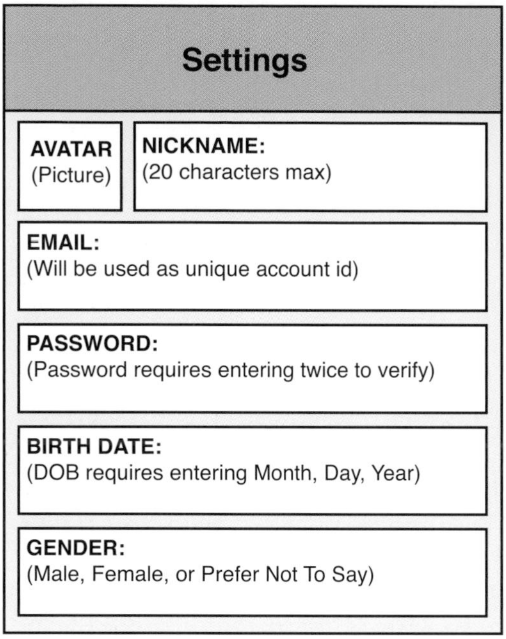

FIGURE 13.1
Rough design for
the Been There,
Done That! avatar
feature.

FIGURE 13.1
Rough design for the Been There, Done That! avatar feature.

Space is at a premium in a mobile application, and you want to keep the settings screen for the Been There, Done That! application as easy to use as possible. The avatar feature has two requirements: The user must be able to set the avatar from a custom graphic, and the graphic chosen must be displayed on the settings screen. Of the various controls available in Android, the `ImageButton` control would be able to handle both tasks.

To incorporate your avatar design changes into the `/res/layout/settings.xml` layout file, you need to modify the region of the screen where the nickname controls reside.

Because you want to add a control to the left of the nickname controls, you need to encapsulate all three controls (the avatar `ImageButton`, nickname label `TextView`, and nickname `EditText` controls) inside a child layout control such as a nested `LinearLayout` Control (horizontally oriented). By nesting the nickname controls in their own vertically oriented `LinearLayout` control, you get the intended results. Figure 13.2 shows the layout updates required by the avatar feature.

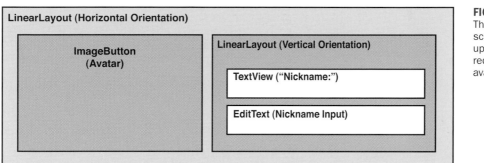

FIGURE 13.2
The settings
screen layout
updates
required for the
avatar feature.

But wait! You want the user to be able to configure the avatar by using the camera (to take a new picture) or by choosing an image already saved on the device. No problem. You can do this by handling clicks and long-clicks on the same Button control. The user can click the ImageButton control to launch the camera or long-click the same ImageButton control to launch the image picker.

Adding an Avatar to the Settings Screen Layout

To update the settings screen, you begin by adding new resources to the project, and then you update the settings.xml layout resource to reflect the new settings screen design.

To enable the avatar feature in the Been There, Done That! application, you need to add some new resources, including any String, Dimension, Color, and Drawable resources you might need. For example, you should add a new graphic resource to show as the default avatar.

Updating the Settings Screen Layout

The settings.xml layout file dictates the user interface of the settings screen. You need to reopen this layout file in the Eclipse layout resource editor and make the following changes:

1. First, find the TextView control called TextView_Nickname in the file. Above this control and inside the ScrollView control, add a new LinearLayout control and set its orientation attribute to horizontal. Set the layout_width and layout_height attributes to fill_parent.

2. Within the LinearLayout control, add an ImageButton control called ImageButton_Avatar. Set the layout_width and layout_height attributes to wrap_content. You need to be able to scale the avatar graphic while preserving its aspect ratio, so set its adjustViewBounds attribute to true and its scaleType attribute to fitXY. You will also want to set its maxHeight and minHeight attributes to a dimension that gives the graphic reasonable bounds for the settings screen (for example, 75px).

3. Below the ImageButton control, add another LinearLayout control. Set its orientation attribute to vertical. Set the layout_width and layout_height attributes to fill_parent. Now move the nickname controls (the TextView control called TextView_Nickname and the EditText control called EditText_Nickname) into this layout.

At this point, save the settings.xml layout file. If you rerun the application in the emulator, the settings screen should now look like Figure 13.3.

FIGURE 13.3
The settings
screen with the
avatar feature.

Working with ImageButton **Controls**

The ImageButton control is a special type of button that displays a Drawable graphic instead of text. Figure 13.3 showed an ImageButton control used to display an avatar graphic as part of the settings screen.

The ImageButton and Button controls are both derived from the View class, but they are unrelated to each other otherwise. The Button class is actually a direct subclass of TextView (think of it as a line of text with a background graphic that looks like a button), whereas the ImageButton class is a direct subclass of ImageView.

> Any graphics displayed within an ImageButton control should be stored locally on the handset. Attempting to use remote Uri addresses is not recommended due to decreased application performance and responsiveness.

By the Way

Setting the Image of an ImageButton **Control**

As with an ImageView control, there are several different ways to set the graphic shown in an ImageButton control, including the following:

▶ setImageBitmap()—Use this method to set the graphic shown on the ImageButton control to a valid Bitmap object.

▶ setImageDrawable()—Use this method to set the graphic shown on the ImageButton control to a valid Drawable object.

▶ setImageResource()—Use this method to set the graphic shown on the ImageButton control to a valid Resource identifier.

▶ setImageURI()—Use this method to set the graphic shown on the ImageButton control to a valid Uri address.

> In some circumstances, the ImageButton control will cache the graphic it is displaying, and continue to do so even if you use one of the methods to change the graphic. One workaround for this is to call setImageURI(null) to flush the previous graphic and then call setImageURI() again with a Uri set to the new graphic to display the ImageButton control.

Watch Out!

Here's a handy trick for accessing application resources such as Drawable resources, using a specially constructed Uri address. This trick allows you to use the setImageURI() method of the ImageButton for both image resources and other graphics on the handset. Resource URIs can be referenced by resource identifier or by resource type/name. The `Uri` address format for the resource identifier method is as follows:

```
android.resource://[package]/[res id]
```

For example, you could use the following `Uri` to access a `Drawable` resource called `avatar.png` by its resource identifier:

```
Uri path =
    Uri.parse("android.resource://com.androidbook.triviaquiz13/" +
    R.drawable.avatar);
```

The `Uri` address format for the resource type/name method is as follows:

```
android.resource://[package]/[res type]/[res name]
```

For example, you could use the following `Uri` to access a `Drawable` resource called `avatar.png` by its resource type/name:

```
Uri path = Uri.parse(
    "android.resource://com.androidbook.triviaquiz13/drawable/avatar");
```

When you have a valid `Uri` for the `Drawable` resource, you can use it with the `setImageURI()` method of an `ImageButton` control as follows:

```
ImageButton avatarButton = (ImageButton) findViewById(R.id.ImageButton_Avatar);
avatarButton.setImageURI(path);
```

Handling `ImageButton` Events

You handle `ImageButton` events such as clicks exactly the same way as you would with any `View` control—by using click listeners. For the avatar `ImageButton` control, you want to handle clicks and long-clicks.

Handling Clicks with `setOnClickListener`

To listen and handle when a user clicks on the avatar `ImageButton` control, you must implement the `View.OnClickListener()` method:

```
avatarButton.setOnClickListener(new View.OnClickListener() {
    @Override
    public void onClick(View v) {
        // TODO: Launch the Camera and Save the Photo as the Avatar
    }
});
```

This should look familiar because you've already implemented a number of listeners for `Button` controls.

Handling Long-Clicks with `setOnLongClickListener`

A long-click is a special type of click available on the Android platform. Basically, a long-click event is when a user clicks on a control for about one second. This type of click is handled separately from a regular, "short" click.

To handle long-clicks, you need to implement the `View.OnLongClickListener` class and pass it into the `ImageButton` control's `setOnLongClickListener()` method. `OnLongClickListener` has one required method you must implement: `onLongClick()`. Here is a sample implementation of `OnLongClickListener` for the avatar `ImageButton` control:

```
avatarButton.setOnLongClickListener(new View.OnLongClickListener() {
    @Override
    public boolean onLongClick(View v) {
    // TODO: Launch Image Picker and Save Image as Avatar
        return false;
    }
});
```

The `onLongClick()` method looks much like the `onClick()` method of the `OnClickListener` class. However, it has a return value, which should be `true` if long-click events are handled.

Try It Yourself ▼

Take a moment to try out clicks and long-clicks with an `ImageButton` control:

1. Navigate to the `QuizSettingsActivity.java` class file and add a click listener and a long-click listener to the `ImageButton_Avatar` control.

2. Within the `onClick()` method of `OnClickListener`, add a Toast message that says `Short click`.

3. Within the `onLongClick()` method of `OnLongClickListener`, add a Toast message that says `Long click`.

4. Save your work and re-launch the application. Click the avatar `ImageButton` control on the settings screen and note when click and long-click events occur.

▲

Working with Image Media

Now that you have the avatar `ImageButton` control configured, you can work on handling the user click actions. When the user clicks the avatar button, you want to launch the appropriate activity (via `Intent`) and then handle the resulting image and set it as an avatar.

For now, you can save the avatar image locally on the handset. You also need to add a new preference to the application SharedPreferences. You begin by defining this new preference in the QuizActivity.java class, as follows:

```
public static final String GAME_PREFERENCES_AVATAR = "Avatar";
```

Launching Activities and Handling Results

If you think back to Hour 3, "Building Android Applications," when we talked about application life cycle, you will recall that there are several ways to launch an activity. Specifically, there is a method called startActivityForResult() that allows you to launch an activity using an intent and then handle the result by implementing the calling activity class's onActivityResult() method.

The startActivityForResult() method takes two parameters: the intent to launch and a developer-defined request code. In this case, the calling activity is QuizSettingsActivity. You have two instances in which you want to start a new activity. The first instance is when the user clicks on the ImageButton control to start the camera capture activity. The second instance is when the user long-clicks on the ImageButton control to start the image gallery. Therefore, you need to define two request codes within QuizSettingsActivity:

```
static final int TAKE_AVATAR_CAMERA_REQUEST = 1;
static final int TAKE_AVATAR_GALLERY_REQUEST = 2;
```

We will talk more about the startActivityForResult() method in a moment, but for now, let's focus on how the QuizSettingsActivity handles the results returned when the launched activity completes. You handle the result returned by the activity by implementing the onActivityResult() method of the QuizSettingsActivity class. Because you have more than one request code, you add a switch statement with two cases, one for camera results and one for image picker results:

```
protected void onActivityResult(int requestCode, int resultCode, Intent data) {
    switch(requestCode) {
    case TAKE_AVATAR_CAMERA_REQUEST:
        if (resultCode == Activity.RESULT_CANCELED) {
            // Avatar camera mode was canceled.
        } else if (resultCode == Activity.RESULT_OK) {
            // TODO: HANDLE PHOTO TAKEN
        }
        break;
    case TAKE_AVATAR_GALLERY_REQUEST:
        if (resultCode == Activity.RESULT_CANCELED) {
            // Avatar gallery request mode was canceled.
        } else if (resultCode == Activity.RESULT_OK) {
            // TODO: HANDLE IMAGE CHOSEN
        }
        break;
    }
}
```

Note that the user might launch an activity and then cancel it. In this case, the resultCode of the onActivityResult() method is Activity.RESULT_CANCELED. However, when the resultCode parameter is Activity.RESULT_OK, you should have a valid result to handle.

Because both cases result in a graphic you want to save as an application avatar, you can create a helper method called saveAvatar(). This method can take a bitmap, save it as a local file, and use it within the Been There, Done That! application. The pseudo-code for the saveAvatar() method looks like this:

```
private void saveAvatar(Bitmap avatar)
{
    // TODO: Save the Bitmap as a local file called avatar.jpg
    // TODO: Determine the Uri to the local avatar.jpg file
    // TODO: Save the Uri path as a String preference
    // TODO: Update the ImageButton with the new image
}
```

Working with the Camera

There are many ways to incorporate camera hardware into your application. You can build camera support directly into your application, or you can integrate existing camera support functionality into your application by using the Intent mechanism.

By far, the simplest way to include photo-taking abilities in an application is by launching the ACTION_IMAGE_CAPTURE intent. For example, you could add the following code to the onClick() method of the avatar ImageButton control's OnClickListener:

```
Intent pictureIntent = new Intent(
    android.provider.MediaStore.ACTION_IMAGE_CAPTURE);
startActivityForResult(pictureIntent, TAKE_AVATAR_CAMERA_REQUEST);
```

There is no camera available on the Android emulator. Instead, a mock camera screen is shown, and a fixed graphic is saved whenever the user chooses to take a picture. This is helpful for testing camera functionality using the Android emulator. When you run the application and click the avatar ImageButton control, the emulator screen should look something like Figure 13.4.

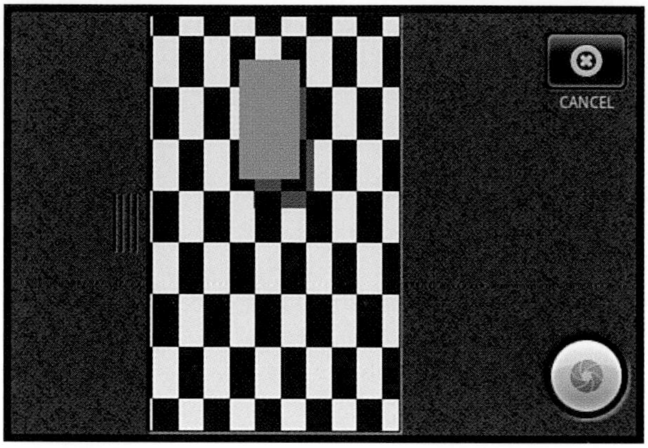

FIGURE 13.4
Taking a photo-
graph using the
camera applica-
tion in the
Android emulator.

Did you Know?

When launching a "remote" activity—that is, an activity that is not necessarily part of your application—you are effectively sending out an intent that says, "I want to do this. Who can do it for me?" A number of other applications on the handset may have the ability to handle this operation. The Android operating system attempts to match the most appropriate activity to handle the request. However, if you want the user to be shown a list of applicable activities (or applications) to handle the request, simply wrap your intent within another intent called ACTION_CHOOSER. You often see this mechanism used with common applications such as messaging applications (for example, "Which application do you want to use to send this message?"). You can wrap an intent within a chooser by using the createChooser() method, like this:

```
Intent.createChooser(innerIntent,
    "Choose which application to handle this");
```

Although most handsets have only one image-capturing application, as a developer, you are better off not making assumptions of this sort.

The ACTION_IMAGE_CAPTURE intent action causes the camera application to launch, allows the user to take a photograph, and returns the photo. By default, a small bitmap is returned, and it is suitable for your avatar. Within a specific case statement of the onActivityResult() method for the request code

TAKE_AVATAR_CAMERA_REQUEST, you can retrieve the bitmap by inspecting the
Intent parameter called data, as follows:

```
Bitmap cameraPic = (Bitmap) data.getExtras().get("data");
```

You can then pass the bitmap graphic into your helper method saveAvatar().

Working with the Gallery

Android has a standard intent action called ACTION_PICK that allows the user to
choose from a set. This type of intent is often used in conjunction with a URI, but it
need not be. This kind of intent can also be used to create a set of all data of a given
MIME type on the handset and allow the user to choose an item from the set.

For example, you can create an intent to use within the onLongClick() method to
display all images to the user as follows:

```
Intent pickPhoto = new Intent(Intent.ACTION_PICK);
pickPhoto.setType("image/*");
startActivityForResult(pickPhoto, TAKE_AVATAR_GALLERY_REQUEST);
```

When you run the application and long-click the avatar ImageButton control, a
gallery of images available on the device is displayed (see Figure 13.5).

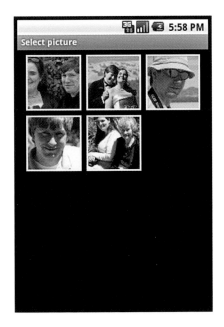

FIGURE 13.5
Choosing an
image from the
gallery on the
Android emulator.

The ACTION_PICK Intent action causes a gallery of all images stored on the handset to launch, allows the user to choose one image, and returns a URI address to the image's location. Therefore, within a specific case statement of the onActivityResult() method for the request code TAKE_AVATAR_GALLERY_REQUEST, you can retrieve the URI by inspecting the Intent parameter called data, as follows:

```
Uri photoUri = data.getData();
```

Then, to convert the Uri to a valid Bitmap object, you can use the following method:

```
Bitmap galleryPic = Media.getBitmap(getContentResolver(), photoUri);
```

You can then pass the bitmap into your helper method called saveAvatar().

Working with Bitmaps

You now have two methods of retrieving a bitmap graphic to save as the application avatar. You can use the Bitmap class (android.graphics.Bitmap) to create, manipulate, and save graphics on the device.

> The Bitmap class encapsulates various bitmap-style graphics formats, including PNG and JPG. Do not confuse this with the bitmap file format (image.bmp). You use the Bitmap class to create and manipulate PNG and JPG graphics on the Android handset.

Saving Bitmap Graphics

You can use the compress() method of the Bitmap class to save a bitmap in various formats. For example, to save the avatar bitmap to a private application JPG file, you could use the following code:

```
String strAvatarFilename = "avatar.jpg";
avatar.compress(CompressFormat.JPEG,
    100, openFileOutput(strAvatarFilename, MODE_PRIVATE));
```

You can determine the URI address of a file by using the fromFile() method of the Uri class. For example, to determine the URI for the avatar graphics file you just saved using the compress() method, you could use the following:

```
Uri imageUri = Uri.fromFile(new File(getFilesDir(), strAvatarFilename));
```

After you have saved the avatar to a file and generated the appropriate URI, you can update the ImageButton control contents with the new image. Now, if you run the application and choose an avatar (via the camera or the gallery), the ImageButton control contents will be updated with the appropriate graphic, as shown in Figure 13.6.

FIGURE 13.6
The Been There, Done That! settings screen with a custom avatar.

Scaling Bitmap Graphics

You can use the createScaledBitmap() method of the Bitmap class to generate thumbnails and such.

> Make sure to calculate the destination height and width appropriately to retain the original bitmap image's aspect ratio. Otherwise, the scaled graphic will be stretched and shrunk in odd ways, which lessens its appeal.

Watch
Out!

Generating Bitmap Graphics from Various Sources

You can use the BitmapFactory class (android.graphics.BitmapFactory) to decode bitmap objects from various sources, including files, byte arrays, streams, and resources.

Performing Bitmap Image Transformations

You can perform various image transformations, such as rotation operations, on bitmap objects by using the Matrix class (`android.graphics.Matrix`). This class manages a 3×3 image matrix that can be used for image translations.

Summary

In this hour, you implemented a new avatar feature on the Been There, Done That! settings screen. The user can set an avatar by taking a picture with the built-in camera or by choosing an existing image from the device. You learned how to launch an activity and retrieve its results by using the `startActivityForResult()` and `onActivityResult()` methods. Finally, you learned about some of the graphics classes available in the Android SDK.

Q&A

Q. *By default, the* `ACTION_IMAGE_CAPTURE` *intent returns a small bitmap graphic of the photo taken by the camera. However, the full-size graphic captured by the camera is much larger. Can I access this photograph data?*

A. You can control the data returned by camera application by supplying some extra data (specifically, the `EXTRA_OUTPUT` field) to the intent.

Q. *How can I maintain aspect ratio when scaling a* `Bitmap` *graphic?*

A. To maintain the aspect ratio of a graphic, simply scale each axis (x and y) by the same percentage. Don't forget that if you apply scaling to all graphics, some may be down-scaled while others may be up-scaled, using the same code.

Workshop

Quiz

1. Activity results handled by the `onActivityResult()` method are differentiated from one another using which parameter?

   A. `requestCode`

   B. `resultCode`

   C. `data`

2. True or False: The `ImageButton` control is a subclass of the `Button` control.

3. True or False: The `Bitmap` class only creates traditional bitmap graphics with the `.bmp` extension.

Answers

1. A. The developer-defined `requestCode` is used to determine which activity (started with the `startActivityForResult()` method) is returning a result. `resultCode` provides information about that activity, such as whether it completed successfully or was canceled by the user.

2. False. The `ImageButton` control is actually a subclass of `ImageView`. However, a `Button` control behaves in a very similar fashion to an `ImageButton` control because they are both derived from the `View` class.

3. False. The `Bitmap` class encapsulates all bitmap-style graphics formats—specifically PNG (recommended) and JPG (supported).

Exercises

1. Use the `Bitmap` class to modify an avatar in some way before saving it to the application file. For example, use the `Matrix` class to invert all the colors in the graphic (inversion).

2. Use the `createScaledBitmap()` method of the `Bitmap` class to generate a scaled version (thumbnail) of a avatar graphic.

HOUR 14

Adding Support for Location-Based Services

What You'll Learn in This Hour:

▶ Designing the favorite place feature
▶ Using location-based services
▶ Using geocoding services
▶ Working with maps

In this hour, you add a new feature to the Been There, Done That! application—the ability for the user to set his or her favorite place in the world from the settings screen. The user can set this information in two ways: by using the current location provided by location-based services (LBS) on the handset or by supplying a place name that can be resolved into the corresponding GPS coordinates using the geocoding functionality provided in the Android SDK.

Designing the Favorite Place Feature

Mobile users are always on the go, and mobile applications that include integration with LBS have become incredibly popular. The Android platform makes it simple to add LBS support to applications. The degree to which LBS support is incorporated into an application is a design choice for the developer, and there are a number of options.

Because the Been There, Done That! application is primarily a game, you want to include some of the most common LBS features. You do this by adding a favorite place feature to the settings screen. As you build this feature, you will learn about some of the other options available for building more powerful LBS applications.

On the settings screen, the user will be able to choose to label and save the handset's last known location as his or her favorite place or type in a place name, such as an address, a city, or a landmark (for example, New York City, Iceland, Yellowstone National Park, 90210). The application then uses any geocoding service providers available to resolve these locations into the appropriate GPS coordinates.

To incorporate this kind of feature into the Been There, Done That! Settings screen, you need to modify the screen design slightly to include the new favorite place feature. Figure 14.1 shows a rough design of how the favorite place feature will be incorporated into the settings screen.

FIGURE 14.1
Rough design of the favorite place feature.

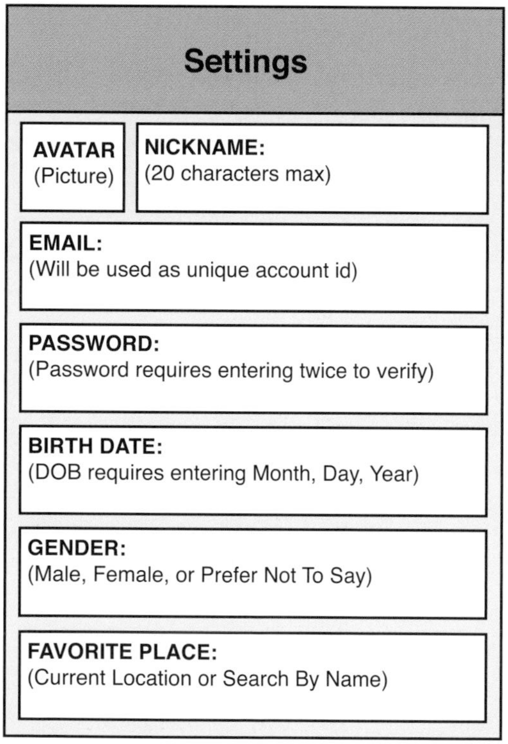

Settings		
AVATAR (Picture)	**NICKNAME:** (20 characters max)	
EMAIL: (Will be used as unique account id)		
PASSWORD: (Password requires entering twice to verify)		
BIRTH DATE: (DOB requires entering Month, Day, Year)		
GENDER: (Male, Female, or Prefer Not To Say)		
FAVORITE PLACE: (Current Location or Search By Name)		

Determining Favorite Place Feature Layout Updates

Recall that the fields displayed on the settings screen are encapsulated within a ScrollView control. This makes it easy to add a new setting at the bottom of the screen. The favorite place feature will function much like the date of birth and password settings.

To incorporate the favorite place design changes into the /res/layout/settings.
xml layout file, you need to add a new region to the settings screen below the gender
Spinner control.

You begin by adding a TextView control to display the label of the new setting.
Then you add an inner LinearLayout control with a Button control to launch the
dialog and a TextView control to display the resulting Favorite Place name.

Figure 14.2 shows the layout updates required by the favorite place feature.

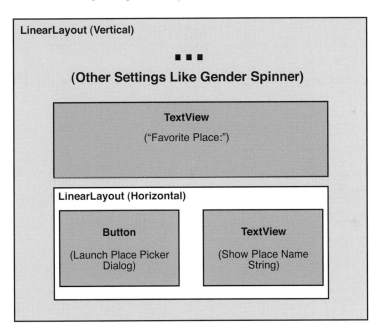

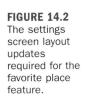

FIGURE 14.2
The settings
screen layout
updates
required for the
favorite place
feature.

Designing the Favorite Place Dialog

You need to give some thought to the custom favorite place picker dialog. Again,
you will build a custom dialog from the AlertDialog class.

The favorite place setting will be stored internally in three parts:

▶ The name of the location (a String value)

▶ The latitude of the location (a float value)

▶ The longitude of the location (a float value)

*By the
Way*

Technically, you could also retrieve and store the altitude of the location, but with most map applications these days, people want a bird's eye view on a two-dimensional space.

To keep the dialog simple, you can offer the user two choices: use the last known location (provided that the handset GPS provider exists and has this information) or enter a string into an `EditText` control, which the geocoding functionality available in the Android SDK translates into GPS coordinates. When you have latitude and longitude information on the location, you can include the ability to launch into the Maps application, if it is available on the device. Figure 14.3 shows a rough design of the favorite place dialog.

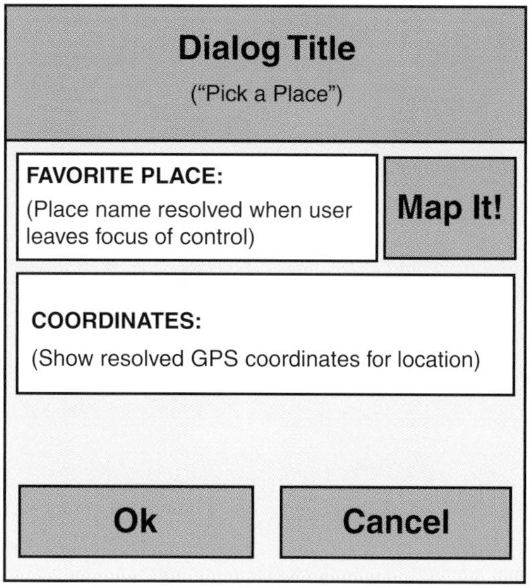

FIGURE 14.3
Rough design of the favorite place dialog.

Implementing the Favorite Place Dialog Layout

You need to create a new layout file where you can store the favorite place dialog layout. For this purpose, you add a new layout resource called `/res/layout/fav_place_dialog.xml` to the project.

This layout is pretty straightforward. All custom dialog controls are encapsulated within a vertically oriented `LinearLayout` control. First, you have a `TextView` control to display the label for choosing a favorite place. Next, you need to display the

EditText input control for the user to type the place name, next to a Button control to allow the user to launch the Map application. You can easily organize the EditText and the Button controls side-by-side, using RelativeLayout. Finally, you include two TextView controls: one to display the label for the GPS coordinates and one to show the actual GPS coordinate data (which is read-only in the Been There, Done That! application).

Figure 14.4 shows the layout for the Favorite Place picker dialog.

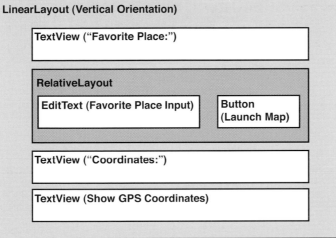

FIGURE 14.4
The favorite place dialog layout.

Implementing the Framework for the Favorite Place Feature

Before you can turn your attention to the more interesting aspects of adding LBS support to the Been There, Done That! application, you need to leverage many of the skills discussed in previous hours to develop the framework for the favorite place feature. This is a great way to exercise some of your new skills. To implement the feature, follow these steps:

1. Add any new String, Dimension, Color, or Drawable resources needed to support the layouts used by the feature.

2. Update the /res/layout/settings.xml layout file to add the new region at the bottom of the settings screen for launching the favorite place dialog and displaying the favorite location, if one is set, as shown in Figure 14.5.

FIGURE 14.5
The settings
screen with the
favorite place
feature.

3. Add the /res/layout/fav_place_dialog.xml layout file to the project and implement the TextView, EditText, and Button controls the dialog requires, as shown in Figure 14.6.

4. Define three new game preference String values in the QuizActivity class. These preferences will be used by the application's SharedPreferences to store the user's favorite location name (String) as well as that location's latitude (float) and longitude (float).

5. Update the QuizSettingsActivity class to include a new dialog. First, define a dialog identifier (for example, PLACE_DIALOG_ID) in the class. Then update the onCreateDialog() and onPrepareDialog() methods of the class to build, initialize, and manage the new favorite place picker dialog.

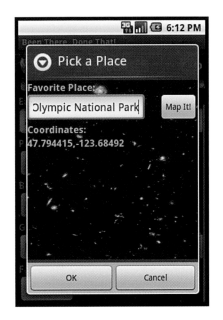

FIGURE 14.6
The favorite place picker dialog.

Because each of these tasks has been covered in a previous hour, we do not go into too much detail here. However, here are a couple hints for getting things up and running:

▶ Add a helper method called `initFavoritePlacePicker()` to display the favorite place name (if it exists) and handle `Button` clicks that launch the favorite place picker dialog. This method should closely resemble the `initPasswordChooser()` and `initDatePicker()` methods.

▶ Build the new favorite place picker dialog much like the password dialog you implemented earlier. One of the key differences between this new dialog and the password dialog is that the new dialog contains a `Button` control for launching the Map application.

▶ Build the favorite place picker `Dialog` one step at a time. Begin by having the `Dialog` save the text inputted as the favorite place name. Next, to save some mock latitude and longitude information, along with the place name. When this is all working, add a `View.OnClickListener()` method for the map `Button` control and have it display a `Toast` message that says something like Map Button Clicked.

> The full implementation of these hints is available in the code provided at the book's website.

After you have implemented the framework to support the favorite place feature, you can turn your attention to more interesting matters, such as calculating the user's last known location and mapping GPS coordinates on a map.

Using Location-Based Services

Developers who enable LBS support in applications need to be aware of a number of issues. First and foremost, a user's location is personal information and subject to privacy concerns. Second, using LBS on a handset takes a toll on the device in terms of network data usage and battery life.

The Android system addresses these issues, in part, through permissions. That said, some of the burden of managing the impact of LBS features on the user and the user's device does fall on the developer. Therefore, here are some guidelines for using services such as LBS:

- ▶ Enable LBS features only when they are needed and disable them as soon as they are no longer required.

- ▶ Inform the user when collecting and using sensitive data, as appropriate. Many users consider their present or past locations to be sensitive.

- ▶ Allow the user to configure and disable features that might adversely affect their experience when using your application. For example, develop a "roaming" mode for your application to allow the user to enjoy your application without incurring huge fees.

- ▶ Handle events such as low-battery warnings and adjust how your application runs accordingly.

- ▶ Consider including a custom privacy message as part of your application's usage terms, to explain how any data collected from the user, including the user's name and location information, will and will not be used.

Watch Out!

> Not every Android device will have LBS hardware, so you should not assume that all devices will be able to provide location information.

A number of LBS features are available as part of the Android SDK, but some of the most exciting features are actually part of the Google APIs add-on. This add-on allows you to incorporate powerful features such as Google Maps functionality directly into Android applications. Developers using the Google APIs add-on must register for a special Google developer account and use a special API key.

Enabling Location Testing on the Emulator

Many LBS features are available to developers without the special Google developer accounts and API keys. For example, you need a special API key to use Google Maps within an application, but you do not need any special permission to launch an Intent object to view a location that can be matched to any Map applications on the device.

Creating an AVD with Google APIs and Applications

You may have noticed that the basic Android installation (the target platform chosen when creating an AVD for use with the emulator) does not include the Maps application. To use the Android Maps application (developed by Google) with the Emulator, you need to create an Android AVD with the Google APIs target platform. Because you want to add some mapping features to the Been There, Done That! application, you need to create a new AVD for this target platform.

Configuring the Location of the Emulator

Unfortunately, the Android emulator just pretends to be a real device—that is, it doesn't actually have any hardware internals, so it cannot, for example, determine its current location via satellites. Instead, you have to seed the location information to the specific emulator instance. The easiest way to configure your emulator is to use the DDMS perspective in Eclipse. You need the latitude and longitude of the location you want the emulator to use.

You can use Google Maps to determine GPS coordinates. To find a specific set of coordinates, go to http://maps.google.com and navigate to the location you desire. Center the map on the location by right-clicking the map and then choose the option to link to the map (usually in the top right corner of the screen, above the map). Copy the link URL—which has the GPS coordinates as part of the query string—to a text file. Find the last ll query variable, which should represent the latitude and longitude of the location. For example, the west edge of Yellowstone Lake in Yellowstone National Park has the ll value 44.427896,-110.585632. The ll value 44.427896,-110.585632 stands for latitude 44.427896 and longitude -110.585632. You can double-check these coordinates by pasting them into Google Maps again and seeing if the map pinpoints the same place location again.

To seed the emulator with a latitude and longitude, follow these steps:

1. Launch the emulator. If you're running an application, click the Home button.

2. Launch the Maps application.

3. Click the Menu button.

4. Choose the My Location menu item (see Figure 14.7).

FIGURE 14.7
The Maps application in the Android emulator.

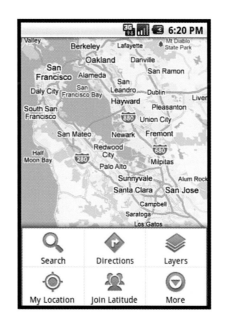

5. Open Eclipse and click on the DDMS perspective.

6. Choose the emulator instance you want to send a location fix to.

7. In the Emulator Control pane, scroll down to the location control.

8. Enter the longitude and latitude of your desired location. Try the coordinates for Yellowstone National Park: latitude 44.427896 and longitude -110.585632 (see Figure 14.8).

9. Click Send.

FIGURE 14.8
Setting the location of the emulator to Yellowstone National Park with DDMS.

Back in the emulator, you'll notice that the Google map is now showing the location you seeded. Your screen should now display your location as Yellowstone National Park, as shown in Figure 14.9.

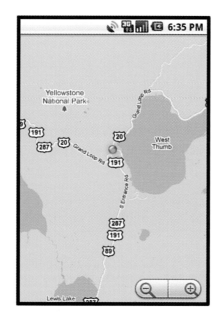

FIGURE 14.9
Setting the location of the emulator to Yellowstone National Park.

You can also use the emulator console command-line tool to send a location fix with the `geo fix` command.

Accessing the Location-Based Services

To access the LBS service on an Android device, you must have the appropriate permissions. Location-based services cannot be used by an Android application unless it is granted the appropriate <uses-permission> settings configured in the Android manifest file.

The most common permissions used by applications leveraging LBS are android.permission.ACCESS_FINE_LOCATION and android.permission.ACCESS_COARSE_LOCATION. To use the GPS provider, you use android.permission.ACCESS_FINE_LOCATION.

When you have registered the appropriate permission, you can access the LocationManager class by using the getSystemService() method, as follows:

```
LocationManager locMgr =
        (LocationManager) getSystemService(LOCATION_SERVICE);
```

The LocationManager class allows you to access the LBS functionality available on the device.

Working with Providers

There may be any number of LBS providers for a device. You can get a list of all providers by calling the getProviders() method of the LocationManager class. You can limit the providers returned to only those that are enabled, or you can provide criteria for returning only providers with certain features (such as fine accuracy). You can also use the getBestProvider() method to return the most appropriate provider for a given set of criteria.

Each of these provider retrieval methods returns a list of names of location providers. The best location provider for given set of criteria can be returned by name, using the getProvider() method. You can use the LocationProvider class to inspect a given provider and see what features it has, such as whether it supports altitude, bearing, and speed information and whether using it may incur a monetary cost to the user.

Getting the Last Known Location

You can retrieve the last known location of the device (as calculated by a specific provider) by using the `getLastKnownLocation()` method of the `LocationManager` class. This location may not be current, but it often gives you a good starting point, and this data is returned quickly, whereas trying to get a current satellite fix can often take quite some time.

You need not start the provider to get the last known location; you simply need to request its last known result. The `getLastKnownLocation()` method returns a `Location` object:

```
Location recentLoc =
    locMgr.getLastKnownLocation(LocationManager.GPS_PROVIDER);
```

The `Location` object can contain a number of interesting pieces of information regarding a location. The information available depends on the abilities of the LBS provider. For example, most providers return latitude and longitude, but not all can calculate altitude. You use the `getLatitude()` and `getLongitude()` methods to retrieve the coordinates from the `Location` object.

Receiving Location Updates

When you need more current information and want to know when the location changes, you can register for periodic location updates by using the `requestLocationUpdates()` method of the `LocationManager` class. This method allows an activity to listen to events from a specific provider (for example, the best provider given your criteria). This frequency of notifications can be adjusted by specifying the minimum time (in milliseconds) and the minimum distance interval (in meters) between updates.

To receive a notification when the location changes, you should have the interested activity implement the `LocationListener` (`android.location.LocationListener`) interface. This interface has a number of helpful callback methods, which allow the activity to react when the provider is enabled and disabled, when its status changes, and when the location changes.

> Resolving the current location can take some time. Therefore, you'll want to consider putting most LBS calls in a worker thread separate from the main UI thread (or writing a background service to support your application). We will discuss threading later in this book.

Watch
Out!

Using Geocoding Services

Geocoding is the process of translating a description of a location into GPS coordinates (latitude, longitude, and sometimes altitude). Geocoding enables you to enter a place name such as Eiffel Tower into Google Maps (http://maps.google.com) and get the appropriate spot on the map. Many geocoding services also have reverse-geocoding abilities, which can translate raw coordinates into some form of address (usually a partial address).

Android devices may or may not have geocoding services available, and geocoding obviously requires a back-end service, and the device must have network connectivity to be able to contact this back-end service. Different geocoding services support different types of descriptions, but the following are some of the most common ones:

▶ Names of towns, states, and countries

▶ Various forms of postal-style addresses (full and partial)

▶ Postal codes

▶ Airport codes (for example, LAX, LHR, JFK)

▶ Famous landmarks

Of course, most geocoding services also allow input of raw coordinates (latitude and longitude) as well. Geocoding services are often localized.

Geocoded addresses are often ambiguous, so a geocoding service may return multiple records. For example, if you were to try to resolve the address "Springfield," you would likely get quite a few results because there is a town called Springfield in about 35 states in the United States, and there are even more Springfields abroad. You might also get results for places called East Springfield or Springfield by the Sea, for example. For the best results, choose the geocoding address that is the most specific (for example, use Springfield's zip code instead of its name to resolve the coordinates).

Like other network operations, geocoding services are blocking operations. This means that you'll want to put any calls to geocoding services in a thread separate from the main UI thread.

Using Geocoding Services with Android

The Android SDK includes the Geocoder (android.location.Geocoder) class to facilitate interaction with the handset's geocoding and reverse-geocoding services, if they are present. Instantiating a Geocoder is simple:

```
Geocoder coder = new Geocoder(getApplicationContext());
```

When you have a valid Geocoder, you can begin to use any geocoding or reverse-geocoding services available on the device.

Geocoding: Translating Addresses into Coordinates

You can use the Geocoder class getFromLocationName()method to resolve a location into coordinates. This method takes two parameters: the string containing the location information and the number of results you want returned. For example, the following code looks up Springfield and limits the number of results to three:

```
String strLocation = "Springfield";
List<Address> geocodeResults =
    coder.getFromLocationName(strLocation, 1);
```

You can iterate through the Geocoder results by using an iterator:

```
Iterator<Address> locations = geocodeResults.iterator();
while (locations.hasNext()) {
    Address loc = locations.next();
    double lat = loc.getLatitude();
    double lon = loc.getLongitude();
    // TODO: Do something with these coordinates
}
```

Each Address object returned contains information about the location. You can use the getLatitude() and getLongitude() methods of the Address class to access the location's coordinates.

You can also use the getFromLocationName() method to limit the returned address results to a certain range.

Reverse-Geocoding: Translating Coordinates into Addresses

You can use the Geocoder class's getFromLocation() method to translate raw latitude and longitude coordinates into address information. Again, you pass in the coordinates and the number of results to be returned.

Working with Maps

Most map features of Android are provided with the special Google API add-ons. For example, you can use the `MapView` control in your layout files to tightly integrate Google Maps features into applications. You can also integrate with existing Maps applications available on the handset by way of the intent mechanism.

Launching a Map Application by Using an Intent

Location applications such as the Maps application handle the `ACTION_VIEW` intent when supplied with a URI with geographic coordinates. This URI has a special format.

When you have determined the latitude and longitude of a location, you can launch the Maps application (or any application that handles this type of data), using the following URI format string:

```
geo:lat,lon
```

Here's an example:

```
String geoURI = String.format("geo:%f,%f", lat, lon);
```

This special URI can also include a zoom level, which is a number between 1 and 23, where zoom level 1 shows the whole planet, and zoom level 23 zooms in all the way (often way too far for map resolution). To include a zoom level, use the following URI format string:

```
geo:lat,lon?z=level
```

Here's an example:

```
String geoURI = String.format("geo:%f,%f?z=10", lat, lon);
```

When you have a properly formatted URI, you can use the `parse()` method to generate the `Uri` and use it with the `ACTION_VIEW` intent, as follows:

```
Uri geo = Uri.parse(geoURI);
Intent geoMap = new Intent(Intent.ACTION_VIEW, geo);
startActivity(geoMap);
```

If there are applications on the device that handle geo-format URIs, the appropriate application (for example, the Google Maps application) will launch as the new foreground activity and show the location. After the user has looked at the map, he or she can return to the calling application by pressing the Back button.

By using the Geocoder class and an intent to launch the Google Maps application, you can complete the favorite place picker dialog, including the Map It! Button control, as shown in Figure 14.10.

If you press the Menu button in the Maps application, you can change the map mode to satellite and zoom in to see the Great Pyramids, as well as all the tour buses and the Sphinx, as shown in Figure 14.11.

FIGURE 14.11
Using the
Google Maps
application to
zoom in satel-
lite view.

Working with Third-Party Services and Applications

The built-in LBS features of the Android SDK are located in the `android.location` package. Basic LBS functionality, such as getting a location fix from satellite trian-gulation, is built into the Android SDK. However, many of the most interesting and powerful mapping and LBS-related features on Android phones are not actually built into the basic Android SDK but are part of the Google APIs that ship along with the Android SDK.

Working with Google APIs and Advanced Map Features

Map features can be built into applications using the Google API add-on. The following are some of the features available in the `com.google.android.maps` package:

► A `MapView` control for displaying an interactive map within a layout

► A `MapActivity` class to simplify `MapView` controls on a screen

▶ The `GeoPoint` class, which encapsulates position information

▶ Classes to support map overlays (drawing on top of the map)

▶ Classes for working with position projections and handling other common LBS-related tasks

For some Google APIs and features, you must sign up for a special account, agree to further terms of service, and receive an API key to use those services. These features are exciting and powerful, but they are unfortunately beyond the scope of this book. Once you have mastered the basics of Android LBS support, consider consulting a more advanced Android manual, such as our book *Android Wireless Application Development* (Addison-Wesley Developer's Library), which contains extensive examples using the Google APIs. You can read more about these classes at the Google APIs Add-On Reference website: http://code.google.com/android/add-ons/google-apis/reference/index.html.

Summary

In this hour, you implemented a new favorite place feature on the Been There, Done That! settings screen. In this hour, you learned how to use built-in location-based services to determine the current location, as well as how to translate addresses into geographical coordinates. You also learned how to launch the Maps application and view a specific location. Finally, you learned about some of the advanced features of the location-based services functionality available within the Android SDK.

Q&A

Q. *I want to use the* `MapView` *control. Where do I get a Google API key?*

A. Start at the Google API add-ons website, which lists all the steps you need to follow to register for the key: http://code.google.com/android/add-ons/google-apis/mapkey.html. As part of this process, you need to set up a Google account if you do not have one already.

Q. *How do I design an application that needs more robust location information, such as an update when the location changes?*

A. There are a number of ways to design LBS applications. For starters, the `LocationManager` object allows you to register an activity for periodic updates of location information, including the ability to launch an intent when a specific location event occurs. Make sure you move all LBS tasks off the main UI thread, as they are time-intensive; use a worker thread, the `AsyncTask` class, or a background process instead. Also, only listen for location events when you must, to avoid performance issues on the device.

Workshop

Quiz

1. Developers need to consider which of the following when working with location-based services?

    A. The user's privacy

    B. The user's phone bill

    C. The device's battery life

    D. The accuracy and validity of the information provided by LBS and geocoding services

    E. The time it takes for location information to be resolved

    F. All of the above

2. True or False: In addition to the `Button` controls provided with `AlertDialog`, other `Button` controls can be used as part of a custom layout.

3. Which services are provided as part of the Android SDK?

    A. Location-based services

    B. Geocoding and reverse-geocoding services

    C. Mapping services

4. True or False: Because the emulator is not the real device, there is no way to use LBS on the emulator.

Answers

1. F. Developers need to take all these concerns into account when developing LBS-enabled applications.

2. True. `Button` controls included as part of a custom layout for a dialog are acceptable. You should provide the appropriate `View.OnClickListener` click handlers as part of the dialog-building process. Note that this is slightly different from the `DialogInterface.OnClickListener` click handlers required to handle the basic three dialog buttons available with `AlertDialog`.

3. A and B. The Android SDK includes support for LBS, geocoding, and reverse-geocoding. The services provided by specific devices vary. Mapping services are provided as part of the Google API add-on, not as part of the stock Android SDK.

4. False. The emulator provides support for LBS services (for some services, the Google add-on is needed), and DDMS can be used to change location.

Exercises

1. Modify the favorite place picker dialog to take GPS latitude and longitude data that the user inputs.

2. Modify the favorite place picker dialog to allow the user to configure the zoom level of the map shown.

3. Modify the Been There, Done That! application to save altitude information along with the latitude and longitude settings.

HOUR 15

Adding Network Support

What You'll Learn in This Hour:

▶ Designing network applications
▶ Running tasks asynchronously
▶ Working with progress bars
▶ Downloading data from an application server

In the next two hours, you enable the Been There, Done That! application to handle two-way network communication. In this hour, you concentrate your attention on downloading data from the Internet. Specifically, you modify the application to retrieve batches of quiz questions and live score data from a remote application server.

Designing Network Applications

Although mobile devices have come a long way in terms of computing speed and data storage, servers can still provide valuable processing power for backing up data or for providing ease of data portability between devices or access to portions of larger datasets that can't be retained on the local device. Luckily, mobile devices have also come a long way in terms of their ability to connect to networks and the Internet. Most Android devices can connect to the Internet in multiple ways, including through 3G (and beyond) networks or Wi-Fi connections. Android applications can use many of the most popular Internet protocols, including HTTP, HTTPS, TCP/IP, and raw sockets.

So far, you have supplied only mock XML data in the Been There, Done That! application. Now it's time to modify the application to contact a remote application server to get live data. To do this, you need to learn about the networking features available on the Android platform, as well as how to offload tasks from the main UI thread and execute them asynchronously.

Two classes of the Been There, Done That! application need to download information from an application:

▶ QuizScoresActivity—This class needs to download score information.

▶ QuizGameActivity—This class needs to download each batch of trivia questions.

To enable the Been There, Done That! application to handle live data, you need to access an application server as well as add networking functionality to the client Android application.

By the
Way

> The full implementation of the networking code provided in this hour is available on the book's website, http://www.informit.com/title/9780321673350.

Working with an Application Server

Network-enabled applications often rely on an application server. The application server provides centralized data storage (a database) and high-performance processing power. Using a centralized server also allows the developer to develop a single server side with multiple client applications. For example, you could easily write iPhone, BlackBerry, and web versions of the Been There, Done That! application that use the same back-end application server. Scores and friends could then be shared across multiple client environments easily.

There are many ways to develop an application server. This implementation leverages a very simple, scalable server that uses Google App Engine (http://code.google.com/appengine/) with Java and servlets. The Google App Engine technology stores information using a schemaless object datastore, with a query engine and support for atomic transactions. While the implementation details of the application server are beyond the scope of this book, it can be helpful to understand how it was designed.

Think of this example's application server as a black box with the following attributes:

▶ The application server is always on and available for users.

▶ The application server is remotely accessed via HTTP.

▶ The application server stores data, such as player settings, scores, and trivia questions.

▶ The application server can be queried for information, such as top scores or batches of questions.

▶ The application server uses JavaServer Pages (JSP) to handle HTTP requests and return the appropriate results in the XML format that the Android application expects.

By the Way

The application server developed for use with this book is not part of the code on the website for this book. However, it is available for your use, in open source form, at http://code.google.com/p/triviaquizserver/.

You could create an application server that has different characteristics than the one described here. For example, you could create a SQL database-driven application server using MySQL and PHP instead, or you could use a number of other technologies.

Informing the User of Network Activity

In this hour, we're most interested in how to query the application server and retrieve the XML returned from a query. Networking support does not necessitate any specific user interface or layout updates to the Been There, Done That! application. However, any time the user is required to wait for an operation that takes time—for example, for XML data to be downloaded from a server and parsed—it is important to inform the user that something is happening, using a visual mechanism such as an indeterminate ProgressBar control, as shown in Figure 15.1. Otherwise, the user might abandon the application due to lack of response.

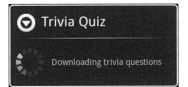

FIGURE 15.1
Using an indeterminate progress bar to inform the user about a lengthy operation.

Developing Network Applications

Developers who enable network support in applications need to be aware of a number of issues. These issues are very similar to those faced when enabling Location-Based Services (LBS) features in an application. User privacy concerns, device performance degradation, and unwanted network data charges are all common points to consider when developing network applications. Also, network connectivity (availability, strength, and quality) is not guaranteed, so enabling network support gives your application a variety of opportunities to fail.

The Android system addresses these issues, in part through permissions, but much of the burden of managing the impact of network features and performance falls upon the developer. Here are some guidelines for developers leveraging network features within applications:

▶ Use network services only when they are needed and cache data locally whenever possible.

▶ Inform the user when collecting and using sensitive data, as appropriate.

▶ Allow the user to configure and disable features that might adversely affect his or her experience when using your application. For example, develop an airplane mode for your application to allow the user to enjoy your application without accessing a remote server.

▶ Gracefully handle events such as no network coverage. Your application is more valuable to the user if it is useful even without an Internet connection.

▶ Consider including a privacy message as part of your application's terms of use. Use this opportunity to inform the user about what data is collected from the user, how it will and will not be used, and where it is stored (for example, on a remote application server).

> Most Android devices on the market at this time are Internet-enabled phones and tablets, but the Android platform is not limited to just mobile devices. Not every Android device is guaranteed to have network support, although it's generally a pretty safe bet that some form of access to the Internet will be available. Keep this fact in mind when making assumptions about how much your application will rely on a network.

Enabling Network Testing on the Emulator

You do not need to make any changes to the emulator to write network-enabled applications. The emulator will use the Internet connection provided by your development computer and simulate true network coverage. Also, the emulator has a number of settings for simulating network latency and network transfer speeds, which can give you a better idea of the actual experience a user would have. For details on the network debugging features of the emulator, see the Android emulator documentation.

> Because the emulator uses your desktop Internet connection, it is likely to be higher speed than a true Android device Internet connection will be.

Testing Network Applications on Hardware

As usual, the best way to test network-enabled applications is on the target Android device. There are a number of network-related settings on an Android device. You configure these settings through the Settings application on the device:

▶ **Airplane Mode**—This mode will block all network activity according to most in-flight regulations.

▶ **Wi-Fi**—There are a number of Wi-Fi settings for when wireless networks are available for use.

▶ **Mobile Networks**—There are several settings for handling data services when roaming.

You can also find a lot of information about the phone service by clicking on the Settings application from the application tray and choosing About Phone (or About device) and then Status from the menus. Here, you will find important phone service information, such as the following:

▶ Phone number (for example, 888-555-1212)

▶ Wireless network (for example, Verizon, T-Mobile)

▶ Network type (for example, CDMA EVDO rev. A, or EDGE)

▶ Signal strength (for example, -81 dBm 0 asu)

▶ Service state (for example, In service)

▶ Roaming state (for example, Roaming or Not roaming)

▶ Mobile network state (for example, Connected)

You can cause a mobile device to lose its signal by placing it inside a cookie tin, refrigerator, microwave, or in any other shielded area. Doing so can be helpful for testing signal and network service loss. Just don't leave a handset in the cold too long, or you will drain the battery. And don't *use* the microwave with the phone inside (common sense for all!).

Accessing Network Services

The Android platform has a wide variety of networking libraries. Those accustomed to Java networking will find the `java.net` package familiar. There are also some helpful Android utility classes for various types of network operations and protocols. Developers can secure network communication by using common technologies such as SSL and HTTPS.

To access a network, an Android application must have the appropriate permissions granted within the Android manifest file. Network tasks are blocking operations, and mobile networks can be very slow, so it is imperative that all network operations be handled asynchronously.

Watch Out!

> Network operations can take some time. Therefore, all network-related calls should be handled asynchronously, separately from the main UI thread. This can be accomplished by using the Java `Thread` class or by using the Android `AsyncTask` class, which is discussed later in this hour.

Setting Network Permissions

To access network services on an Android device, you must have the appropriate permissions. An Android application can use most networking services only if it is granted the appropriate `<uses-permission>` settings configured in the Android manifest file.

The following are some common permission values used by applications leveraging the network:

▶ `android.permission.INTERNET`

▶ `android.permission.ACCESS_NETWORK_STATE`

There are a number of other permissions related to networking, including those that allow access and changes to Wi-Fi state and network state. You might also want to look at `android.permission.WAKE_LOCK`, to keep the device from sleeping.

Checking Network Status

The Android SDK provides utilities for gathering information about the current state of a network. This is useful for determining whether a network connection is available before trying to use a network resource. By validating network connectivity before attempting to make a connection, you can avoid many of the failure cases common in mobile device networking applications and provide your end users with a more pleasant user experience.

Retrieving Network Status Information Programmatically

Applications need to register the `android.permission.ACCESS_NETWORK_STATE` permission in the Android manifest file to read the network status of the device. To alter the network state of the device, the application must also have the `android.permission.CHANGE_NETWORK_STATE` permission.

Developers can leverage the `ConnectivityManager` class (`android.net.ConnectivityManager`) to access network status information about the device programmatically. You can get an instance of `ConnectivityManager` by using the familiar `getSystemService()` method of the application's `Context` object:

```
ConnectivityManager conMgr = (ConnectivityManager)
    getSystemService(Context.CONNECTIVITY_SERVICE);
```

When you have a valid instance of `ConnectivityManager`, you can request the mobile (cellular) network information by using the `getNetworkInfo()` method:

```
NetworkInfo netInfo =
    conMgr.getNetworkInfo(ConnectivityManager.TYPE_MOBILE);
```

The `NetworkInfo` class (`android.net.NetworkInfo`) has a number of methods for retrieving important information about the network state, including whether the network is available, connected, and roaming:

```
boolean isMobileAvail = netInfo.isAvailable();
boolean isMobileConn = netInfo.isConnected();
boolean isRoamingConn = netInfo.isRoaming();
```

The `NetworkInfo` class also has many other methods for determining fine-grained network status information. These can be read about in the documentation.

Checking Server Availability Programmatically

Even if a network is available and connected, there is no guarantee that the remote server you want to communicate with is accessible from the network. However, `ConnectivityManager` has a handy method called requestRouteToHost() that allows you to attempt to validate traffic, using a given network type (for example, mobile network, Wi-Fi) and IP address is possible.

Using HTTP Networking

The most common network transfer protocol is Hypertext Transfer Protocol (HTTP). Most commonly used HTTP ports are open and available for use on phone networks.

A fast way to get to a network resource is by retrieving a stream to the content. Many Android interfaces for reading data accept streams. One such example is XmlPullParser. The setInput() method of XmlPullParser class takes an InputStream. Previously, you retrieved this stream from the resources. Now, however, you can get it from a network resource, using the simple URL class, as shown here:

```
URL xmlUrl = new URL(xmlSource);
XmlPullParser questionBatch =
    XmlPullParserFactory.newInstance().newPullParser();
questionBatch.setInput(xmlUrl.openStream(), null);
```

From here, the parsing of the XML is unchanged because the XML format is the same, and the XmlResourceParser used previously was derived from the XmlPullParser class. Because the parsing may take longer now, you will move it off the main thread later in the hour.

Once you have the question batches and score data downloading from the remote server, you can remove the mock XML resources from the project and the code that retrieves the XML resources.

Did you Know?

> If your application wants to retrieve and display web content, you can use the WebView control, which leverages the WebKit rendering engine to draw HTML content onscreen. You can use the WebView control to display local or remote content.

Indicating Network Activity with Progress Bars

Network-enabled applications often perform tasks such as connecting to remote servers and downloading and parsing data. These tasks take processing time, and the user should be aware that these activities are taking place. A great way to indicate that an application is doing something is to show some sort of progress indicator. The Android SDK provides two basic styles of the ProgressBar control to handle determinate and indeterminate progress.

Displaying Indeterminate Progress

The simplest `ProgressBar` control style is a circular indicator that animates (see Figure 15.2). This kind of progress bar does not show progress per se but informs the user that something is happening. You want to use this style of progress bar when the length of the background processing time is indeterminate.

http://perlgurl.org/

Displaying Determinate Progress

When you want to inform the user of specific milestones in progress, you can use the determinate progress bar control. This control displays as a horizontal progress bar that can be updated to show incremental progress toward completion (see Figure 15.3). To use this progress indicator, you use the `setProgress()` method of the `ProgressBar` control.

As described later in this hour, you can put progress bars in the application's title bar. This can save valuable screen space. You often see this done on screens displaying web content.

Displaying Progress Dialogs

You may want to indicate progress in a dialog window, as opposed to adding a `ProgressBar` control to the layout of an existing screen. You can use the special `Dialog` class called `ProgressDialog` for this purpose. For example, you can use `ProgressDialog` windows (see Figure 15.4) in the Been There, Done That! application to inform the user that data is being downloaded and parsed before displaying the appropriate screen of the application.

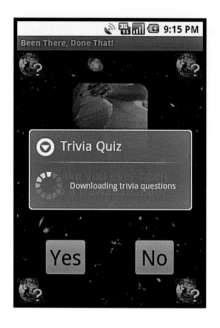

Here is the code needed to programmatically create and display the `ProgressDialog` class:

```
ProgressDialog pleaseWaitDialog = ProgressDialog.show(
    QuizGameActivity.this,
    "Trivia Quiz",
    "Downloading trivia questions…",
    true);
```

You can use the `dismiss()` method to dismiss `pleaseWaitDialog` control when you have completed any background processing:

```
pleaseWaitDialog.dismiss();
```

By the Way

> The `pleaseWaitDialog` control can be cancelled by the user if a fifth parameter is added to the show() method and set to true. In this case, we don't allow the user to cancel the dialog because we want it showing during the entire download. In the example code, which shows the final results for this hour, you'll see we do allow it to be cancelled, and you can read about it later in this hour.

Now you know how to create progress bars and display them in dialog windows using `ProgressDialog control`. Because the progress you want to indicate should actually be taking place asynchronously, it's time to turn our attention to background processing.

Running Tasks Asynchronously

Despite rapidly evolving technology, mobile wireless networks still provide relatively slow Internet connections compared to those found in personal computers. Your Android applications must be responsive, so you must always move all network operations off the main UI thread and onto a secondary, "worker," thread. The Android platform provides two methods for doing this:

▶ AsyncTask—This abstract class can be used to offload background operations from the UI thread easily. This class is the first choice when handling operations that require some time and thus might affect the performance and responsiveness of your application.

▶ Thread and Handler—These classes can be used together to handle concurrent processing and communicating with the UI thread's message queue. This advanced method allows more flexibility in terms of implementation, but you, as the developer, are responsible for managing thread operations appropriately.

For the Been There, Done That! application, the AsyncTask class is most appropriate because it's the most straightforward to implement.

Using AsyncTask

The Android SDK includes the AsyncTask class (android.os.AsyncTask) to help manage background operations that will eventually post back to the UI thread.

Instead of using handlers and creating threads, you can simply create a subclass of AsyncTask and implement the appropriate callback methods:

▶ onPreExecute()—This method runs on the UI thread before background processing begins.

▶ doInBackground()—This method runs in the background and is where all the real work is done.

▶ publishProgress()—This method, called from the doInBackground() method, periodically informs the UI thread about the background process progress. This method sends information to the UI process.

▶ onProgressUpdate()—This method runs on the UI thread whenever the doInBackground() method calls publishProgress(). This method receives information from the background process.

▶ onPostExecute()—This method runs on the UI thread once the background processing is completed.

When launched with the execute() method, the AsyncTask class handles processing in a background thread without blocking the UI thread.

Using Threads and Handlers

When you want to control a thread yourself, you can use the Thread class in conjunction with a Handler object.

The style of networking that has been presented so far causes the thread it's running on to block until the operation is finished. For small tasks, this might be acceptable. However, when timeouts or additional processing time is needed, such as parsing XML, you need to move these time-intensive operations away from the main UI thread by launching a new thread. This provides a smoother experience for the user.

The following code demonstrates how to create and launch an anonymous thread that connects to a remote server, retrieves and parses some XML, and posts a response back to the UI thread, using a Handler object on the main thread to change a TextView control called parsingStatus, which displays the parsing status:

```
import android.os.Handler;
Handler mHandler = new Handler();
// ...
new Thread() {
    public void run() {
        // Instantiate XML parser

        mHandler.post(new Runnable() {
            public void run() {
                parsingStatus.setText("Began Parsing...");
            }
        });

        // XML Parsing loop here
        // Update parsingStatus has needed…

        mHandler.post(new Runnable() {
            public void run() {
                parsingStatus.setText("Finished parsing...");
            }
        });
    }
}.start();
```

The Thread class uses the Handler object called mHandler to post information back to the main UI thread.

Downloading and Displaying Scores

Now let's work through a simple example of using `AsyncTask` within the `QuizSettingsActivity` class to handle the downloading and parsing of XML score information. You begin by creating a subclass called `ScoreDownloaderTask`, which extends the `AsyncTask` class within the `QuizSettingsActivity` class:

```
private class ScoreDownloaderTask extends AsyncTask<Object, String, Boolean> {
    // TODO: Implement AsyncTask callback methods
    TableLayout table;
}
```

Because you will be populating a `TableLayout` control as part of this background task, it makes sense to add a handy member variable within `ScoreDownloaderTask` as well.

Starting `ScoreDownloaderTask`

After you've implemented the `ScoreDownloaderTask` class, you will want to update the `onCreate()` method of the `QuizScoresActivity` class to call the `ScoreDownloaderTask` class's `execute()` method when the screen first loads. The `execute()` method takes two parameters: the server web address and the table to populate with scores (a `TableLayout` control):

```
public static final String TRIVIA_SERVER_BASE =
    "http://tqs.mamlambo.com/";
public static final String TRIVIA_SERVER_SCORES =
    TRIVIA_SERVER_BASE + "scores.jsp";
// ...
allScoresDownloader =
    new ScoreDownloaderTask();
allScoresDownloader.execute(TRIVIA_SERVER_SCORES, allScoresTable);

SharedPreferences prefs =
    getSharedPreferences(GAME_PREFERENCES, Context.MODE_PRIVATE);
Integer playerId = prefs.getInt(GAME_PREFERENCES_PLAYER_ID, -1);

if (playerId != -1) {
    friendScoresDownloader = new ScoreDownloaderTask();
    friendScoresDownloader.execute(
        TRIVIA_SERVER_SCORES + "?playerId="
        + playerId, friendScoresTable);
}
```

Now that you have set up the `ScoreDownloaderTask` class, you can focus on implementing the `AsyncTask` callback methods appropriately.

Don't worry about the `playerId` value just yet. We'll discuss that next hour.

By the Way

Starting the Progress Indicator

Next, you need to implement the onPreExecute() method, which runs on the UI thread before background processing begins. This is the perfect place to demonstrate adding to the title bar an indeterminate progress indicator:

```
@Override
protected void onPreExecute() {
    mProgressCounter++;
    QuizScoresActivity.this.setProgressBarIndeterminateVisibility(true);
}
```

There are two tabs of scores. Each tab's scores are downloaded separately, and you want the progress indicator to display until both are complete. Thus, you can create a counter, mProgressCounter, to track each download. In this way, you could also add a third tab, and the indicator would still hide at the correct time.

In the onCreate() method of the activity, the following line must be added before the indeterminate progress bar indicator will display properly in the title bar:

```
requestWindowFeature(Window.FEATURE_INDETERMINATE_PROGRESS);
```

You must call this method before you call the setContentView() method.

Handling the Background Processing

Now it is time to identify what processing should run asynchronously. For this example, it is the downloading and parsing code. You override the doInBackground() method, which is where all the background processing takes place. The methods called within doInBackground() will not block the main UI thread. Here's a sample implementation of the doInBackground() method, with exception handling removed for clarity:

```
@Override
protected Boolean doInBackground(Object... params) {
    boolean result = false;
    String pathToScores = (String) params[0];
    table = (TableLayout) params[1];
    XmlPullParser scores = null;
    URL xmlUrl = new URL(pathToScores);
    scores = XmlPullParserFactory.newInstance().newPullParser();
    scores.setInput(xmlUrl.openStream(), null);
    if (scores != null) {
        processScores(scores);
    }
    return result;
}
```

Here you simply generate the appropriate URL to the application server and use the openStream() method to access the data stream from a remote application server.

After you call the setInput() method of the XmlPullParser, you can use that XmlPullParser just as you used the one pointed at local resource data.

Now move the processScores() method into the ScoreDownloaderTask class. Now you will want to update the method, which simply takes the XmlPullParser and parses the XML, to publish scores as they are parsed, using the publishProgress() method:

```
private void processScores(XmlPullParser scores)
    throws XmlPullParserException, IOException {
    int eventType = -1;
    boolean bFoundScores = false;

    // Find Score records from XML
    while (eventType != XmlResourceParser.END_DOCUMENT) {
        if (eventType == XmlResourceParser.START_TAG) {

            // Get the name of the tag (eg scores or score)
            String strName = scores.getName();

            if (strName.equals("score")) {
                bFoundScores = true;
                String scoreValue =
                    scores.getAttributeValue(null, "score");
                String scoreRank =
                    scores.getAttributeValue(null, "rank");
                String scoreUserName =
                    scores.getAttributeValue(null, "username");
                publishProgress(scoreValue, scoreRank, scoreUserName);
            }
        }
        eventType = scores.next();
    }

    // Handle no scores available
    if (bFoundScores == false) {
        publishProgress();
    }
}
```

The publishProgress() method can be called anytime within the doInBackground() method to cause the onProgressUpdate() callback method to be called. This allows the background process to communicate with the UI thread.

Handling Progress Updates

You can update the UI thread with background progress information by overriding the onProgressUpdate() method. Here, you grab the new score just parsed from the method parameters and insert a new row in the score TableLayout control:

```
@Override
protected void onProgressUpdate(String... values) {
    if (values.length == 3) {
```

```
        String scoreValue = values[0];
        String scoreRank = values[1];
        String scoreUserName = values[2];
        insertScoreRow(table, scoreValue, scoreRank, scoreUserName);
    } else {
        final TableRow newRow =
            new TableRow(QuizScoresActivity.this);
        TextView noResults =
            new TextView(QuizScoresActivity.this);
        noResults.setText(
            getResources().getString(R.string.no_scores));
        newRow.addView(noResults);
        table.addView(newRow);
    }
}
```

The insertScoreRow() method simply creates a new TableRow control and adds it to the TableLayout control. The array of values must be passed in the same order each time. This is because of how the AsyncTask Java template works.

Clearing the Progress Indicator

Next, you implement the onPostExecute() method, which runs on the UI thread after background processing completes. Specifically, when you have completed all parsing and displaying, you can hide the progress indicator shown in the title bar if all the tasks are complete, as determined by mProgressCounter.

```
@Override
protected void onPostExecute(Boolean result) {
    Log.i(DEBUG_TAG, "onPostExecute");
    mProgressCounter—;
    if (mProgressCounter <= 0) {
        mProgressCounter = 0;
        QuizScoresActivity.this.
            setProgressBarIndeterminateVisibility(false);
    }
}
```

Handling Cancellation

You can handle cancellation of the background processing by overriding the onCancelled() method. The onCancelled() method runs on the UI thread and, if it's called, it means that the onPostExecute() method will not be called. Thus, any cleanup must be performed here. For this example, we perform the following operation:

```
@Override
protected void onCancelled() {
    Log.i(DEBUG_TAG, "onCancelled");
    mProgressCounter—;
    if (mProgressCounter <= 0) {
```

```
        mProgressCounter = 0;
        QuizScoresActivity.this.
            setProgressBarIndeterminateVisibility(false);
    }
}
```

The `onCancelled()` method is called when the `cancel()` method of `AsyncTask` is called. This does not happen automatically. Instead, good practice is to cancel tasks when they are no longer needed. For the scores screen, you'll want to cancel the tasks if they're still running when the user leaves the screen for any reason. That is, you cancel them in the `onPause()` method of the `Activity`, as shown here:

```
@Override
protected void onPause() {
    if (allScoresDownloader != null &&
        allScoresDownloader.getStatus() !=
        AsyncTask.Status.FINISHED) {
        allScoresDownloader.cancel(true);
    }
    if (friendScoresDownloader != null &&
        friendScoresDownloader.getStatus() !=
        AsyncTask.Status.FINISHED) {
        friendScoresDownloader.cancel(true);
    }
    super.onPause();
}
```

Downloading and Parsing Question Batches

Now that you understand how to download data asynchronously, you can use `AsyncTask` to handle downloading and displaying the question batches on the game screen. This process is very similar to the process involved in downloading score data. However, you will not publish progress as you go; instead, you will simply display a progress bar until all questions in a given batch are downloaded.

Begin by creating a subclass called QuizTask that extends the `AsyncTask` class within the QuizGameActivity class, like this:

```
private class QuizTask extends AsyncTask<Object, String, Boolean> {
    // TODO: Implement AsyncTask callback methods
}
```

> You might want to add a custom `DEBUG_TAG` member variable to the `QuizTask` class. This allows you to differentiate between debugging information from the background thread and UI thread.

By the Way

The `QuizTask` class also needs member variables for the starting question number and a `ProgressDialog` to display background processing progress to the user:

```
int startingNumber;
ProgressDialog pleaseWaitDialog;
```

Once you've implemented the `QuizTask` class, you can update the `onCreate()` method of the `QuizGameActivity` class to call the `QuizTask` class's `execute()` method when the screen first loads. The `execute()` method takes two parameters: the server web address for question downloads and the starting question number (an `Integer`) for the batch to download:

```
public static final String TRIVIA_SERVER_QUESTIONS =
    TRIVIA_SERVER_BASE + "questions.jsp";
// ...
QuizTask downloader = new QuizTask();
downloader.execute(TRIVIA_SERVER_QUESTIONS, startingQuestionNumber)
```

Starting the Progress Dialog

Now you need to implement the `onPreExecute()` method. This is the perfect place to display a progress dialog that tells the user that the trivia questions are being downloaded. The user won't be able to do anything until the questions are downloaded. Although you put the indicator in the title bar when downloading the scores earlier, you want to put the progress dialog over the game screen:

```
@Override
protected void onPreExecute() {
    pleaseWaitDialog = ProgressDialog.show(
        QuizGameActivity.this, "Trivia Quiz",
        "Downloading trivia questions", true, true);
    pleaseWaitDialog.setOnCancelListener(new OnCancelListener() {
        public void onCancel(DialogInterface dialog) {
            QuizTask.this.cancel(true);
        }
    });
}
```

Although we've used hardcoded strings here for clarity, a well-written application would use string resources for easy localization. A cancel listener is added. This allows the user to press the back button to cancel the dialog. When this happens, the `AsyncTask` `cancel()` method is called. This means that cancelling the dialog will now cancel the task, which will cancel the network activity.

Handling the Background Processing

Now you need to identify what processing should run asynchronously. Again, this is the downloading and parsing code. The following code (with exception handling removed for clarity) shows how to override the `doInBackground()` method:

```
@Override
protected Boolean doInBackground(String... params) {
    boolean result = false;
    startingNumber = (Integer)params[1];
    String pathToQuestions = params[0] +
        "?max=" + QUESTION_BATCH_SIZE + "&start=" + startingNumber;
    result = loadQuestionBatch(startingNumber, pathToQuestions);
    return result;
}
```

Here, the background processing simply involves determining the appropriate question batch to download and calling the helper method `loadQuestionBatch()`. This method must be moved into the `QuizTask` class and updated to contact the application server. Again, this is simply a matter of generating the appropriate URL, opening the stream to the remote application server, and using the `setInput()` method of `XmlPullParser`.

> For the full code to the implementation, please see the sample code provided on this book's website.

Dismissing the Progress Dialog

Next, you implement the `onPostExecute()` method. Now that the background processing has taken place, you can just drop in the code you originally used to display the screen. This is also the perfect place to dismiss the progress dialog:

```
@Override
protected void onPostExecute(Boolean result) {
    Log.d(DEBUG_TAG, "Download task complete.");
    if (result) {
        displayCurrentQuestion(startingNumber);
    } else {
        handleNoQuestions();
    }

    pleaseWaitDialog.dismiss();
}
```

> For the full code to the implementation, please see the sample code provided on this book's website.

Summary

In this hour, you modified the Been There, Done That! application to download data, including the quiz question batches and user scores, from a remote application server. You learned how to use the `AsyncTask` class to handle background processing and keep your application responsive. You also learned about many of the issues to be aware of when developing network-enabled mobile applications.

Q&A

Q. *What is the optimum batch size for downloads?*

A. This is a tricky question. The short answer is: not so much data that the user is tapping his or her foot, waiting for the application to run, but enough so that the user doesn't have to wait for downloads too often. Ideally, all downloading would take place behind the scenes, while the user is doing something else, such as answering the questions that have downloaded.

Q. *Where can I find out more about the network protocol support available on the Android platform?*

A. Three good networking packages to browse within the Android SDK are `android.net`, `java.net`, and `org.apache`.

Workshop

Quiz

1. Where can you find out information about an Android handset's network status?

   A. On the status bar

   B. In the Android Settings application

   C. By calling the `getHandsetNetworkStatus()` method of the `NetStatus` class

2. True or False: The Android emulator cannot simulate network speed and latency similar to that found on real Android devices.

3. True or False: You must use Google App Engine for Android application servers.

4. Which of the following is a not a network protocol or technology that Android can use?

   A. HTTP

   B. HTTPS

   C. TCP

   D. IP

   E. Raw Sockets (RS)

Answers

1. A and B. Some basic information about the device's network status is indeed shown on the status bar, but you can get detailed network status information from the Android Settings application.

2. False. The Android emulator has a number of settings for simulating network speed and latency.

3. False. You can use any server technology standard you want to implement an application server to interact with the Android application. Google App Engine is only one of many such technologies.

4. Trick question! All of the listed protocols or network technologies can be used within Android applications. HTTP and HTTPS can be used for web technologies. TCP and IP are lower level network protocols used by Android and there are standard Java APIs for direct network socket use.

Exercises

1. Test the Been There, Done That! application in a variety of network situations. Modify the emulator settings to simulate a slow network and then run the application and view the results.

2. Modify the application to use the `Thread` and `Handler` methods for background processing instead of the `AsyncTask` method.

3. Modify the application to download the next batch of trivia questions in the background prior to running out of existing questions in the batch.

HOUR 16

Adding More Network Support

What You'll Learn in This Hour:

▶ Accessing device telephony information

▶ Using HTTP client services

▶ Performing HTTP GET requests

▶ Performing HTTP POST requests

▶ Adding third-party JAR files to your project

▶ Working with multipart MIME files

In this hour, you enhance the Been There, Done That! application to upload player data such as settings, scores, and avatars to the application server. You also learn how to access information about the device's telephony status. Finally, you add some external libraries to an Android project and work with multipart MIME entities.

Determining Data to Send to the Server

So far, you have only downloaded data within the Been There, Done That! application. Now it's time to upload player information to the application server. To do this, you need to learn how to use the Apache HTTP client features available on the Android platform, as well as how to add extra Apache libraries to the project.

Three features of the Been There, Done That! application need to upload data to the application server:

▶ QuizSettingsActivity—This class needs to create a player record on the application server and upload player settings information.

▶ QuizGameActivity—This class needs to upload the player's score.

▶ QuizSettingsActivity—This class needs to upload the avatar graphic.

To enable the Been There, Done That! application to handle live data, you need to access an application server as well as add networking functionality to the client Android application.

> The full implementation of the networking code provided in this hour is available on the book's website, http://www.informit.com/title/9780321673350.

Accessing Phone Status Information

Some of the Been There, Done That! player settings will be uploaded to the application server. The application server needs to be able to determine which player (or device) it is communicating with. Therefore, the application uses the unique device identifier of each player's handset to differentiate between players. To get this unique identifier, you need to access information available within the TelephonyManager class.

In addition to the wide variety of Android SDK networking libraries you have learned about thus far, you can also access phone status and telephony information by using the TelephonyManager class. The TelephonyManager class allows an Android application to access information about the phone carrier network, cellular data connection, subscriber identity module (SIM), and the device.

> Android devices are not guaranteed to be mobile handsets. Support for telephony service support may vary widely by phone type and service provider or may not be available at all.

Setting Phone State Permissions

To access phone state information, an Android application must have the appropriate permissions granted within the Android manifest file. Phone state information cannot be accessed or modified by an Android application unless it is granted the appropriate <uses-permission> settings configured in the Android manifest file.

The following are common permission values used by applications leveraging phone state information:

▶ android.permission.READ_PHONE_STATE

▶ android.permission.MODIFY_PHONE_STATE

Uploading Data to a Remote Application Server

In Hour 10, "Building Forms to Collect User Input," you created the settings screen and stored the data in SharedPreferences. Now you will modify this screen to upload a copy of the player settings to the server (in addition to storing it in SharedPreferences). With this particular implementation, the client device always has the last word in the data. The application server simply stores a copy of the settings. This particular application does not have two-way synchronization; that would be beyond the scope of this book and take quite a bit longer than an hour to explain.

To communicate with the application server, you can leverage the HttpClient package (org.apache.http) included in the Android SDK. This package provides utilities for handling a wide variety of HTTP networking scenarios within your application.

You will learn how to use HttpGet to post query variables in the same way a web form submission would work, using the HTTP GET method. Then you'll learn how to use HttpPost to post form variables and upload the avatar graphic, in the same way a web form might use the HTTP POST method.

The application server was written with HTML web forms in mind. In fact, the server was tested using a standard HTML form before the Android client was written. By developing a web client before the Android client, you ensure that the client/server communication protocols used are standard and cross-platform compatible. When you use this procedure, you know that any platform—including Android—that can handle web form–style GET and POST methods will be compatible with this application server. This way, the application can rely on the Apache HTTP libraries—primarily the org.apache.http.client package.

The application server developed for use with this book is not part of the code on the website for this book. However, it is available for your use, in open source form, at http://code.google.com/p/triviaquizserver/.

Network upload operations can take some time. Therefore, all network-related calls should be handled asynchronously, separately from the main user interface thread. This can be accomplished by using the Java Thread class or by using the Android AsyncTask class. Also, make sure to inform the user of lengthy operations by using a mechanism such as a ProgressBar control. For more information, see Hour 15.

Uploading Player Data with the HTTP GET Method

The player data is submitted to the application server by using the HTTP GET method via the HttpGet class. Because you are posting form query variables, you want to use the URLEncodedUtils utility with a List container of BasicNameValuePair objects to assist with creating the final URL for the request. Finally, the whole network operation must be wrapped inside the AsyncTask object so that the user interface can continue to respond while the network request is being handled.

Creating an AsyncTask Class to Handle Uploads

To upload the user settings information to the application server, you need to add another AsyncTask subclass called AccountTask to QuizSettingsActivity. The AccountTask class can be run using the execute() method whenever the player changes a setting on the settings screen (see Figure 16.1). You can also run this task when the user first launches the application, to set up a unique player identifier on the application server for this player on this particular device, even if the person has not entered his or her nickname or email address. This could also allow you to retrieve the settings data from the server (via two-way syncing).

FIGURE 16.1
Using an inde-
terminate
progress indica-
tor in the top
right of the
menu bar (faint
circle).

The details of the AccountTask subclass are very similar to those of the other
AsyncTask subclasses you have written over the past two hours. (In the following
example, exception handling has been removed for clarity and brevity.) The only
interesting method here is doInBackground(), which communicates player settings
to the application server:

```
@Override
protected Boolean doInBackground(Object... params) {
    Boolean succeeded = false;

    Integer playerId =
        mGameSettings.getInt(GAME_PREFERENCES_PLAYER_ID, -1);
    String nickname =
        mGameSettings.getString(GAME_PREFERENCES_NICKNAME, "");
    String email =
        mGameSettings.getString(GAME_PREFERENCES_EMAIL, "");
    String password =
        mGameSettings.getString(GAME_PREFERENCES_PASSWORD, "");
    Integer score =
        mGameSettings.getInt(GAME_PREFERENCES_SCORE, -1);
    Integer gender =
        mGameSettings.getInt(GAME_PREFERENCES_GENDER, -1);
    Long birthdate =
        mGameSettings.getLong(GAME_PREFERENCES_DOB, 0);
    String favePlaceName =
        mGameSettings.getString(GAME_PREFERENCES_FAV_PLACE_NAME, "");

    Vector<NameValuePair> vars = new Vector<NameValuePair>();

    if (playerId == -1) {
        TelephonyManager telManager =
```

```
        (TelephonyManager) getSystemService(Context.TELEPHONY_SERVICE);
    String uniqueId = telManager.getDeviceId();
    vars.add(new BasicNameValuePair("uniqueId", uniqueId));

} else {
    vars.add(
        new BasicNameValuePair("updateId", playerId.toString()));
    vars.add(
        new BasicNameValuePair("score", score.toString()));
}

vars.add(new BasicNameValuePair("nickname", nickname));
vars.add(new BasicNameValuePair("email", email));
vars.add(new BasicNameValuePair("password", password));
vars.add(new BasicNameValuePair("gender", gender.toString()));
vars.add(new BasicNameValuePair("faveplace", favePlaceName));
vars.add(new BasicNameValuePair("dob", birthdate.toString()));

String url =
    TRIVIA_SERVER_ACCOUNT_EDIT+ "?" + URLEncodedUtils.format(vars, null);

HttpGet request = new HttpGet(url);
ResponseHandler<String> responseHandler =
    new BasicResponseHandler();
HttpClient client = new DefaultHttpClient();
String responseBody = client.execute(request, responseHandler);

if (responseBody != null && responseBody.length() > 0) {
    Integer resultId = Integer.parseInt(responseBody);
    Editor editor = mGameSettings.edit();
    editor.putInt(GAME_PREFERENCES_PLAYER_ID, resultId);
    editor.commit();
    succeeded = true;
}
return succeeded;
}
```

Don't be overwhelmed by this code. It is actually pretty straightforward: You begin by creating a vector of name/value pairs for each of the player settings (saved in SharedPreferences) that you want to communicate to the server.

If this is the first time these player settings are being communicated to the server, a new record will be created. The new record is basically an empty player record on the server, with only one value: the device's unique identifier. This allows you to have a reasonable identifier for the player, even before he or she begins to enter other settings information. It also makes it possible for the player to change other information, such as his or her nickname, without unforeseen consequences. You should store the resulting identifier because it is used in all future requests.

When you have all the appropriate query variables set, you are ready to generate the request. You can use the handy URLEncodedUtils.format() method to format the vector of variables for the GET request. Finally, you initialize an HttpGet object, pass the GET request string you formulated, and execute it by using an `HttpClient` instance.

The `HttpClient` class provides helper utilities, in the form of the `ResponseHandler` classes, to parse the response. In this case, `BasicReponseHandler` is used to easily retrieve the body of the response as a `String` object. In this case, the `String` object contains the unique player ID, which can be stored in `SharedPreferences` for future use.

It is typically not a good idea to send sensitive data across networks in plain text. For example, the device identifier could be used for nefarious purposes. Because all this application needs is some sort of unique but repeatable identifier, you could use a one-way hashing function, such as Secure Hash Algorithm (SHA), to do secure the device identifier data. The `MessageDigest` class, part of the `java.security` package, conveniently provides this ability:

```
MessageDigest sha = MessageDigest.getInstance("SHA");
byte[] enc = sha.digest(uniqueId.getBytes());
```

The book's website contains the full implementation of this example and sends the hashed value to the server.

By the Way

Handling Player Score Uploads

To upload the player score information to the application server, you might want to add another `AsyncTask` subclass to the `QuizGameActivity` class. But why not just update the existing `QuizTask` to communicate the player's score to the application server each time the game downloads new questions? This can help reduce latency and increase network efficiency.

You can simply add the score information as a query variable of the request being sent to the server within the `doInBackground()` method of the `QuizTask` class. You use the following code to accomplish this:

```
SharedPreferences settings =
    getSharedPreferences(GAME_PREFERENCES, Context.MODE_PRIVATE);
Integer playerId = settings.getInt(GAME_PREFERENCES_PLAYER_ID, -1);
if (playerId != -1) {
    Log.d(DEBUG_TAG, "Updating score");
    Integer score = settings.getInt(GAME_PREFERENCES_SCORE, -1);
    if (score != -1) {
        pathToQuestions +=
            "&updateScore=yes&updateId="+playerId+"&score="+score;
    }
}
```

The code is added right after the `pathToQuestions` URL is created but before it's used so it can be updated.

Did you
Know?

> You could also use a List container of BasicNameValuePair objects in conjunc-
> tion with the URLEncodedUtils.format() method. However, for primitive values,
> such as integers, no additional encoding is needed.

Uploading Player Avatars with HTTP POST

To upload binary data such as an avatar image, you need to consider using an
HTTP POST request, as opposed to a GET request. This allows you to submit the
avatar content much as you would in an HTML web form. The application server
can then handle the POST request appropriately and save a copy of the player
avatar (see Figure 16.2).

FIGURE 16.2
Uploading the
avatar.

Watch
Out!

> Whenever you are storing non-primitive types of data, consider the best practices
> for the datastore your application server relies upon. For example, one common
> practice for SQL databases is to store the *address* to the image in the database
> but not store the binary data (as a blob).

Adding JAR Files to Your Android Project

Ideally, you want to use the HttpClient class to upload a multipart MIME message
containing the avatar and some other important information for the application
server. However, as of this writing, Apache HttpClient support within the Android

SDK is incomplete. The Android SDK does not yet contain multipart MIME support, but this is likely to change in a future version of the SDK. For now, if you want to include multipart MIME support, you must add these Apache libraries to your project as JAR files. Specifically, you'll need to add the following JAR files to your project:

▶ Mime4j (http://james.apache.org/mime4j/index.html)

▶ HttpMime 4.0 (http://hc.apache.org/httpcomponents-client/httpmime/index.html)

▶ Apache Commons IO (http://commons.apache.org/io/)

Don't know what multipart MIME is? A great description is available on Wikipedia: http://en.wikipedia.org/wiki/MIME#Multipart_messages. Essentially, multipart MIME is a way of encoding multiple pieces of data—including binary data—in a single text message. Multipart MIME messages used with an HTML form correspond to the content encoding type `multipart/form-data`. Multipart MIME is not limited to HTTP. For example, email messages often use multipart MIME.

Did you Know?

Try It Yourself ▼

Adding a JAR File to an Android Project

To add a JAR file to an Android project, follow these steps:

1. Download the JAR file(s) you want to include in your project.

2. Create a directory called /libs in your project. This folder should be at the same level as the /src and /res folders.

3. Copy the JAR file(s) to the /libs directory.

4. Under Android Project Properties, select the Java Build Path menu option and navigate to the Libraries tab.

5. Click the Add JARs button and choose the JAR files you want to add to the project. Click OK.

6. Refresh the project, if necessary. Code away!

To have full multipart MIME support in the Been There, Done That! application, you need to add all three JAR files listed earlier. These packages also add some other interesting utilities, such as the IOUtils class, which provides a number of handy methods for dealing with data streams.

▲

Creating an `AsyncTask` **Class to Handle Avatar Uploads**

To upload the avatar graphic to the application server, you need to add another `AsyncTask` subclass called `ImageUploadTask` to the `QuizSettingsActivity` class. The `ImageUploadTask` class can be run using the `execute()` method whenever the player sets a new avatar on the settings screen.

The details of the `ImageUploadTask` class are very similar to those of the other `AsyncTask` subclasses you have written over the past two hours. The only really interesting part to this new task is the avatar file handling code needed within the `doInBackground()` method (exception handling removed for clarity and brevity):

```java
@Override
protected Boolean doInBackground(Object... params) {
    String avatar =
        mGameSettings.getString(GAME_PREFERENCES_AVATAR, "");
    Integer playerId =
        mGameSettings.getInt(GAME_PREFERENCES_PLAYER_ID, -1);

    MultipartEntity entity =
        new MultipartEntity(HttpMultipartMode.BROWSER_COMPATIBLE);
    File file = new File(avatar);
    FileBody encFile = new FileBody(file);
    entity.addPart("avatar", encFile);
    entity.addPart("updateId", new StringBody(playerId.toString()));

    HttpPost request = new HttpPost(TRIVIA_SERVER_ACCOUNT_EDIT);
    request.setEntity(entity);

    HttpClient client = new DefaultHttpClient();
    ResponseHandler<String> responseHandler =
        new BasicResponseHandler();
    String responseBody = client.execute(request, responseHandler);

    if (responseBody != null && responseBody.length() > 0) {
        Log.w(DEBUG_TAG,
            "Unexpected response from avatar upload: " + responseBody);
    }
    return null;
}
```

You need to create a browser-compatible multipart MIME object by using the `MultipartEntity` class and add two parts: one for the avatar file contents and one for the unique player identifier that the avatar belongs to. Next, you generate an `HttpPost` object with the URL to the application server. Finally, you set the entity within the `HttpPost` object by using the `setEntity()` method. To send the request and retrieve the response, you use the `HttpClient` and `ResponseHandler` classes as usual.

Summary

In this hour, you modified the Been There, Done That! application to upload game data—including player settings, avatar, and scores—to a remote application server. You also learned how to retrieve telephony information, such as network type and roaming information, via `TelephonyManager`. In addition, you learned how to use the HTTP GET and POST methods with `HttpClient` when uploading data to a server.

Q&A

Q. *How can I avoid uploading user data in plain text?*

A. There are many ways you can protect user data during transmission. For example, you can encrypt all data being sent over HTTP via SSL, using HTTPS. Passwords that have already been shared through a secured channel can be sent in hashed form, using `MessageDigest`.

Q. *Is JavaScript Object Notation (JSON) support available on the Android platform?*

A. Yes, you can find JSON libraries in the `org.json` package in the Android SDK.

Workshop

Quiz

1. Which of the following can the `TelephonyManager` class provide information about?

    A. Call State

    B. Network Type

    C. UserName

2. True or False: The Android SDK comes complete with full multi-part MIME handling support.

3. True or False: Network operations should always be performed on the UI thread so they are as fast as possible.

4. Which of the following are classes or objects that cannot be used to perform tasks in the background?

   A. BackgroundTask

   B. AsyncTask

   C. Thread

   D. AsyncActivity

Answers

1. A and B. The `TelephonyManager` can provide Call State and Network Type information.

2. False. There is no built-in MIME support. Instead, this hour demonstrates how to add external libraries that have MIME support.

3. False. Lengthy operations, such as networking operations, should never be performed on the UI thread to keep the handset as responsive as possible.

4. A and D. An AsyncTask is really a helper class that simplifies the use of a Thread. Both classes can be used. The other two are not SDK provided classes, if they exist at all.

Exercises

1. Use the hashed unique device ID and the URL http://tqs.mamlambo.com/get-player to perform a GET request to retrieve player info and load up the settings with the data from the server. Pass in just the `playerId` to get public data or pass in `playerId` and `password` to get all the data (this is what you'll need for a full recovery).

2. Add a new feature to the application to allow players to suggest for new trivia questions via SMS to the developer.

3. Add a new feature to the application that allows players to suggest new trivia questions—with images—by uploading them via multipart MIME POST to http://tqs.mamlambo.com/suggest, with a player identifier form field (`playerId`), question text form field (`question`), and question image form field (`questionImage`), with the image data done in the same way as for the avatar image used in this hour.

HOUR 17

Adding Social Features

What You'll Learn in This Hour:

▶ Enhancing applications with social features
▶ Adding friend request support
▶ Displaying friends' scores
▶ Integrating with third-party social networking services

In this hour, you enhance the Been There, Done That! application by adding some social integration. Specifically, you modify the application to allow the user to keep track of other players' scores. You also review the many ways in which Android applications can use social features and third-party social networking sites to improve the game experience for users.

Enhancing Your Application with Social Features

The Been There, Done That! application has really taken shape over the past few hours. However, it's not terribly fun to play a game all alone. Ideally, users want to be able to share the game experience with other players. Applications that allow some sort of user interaction are more likely to become viral and more popular, thus ensuring success.

Social applications can be roughly divided into two categories: those that are designed to access social networks, such as MySpace or Facebook, directly and applications that use social information to enhance the user's game experience. The Been There, Done That! game is ideal for this latter use.

Tailoring Social Features to Your Application

Determining what social and interactive features to build into your application can be tricky business. As an application designer, you might ask yourself questions like the following:

▶ What social features, if any, make sense in my application? Will the application use social features to encourage competition (high score comparisons, notifications when a friend surpasses the user's high score, and so on)? Will the application use social networking features to broadcast game activity (post game wins to Facebook or a Twitter feed) and thus enable free promotional opportunities for the application?

▶ How can my end user invite contacts to play my application? Will users enter their friends' email addresses, phone numbers, or user names to connect with them? Will invitations be delivered via email? SMS? Will player relationships, like friendships, need to be confirmed by both sides?

▶ What existing social networking sites (Facebook, Twitter, and so on) are my target users a part of, and does it make sense for my application to integrate any of these sites' features?

▶ How will my application protect its users' (and their friends') privacy? What guidelines will I use to determine what the application (and my company) can and cannot do with private user data?

Supporting Basic Player Relationships

Social applications rely on relationships between users. Different applications describe these relationships using different terminology. The terms *contact* and *friend* are the most widely used terms to describe user relationships, but some sites use unique terminology, such as *user's circle* or *follower*. Clever applications sometimes refer to friends or contacts within the theme of the game. For example, a clever war-themed game might use the phrase "recruit fellow warriors for the mission" instead of the more generic "invite your friends to play the game by giving us their email addresses."

Adding Friend Support to Your Application

For the Been There, Done That! application, you will add some light social integration to allow players to follow other players' game scores. This is a relatively simple way to encourage game play. By sharing only "public" score information, you can avoid having to build in support for friend validation and confirmation.

The simple social feature you will add in this hour works as follows:

1. A player adds a friend's email address to mark the person as a friend.

2. If the email address matches that of another player on the application server, a friendship link is established.

3. The players now see each other's scores on the Scores of Friends tab of the scores screen.

> The full implementation of the code provided in this hour is available at this book's website, http://www.informit.com/title/9780321673350.

By the Way

Enabling Friend Requests on the Settings Screen

To add friend support to the Been There, Done That! application, you need to update QuizSettingsActivity to allow the user to input friend email addresses. Specifically, you need to do the following:

▶ Add a button to the settings screen to launch a new dialog.

▶ Implement the dialog to QuizSettingsActivity to allow the user to input a friend's email address.

▶ Add some networking code to communicate the friend request to the application server.

Updating the Settings Screen Layout

You need to update the user interface of the Been There, Done That! application to allow a player to enter friends' email addresses. There are a number of ways you could go about doing this, of course. You could add a new activity and update the menu screen, allowing for a whole new screen in the application, or you could just update the settings screen with a new area.

To keep things simple, you can just add a new section at the bottom of the settings screen that acts much like the other settings that rely on a dialog (see Figure 17.1).

FIGURE 17.1
The settings
screen updated
to allow for
friend requests.

For example, you could add the following just below the favorite place layout
controls:

```
<TextView
    android:id="@+id/TextView_Friend_Email"
    android:layout_width="wrap_content"
    android:layout_height="wrap_content"
    android:text="@string/settings_friend_email_label"
    android:textSize="@dimen/help_text_size"
    android:textStyle="bold"></TextView>
<LinearLayout
    android:id="@+id/LinearLayout_Friend_Email"
    android:orientation="horizontal"
    android:layout_height="wrap_content"
    android:layout_width="fill_parent">
    <Button
        android:id="@+id/Button_Friend_Email"
        android:layout_width="wrap_content"
        android:layout_height="wrap_content"
        android:text="@string/settings_button_friend_email"></Button>
    <TextView
        android:layout_width="fill_parent"
        android:layout_height="fill_parent"
        android:textSize="@dimen/help_text_size"
        android:textStyle="bold"
        android:gravity="center"
        android:id="@+id/TextView_Friend_Email_Tip"
        android:text="@string/settings_friend_email_tip"></TextView>
</LinearLayout>
```

Like other settings on this screen, the layout updates involve adding several
TextView labels and a Button control called Button_Friend_Email. Clicking this
button will launch a new dialog. Therefore, you need to add a new layout resource
to describe the dialog layout (see Figure 17.2).

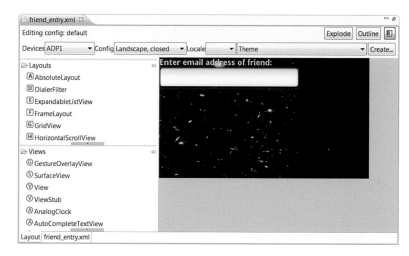

FIGURE 17.2
Preview of the
friend request
dialog layout.

This layout should be defined as follows in the XML layout file called /res/
layout/friend_entry.xml:

```xml
<?xml version="1.0" encoding="utf-8"?>
<LinearLayout
    xmlns:android="http://schemas.android.com/apk/res/android"
    android:id="@+id/root"
    android:orientation="vertical"
    android:layout_width="wrap_content"
    android:layout_height="wrap_content"
    android:background="@drawable/bkgrnd">
    <TextView
        android:id="@+id/TextView_Friend_Email"
        android:layout_width="wrap_content"
        android:layout_height="wrap_content"
        android:textSize="@dimen/help_text_size"
        android:textStyle="bold"
        android:text="@string/settings_friend_email"></TextView>
    <EditText
        android:id="@+id/EditText_Friend_Email"
        android:layout_height="wrap_content"
        android:maxLength="50"
        android:layout_width="fill_parent"
        android:maxLines="1"
        android:inputType="textEmailAddress"></EditText>
</LinearLayout>
```

The contents of this layout are straightforward. The layout is a LinearLayout container with two controls: a TextView label that prompts the user to enter an email
address and an EditText control to receive the email address string from the user.

Launching the Friend Request Dialog

Clicking the Button control called Button_Friend_Email launches a dialog that allows the user to enter a friend's email address. This dialog is launched much the same as any other dialog in the settings screen:

```
Button addFriend = (Button) findViewById(R.id.Button_Friend_Email);
addFriend.setOnClickListener(new View.OnClickListener() {
    public void onClick(View v) {
        showDialog(FRIEND_EMAIL_DIALOG_ID);
    }
});
```

You need to update the onCreateDialog() method of the QuizSettingsActivity class to include a case statement for this new dialog:

```
case FRIEND_EMAIL_DIALOG_ID:

    final View friendDialogLayout = layoutInflater.inflate(
        R.layout.friend_entry, (ViewGroup) findViewById(R.id.root));

    AlertDialog.Builder friendDialogBuilder =
        new AlertDialog.Builder(this);
    friendDialogBuilder.setView(friendDialogLayout);
    final TextView emailText = (TextView)
        friendDialogLayout.findViewById(R.id.EditText_Friend_Email);

    friendDialogBuilder.setPositiveButton(
        android.R.string.ok, new DialogInterface.OnClickListener() {

        public void onClick(DialogInterface dialog, int which) {

            String friendEmail = emailText.getText().toString();
            if (friendEmail != null && friendEmail.length() > 0) {
                doFriendRequest(friendEmail);
            }
        }
    });
    return friendDialogBuilder.create();
```

This dialog implementation should look quite familiar. Again, you are building up an AlertDialog control by inflating a layout resource. When the user clicks the OK button in the dialog (see Figure 17.3), the email address is communicated to the application server asynchronously, using the FriendRequestTask class. (We'll talk more about this in a moment.) The application server is responsible for setting up the friend relationship if the friend's email address exists in the datastore.

FIGURE 17.3
The friend
request dialog.

Creating an `AsyncTask` Subclass to Handle Friend Requests

To send friend requests to the application server, you need to add another
AsyncTask subclass called `FriendRequestTask` to `QuizSettingsActivity`. The
FriendRequestTask class can be run using the `execute()` method whenever the
player inputs a friend's email address in the friend request dialog and presses OK.

The details of the `FriendRequestTask` class are very similar to those of the other
AsyncTask subclasses you have written over the past few hours. (In the following
example, exception handling has been removed for clarity and brevity.) The only
really interesting part to this new task is the friend request code within the
doInBackground() method:

```
@Override
protected Boolean doInBackground(String... params) {
    Boolean succeeded = false;
    String friendEmail = params[0];
    SharedPreferences prefs =
        getSharedPreferences(GAME_PREFERENCES, Context.MODE_PRIVATE);
    Integer playerId = prefs.getInt(GAME_PREFERENCES_PLAYER_ID, -1);

    Vector<NameValuePair> vars = new Vector<NameValuePair>();
    vars.add(new BasicNameValuePair("command", "add"));
    vars.add(new BasicNameValuePair("playerId", playerId.toString()));
    vars.add(new BasicNameValuePair("friend", friendEmail));
    HttpClient client = new DefaultHttpClient();
    HttpPost request = new HttpPost(TRIVIA_SERVER_FRIEND_EDIT);
    request.setEntity(new UrlEncodedFormEntity(vars));
    ResponseHandler<String> responseHandler = new BasicResponseHandler();
```

```
String responseBody = client.execute(request, responseHandler);
if (responseBody != null) {
    succeeded = true;
}
return succeeded;
}
```

Here, you use `HttpClient` to execute an HTTP POST request, using form variables, to the application server. You can form the `HttpPost` request object by combining the appropriate application server URL with the query variables, encoded using the handy `UrlEncodedFormEntity` class, set as the entity for the POST request. When the query is fully formed, you can execute the request by using the `execute()` method of `HttpClient`, as you have in previous examples. Then you simply check the response to determine whether the friend request was successful by checking the resulting `ResponseHandler` object.

Displaying Friends' Scores

Now that players can add friends, you need to update `QuizScoresActivity` to populate the Scores of Friends tab with live data from the application server. Luckily, this feature is straightforward because the application server is the primary handler for friend relationships. Retrieving friends' scores is simply a slightly different query on the application server datastore.

Displaying friends' scores on the scores screen is handled exactly the same way as displaying the all-time-high scores, except that the application server URL for the data request includes the identifier of the player. The application server then knows you want to filter the scores to just those connected to that player.

From an implementation perspective, you can simply create another instance of `ScoreDownloaderTask` to retrieve these scores and populate the Scores of Friends tab (see Figure 17.4). When you have the scores screen working with live data, you can remove the mock XML resource files and any associated code from the project.

FIGURE 17.4
The Scores of
Friends tab.

Enhancing Player Relationships

Enabling friend relationships can greatly enhance the experience for users in a variety of ways above and beyond what you have implemented thus far. Adding friend support may seem like a very lightweight social feature, but imagine how you can build up more social features from this simple starting point. Player relationships allow developers the flexibility to enhance applications in a variety of ways, such as the following:

▶ The application server could send an email invitation to any friend who did not already exist in the database.

▶ Players do not need to be restricted to the Android platform. Other platforms (web, iPhone, BlackBerry, and so on) could easily be added. This means friends could contact the same application server and play each other across platforms.

▶ Friend relationships could be one way or two way (showing up on one or both players' Friends lists). Different trust relationships could be established, allowing players access to different types of information about other players, including friends' answers to questions and their favorite place in the world.

▶ After a friend relationship has been established, more application features could be added, including challenges, messaging, notifications...the sky's the limit. Use your imagination.

The complete implementation of the friends feature as described in this hour may seem incomplete—and it is! Any application incorporating a similar friends features should, at minimum, allow the player to manage (for example, view, delete) his or her existing friend relationships. However, these improvements are left as exercises for the reader.

Integrating with Social Networking Services

Social networking has really come into its own in the past few years, allowing people to connect, keep in touch, and share information (for better or worse) about their lives. Many social networking sites have developed APIs for third-party developers, many of which are web services based on representational state transfer (REST). There has been an explosion in the number of applications available for social networks, such as Facebook.

Android applications can integrate with a social networking site through development programs and the API provided by the specific site or service. The level of integration may range from lightweight to complete. Here are some examples of social networking integration you could consider in an Android application:

▶ Giving the user the option to automatically tweet on Twitter when he or she wins a game.

▶ Writing an application that allows the user to view and update his or her personal blog, Twitter feed, and Facebook status.

▶ Developing a fully featured Twitter client application.

In each case, Twitter features are integrated into the Android application in different ways. Now let's look at adding support for some of the social networking services that are popular today.

Adding Facebook Support

Facebook is a popular social web service where people can connect, share pictures and video, and chat. Facebook provides a portal for developers who want to integrate Facebook functionality into third-party applications at http://developers. facebook.com. You can find out more about the Facebook Platform for Mobile (Facebook Connect, Facebook SMS, and so on) at http://wiki.developers.facebook. com/index.php/Mobile.

Adding Twitter Support

Twitter is a popular social networking service where people share short text messages called *tweets*. Each tweet is only 140 or fewer characters, making Twitter an ideal platform for mobile. Twitter provides a portal for developers, with reference information about the Twitter API, at http://apiwiki.twitter.com.

Working with the OpenSocial Initiative

When you want to target more than one social networking site or reach as many end users as possible, you'll want to look into the OpenSocial APIs: http://wiki.opensocial.org. OpenSocial uses common APIs (instead of site-specific ones) to integrate with many popular social applications and services including the following, which are in alphabetic order:

- ▶ friendster (still popular in Southeast Asia)

- ▶ hi5 (popular in Europe and Central and South America)

- ▶ Hyves (popular in the Netherlands)

- ▶ LinkedIn (business networking)

- ▶ Mail.ru (popular in Russia)

- ▶ mixi (popular in Japan)

- ▶ MySpace (popular in the United States and worldwide)

- ▶ Netlog (popular in Europe and the Middle East)

- ▶ orkut (popular in South America and India)

- ▶ RenRen (formerly Xiaonei, popular with students in China)

- ▶ Yahoo! (popular in the United States and worldwide)

- ▶ XING (business networking, popular in Europe and China)

Each of these social networks has daily and monthly active users in the millions.

Summary

In this hour, you learned how social features can be used to enhance the user experience of a mobile application. You worked through a short example of how to add social features to the Been There, Done That! application by adding the ability for a user to specify friends (by email address) and view friends' scores. Finally, you learned about many of the third-party social networking services you can consider integrating your application with.

Q&A

Q. *How do I determine the best unique identifier to distinguish users?*

A. Despite a number of initiatives to implement single-login services, there is still not a great answer to this question. Some candidates are unique username/password pairings, email addresses, or phone numbers. In the example in this hour, we relied on the email address of the player as a unique identifier, and we allowed the user to set up a password. Many social networking sites use a similar mechanism, but this approach is not without problems—for example, email addresses change, users may have more than one account, and they have to keep track of yet another login and password combination. When you're integrating with a social networking website, you need to use whatever authentication and credentials are required by the site's API.

Q. *What are some of the privacy concerns I should consider when developing social applications?*

A. When it comes to social applications, you should always include information about how you'll use any information supplied by the user. You're going to be safest when you follow these principles: Don't access, use, or store any information your application doesn't require and do assume that any and all information supplied by the user is private. Now, by this definition, even the lightweight friend support you added to the Been There, Done That! application is sharing private data: the user's nickname, score, and avatar. (See the exercises for accessing friends' avatar images from the server.) Technically, if you published this application, you would want to make it very, very clear to the player that this information is going to be uploaded to the application server and accessible to other players.

Q. *How do I find out if my application can integrate with a social network application that's not listed in this hour?*

A. Whether you want to integrate with a social networking service or some other web service (for example, Google, Amazon, eBay), the simplest way to find out if a service has an API is to browse the company's website. There you will often find a link for developers near the information about customer support, contact, and company information or within the customer support FAQ. Most companies require developers to agree to terms of use, and some companies require you to register for a special API key to use the services.

Workshop

Quiz

1. True or False: All Android applications can and should be enhanced using social features.

2. How does the Been There, Done That! application create friend relationships?

   A. By allowing the player to search the application server for friends he or she recognizes

   B. By allowing the player to input a friend's email address

   C. By launching the Contacts application and allowing the player to choose a contact

   D. By allowing the player to input a friend's phone number

3. True or False: The Android SDK has built-in support for social networking sites such as Facebook, Twitter, and MySpace.

Answers

1. False. Adding social features to an application can enhance the experience for users, but this is a design decision that requires thought and planning. Some types of applications benefit greatly from these features, while others may not. Add social features to an application only when doing so provides a clear benefit to both users and the developer.

2. B. Players can add friends in the Been There, Done That! application by inputting their email addresses. The application server tries to match each email address entered to an existing player. If the player exists, then a friend relationship is established.

3. False. You can use the networking features of the Android SDK to access the developer APIs provided by third-party social networking sites such as Facebook, Twitter, and MySpace.

Exercises

1. Modify the Scores of Friends tab of the scores screen to display each friend's avatar as well as each score. (Hint: The URL for each friend's avatar is included in the XML score data downloaded from the application server.)

2. Modify the scores screen to add another tab, showing the scores of players who have added this player as a friend (in other words, players who are watching this player's score). The application server has the appropriate query implemented. Use the same URL but add the variable `followers` and set it to the string `true` (for example, "http://tqs.mamlambo.com/scores.jsp?playerId=##&followers=true").

3. Review the development API documentation of the third-party social networking service of your choice. Consider implementing a simple feature for the Been There, Done That! application which accesses that networking service in an interesting way. For example, you might post a tweet to the player's Twitter feed each time that player answers a quiz question in the affirmative (for example, "Player X has climbed Mount Everest!").

4. Add a feature to send a text message to the user's friend to challenge him or her to beat the user's score.

HOUR 18

Creating a Home Screen App Widget

What You'll Learn in This Hour:

▶ Designing and implementing an App Widget

▶ Handling App Widget user events

▶ Working with services

In this hour, you will create an App Widget for the Been There, Done That! application. Specifically, you will create a simple App Widget control that can be added to the user's Home screen to display the user's avatar, nickname, and score information and remind them to continue playing the game.

Designing an App Widget

The Android SDK provides developers with an interesting way to provide functionality outside the traditional boundaries of a mobile application: by using App Widgets. Developers can use the App Widget API to create mini controls or views that can be added to the user's Home screen. These simple controls can provide a user with information about the application and remind the user to launch the application when necessary.

App Widgets can be useful for certain types of applications, such as those that might need to inform the user of some status or update. A weather application might include an App Widget that displays the current weather conditions at the given location on the Home screen. A task management application might include an App Widget that informs the user of the next task on his or her to-do list or how many tasks are left for the day. A picture gallery application might include an App Widget that acts as a slideshow of all the pictures stored in the gallery.

In this lesson, you will create a simple App Widget for the Been There, Done That! application. This App Widget will do the following:

▶ Display the user's avatar

▶ Display the user's nickname

▶ Display the user's current score

▶ Launch the Been There, Done That! application when clicked

Defining App Widget Properties

App Widget definition and configuration properties are defined in a separate XML file and are then referenced from within the Android manifest file. (We'll get to that in a moment.)

The following are some of the common properties used to define an App Widget:

▶ **Size**—The width and height dimensions of the App Widget, defined in density-independent pixels (dp or dip), which correspond to the number of Home screen grid cells the App Widget will require to display correctly.

> The Android Home screen is organized in grid cells that usually correspond to a square of 74×74 pixels. Only one item, such as an App Widget or application shortcut, can sit in any cell. This way, items on the Home screen do not overlap.

▶ **Update Frequency**—The time (in milliseconds) between system calls to the App Widget provider to update the contents of the App Widget.

▶ **Initial Layout**—A layout file to use when the App Widget is initially added. This can be changed in code later.

▶ **Configuration Activity**—The definition for an activity to launch to configure various aspects of the App Widget before it is first displayed.

To add an App Widget definition for this example, start by adding a new XML file called widget_info.xml under the /res/xml folder. In this file, place the following App Widget definition:

```xml
<?xml version="1.0" encoding="utf-8"?>
<appwidget-provider
    xmlns:android="http://schemas.android.com/apk/res/android"
    android:minWidth="146dp"
```

```
        android:minHeight="146dp"
        android:updatePeriodMillis="10800000"
        android:initialLayout="@layout/widget">
</appwidget-provider>
```

This definition file defines an App Widget that will update every three hours and be 2×2 grid cells in size. If you've done the math, you may have noticed that the 146dp on each edge is not double the 74dp we previously defined a grid cell size to be. Although a grid cell is typically considered 74dp on edge, when calculating the size, you must subtract 2dp from the final result. In this example, we multiplied 74 by 2 to get 148. Then, we subtracted 2 from it to get to the 146 we put in the file. Without this, the App Widget may not draw in the expected number of cells.

This App Widget will receive update calls every 10,800,000 milliseconds, which corresponds to three hours. In addition, this App Widget will initially use a predefined layout, referenced by android:initialLayout="@layout/widget". The contents of this layout file will be discussed shortly.

Updating the Android Manifest File

The Android manifest file needs to be updated to tell the system where to find the definition of the App Widget. An App Widget is a specialized form of a BroadcastReceiver control.

Therefore, a <receiver> definition must be placed within the AndroidManifest.xml file that defines what Intent objects will be received and a couple other pieces of data specific to the App Widget.

To accomplish this task, add the following <receiver> section to the application section of the AndroidManifest.xml file:

```
<receiver
    android:name="QuizWidgetProvider">
    <intent-filter>
        <action
            android:name="android.appwidget.action.APPWIDGET_UPDATE" />
    </intent-filter>
    <meta-data
        android:name="android.appwidget.provider"
        android:resource="@xml/widget_info" />
</receiver>
```

This <receiver> segment of the Android manifest file defines an intent filter for App Widget updates. In addition, it ties the App Widget, and its definition file, to the overall application.

Designing the App Widget Layout

App Widgets have specific layout requirements. To begin with, an App Widget is drawn through the `RemoteViews` interface, which limits the user interface that can be displayed. Next, the App Widget must conform to the size configured in its properties.

A `RemoteViews` object is used when the actual display of a view will be performed from within another process. This is exactly what happens with an App Widget: It is displayed in the App Widget host process, not the application's main process. `RemoteViews` objects are limited in the layout and view objects they may use. Some layout and view objects supported within App Widgets include the following:

- ▶ `LinearLayout`

- ▶ `FrameLayout`

- ▶ `RelativeLayout`

- ▶ `TextView`

- ▶ `ImageView`

- ▶ `Button`

- ▶ `ImageButton`

- ▶ `ProgressBar`

- ▶ `AnalogClock`

- ▶ `Chronometer`

Classes extending these controls cannot be used. This means that the design of the layout is very limited. App Widgets are not meant to display much information, though, and the customary way of enhancing the features of an App Widget is to trigger the launch of full activity when more powerful features or complex screens are required. This functionality could be used to draw an entire screen or be limited to just a popup screen. Either way, activities launched from an App Widget no longer carry the limitations that an App Widget has from the required use of a `RemoteViews` object.

To design a layout for the App Widget, create a new layout file called `widget.xml`, and place the following code in it:

```xml
<?xml version="1.0" encoding="utf-8"?>
<RelativeLayout
    xmlns:android="http://schemas.android.com/apk/res/android"
    android:layout_width="wrap_content"
```

```
        android:layout_height="wrap_content"
        android:id="@+id/widget_view">
    <ImageView
        android:layout_centerInParent="true"
        android:layout_height="fill_parent"
        android:layout_width="fill_parent"
        android:id="@+id/widget_image"></ImageView>
    <TextView
        android:text="@+id/TextView01"
        android:layout_width="wrap_content"
        android:layout_height="wrap_content"
        android:layout_alignParentTop="true"
        android:layout_centerHorizontal="true"
        android:id="@+id/widget_nickname"></TextView>
    <TextView
        android:text="@+id/TextView02"
        android:layout_width="wrap_content"
        android:layout_height="wrap_content"
        android:layout_centerHorizontal="true"
        android:layout_alignParentBottom="true"
        android:id="@+id/widget_score"></TextView>
</RelativeLayout>
```

Implementing an App Widget Provider

Now that the configuration is in place, you need to implement the App Widget. To do this, you need to extend the `AppWidgetProvider` class, which contains five methods that can be overridden:

- ▶ `onUpdate()`—This method is called at each update interval.

- ▶ `onDeleted()`—This method is called each time an App Widget is deleted.

- ▶ `onEnabled()`—This method is called the first time an App Widget is created, but not subsequent times.

- ▶ `onDisabled()`—This method is called when the last instance of an App Widget is deleted.

- ▶ `onReceive()`—This method is called for all received broadcast events; the default implementation calls each of the previous callback methods (e.g. `onUpdate()`, `onDeleted()`, `onEnabled()`, and `onDisabled()`) when necessary. This method can be overridden when advanced behavior is required.

For this example, you only need to override the `onUpdate()` method to update the `RemoteViews` object. No persistent setup is needed, so you don't need to override any of the other methods. That said, here's the implementation of the `AppWidgetProvider` class:

```java
public class QuizWidgetProvider2 extends AppWidgetProvider {
    @Override
    public void onUpdate(Context context,
            AppWidgetManager appWidgetManager,
            int[] appWidgetIds) {
        WidgetData widgetData = new WidgetData("Unknown", "NA", "");
        getWidgetData(widgetData);
        String packageName = context.getPackageName();
        RemoteViews remoteView =
                new RemoteViews(context.getPackageName(), R.layout.widget);
        remoteView.setTextViewText(
                R.id.widget_nickname, widgetData.nickname);
        remoteView.setTextViewText(
                R.id.widget_score, "Score: " + widgetData.score);
        if (widgetData.avatarUrl.length() > 0) {
            URL image;
            try {
                image = new URL(widgetData.avatarUrl);

                Bitmap bitmap =
                        BitmapFactory.decodeStream(image.openStream());
                if (bitmap == null) {
                    Log.w(DEBUG_TAG, "Failed to decode image");
                    remoteView.setImageViewResource(
                            R.id.widget_image, R.drawable.avatar);
                } else {
                    remoteView.setImageViewBitmap(
                            R.id.widget_image, bitmap);
                }
            } catch (MalformedURLException e) {
                Log.e(DEBUG_TAG, "Bad url in image", e);
            } catch (IOException e) {
                Log.e(DEBUG_TAG, "IO failure for image", e);
            }

        } else {
            remoteView.setImageViewResource(
                    R.id.widget_image, R.drawable.avatar);
        }

        try {
            ComponentName quizWidget =
                    new ComponentName(context, QuizWidgetProvider.class);
            AppWidgetManager appWidgetManager =
                    AppWidgetManager.getInstance(context);
            appWidgetManager.updateAppWidget(quizWidget, remoteView);
        } catch (Exception e) {
            Log.e(DEBUG_TAG, "Failed to update widget", e);
        }
    }

    private void getWidgetData(WidgetData widgetData) {
    }
}
```

At this point, you need to get the data that will be displayed in the App Widget. The `getWidgetData()` method handles this by getting the player identifier from `SharedPreferences` and then downloading the data from the server. You handle the operation this way instead of loading this data straight from `SharedPreferences` so that you can switch it later to support loading data from friends or other players.

Next, you build up the `RemoteViews` object. The initialization requires not only the layout to use but also the package for where the layout comes from. Recall that a `RemoteViews` object will not be displayed in the same process, so more information is needed in order for it to access the resources.

You have access to the nickname and score information (or suitable default values), so you can set those via the `setTextViewText()` method, passing in both the identifier from the layout and the value. The code for the avatar image is similar but first verifies that a suitable URL for the avatar is available and that the image can be decoded. Finally, either the `setImageViewBitmap()` or `setImageViewResource()` method is called to apply the avatar image to the `RemoteViews` object.

Finally, you have to actually update the App Widget. You do this via a call to the `updateAppWidget()` method of `AppWidgetManager`. It requires both the `RemoteViews` object and the Android `ComponentName` object of the `QuizWidgetProvider`, retrieved by instantiating that class directly.

If you were paying close attention, you may have noticed that you didn't use two of the `onUpdate()` parameters: `appWidgetManager` and `appWidgetIds`. The `appWidgetManager` parameter isn't used because you'll be moving the code to a different method shortly, where an instance of it will be retrieved separately. The `appWidgetIds` parameter is used when you want to support multiple unique App Widgets that show different data. In that case, the application must track the `appWidgetIds` values, which are assigned by the system, separately and pair them correctly to the data that needs to be shown in each App Widget. Typically, this is done using a distinct configuration activity for each App Widget so the user controls what they want displayed in each different instance of this App Widget.

By the Way

The App Widget should now appear in the Home screen's App Widget interface, as shown in Figure 18.1.

FIGURE 18.1
Adding the App
Widget to the
Home screen.

▼ Try It Yourself

To add an App Widget to the Home screen of an Android phone or the emulator, follow these easy steps:

1. Navigate to the Home screen.

2. Find a suitably empty area of the screen. (Remember that the App Widget needs 2×2 grid cells.)

3. Click and hold your finger (or the mouse button on the emulator) over the area where you want to add the App Widget.

4. When the pop-up menu appears, choose Add to Home Screen, Widgets.

5. Select the App Widget you just created (or any other App Widget) from the list and add it to your Home screen.

At this point, the App Widget looks as shown in Figure 18.2.

FIGURE 18.2
The Been There, Done That! App Widget.

Handling App Widget User Events

As it stands, the App Widget works but isn't terribly interactive. You don't want it to just display information to the user; you want it to also bring the user back to the application. Another area where the App Widget might be improved is to make it handle slow avatar image downloads gracefully.

App Widgets are displayed through `RemoteViews` objects and not within the application where they are created. Instead, they are displayed within an App Widget host. This affects the handling of user input. Recall that the list of views that an App Widget supports did not include any user input fields. Basically, the only event that an App Widget supports is a click event.

> You may have seen a number of App Widgets, such as the Facebook App Widget, present what look like `EditText` fields. However, if you click on them to enter text, you'll notice that in all cases, a different UI comes up to actually take the entry. This method is an excellent way to provide advanced controls within the limitations of the App Widget framework.

By the Way

Because the App Widget isn't displayed in the same process as the application, a new method is needed for getting the click event. The Android SDK provides an

Intent type known as PendingIntent for this purpose. This is an Intent that will basically be sent at a future time and can be sent by another process. To create a PendingIntent, an Intent instance must first be created. Then the PendingIntent is created with some additional information, such as what to do on subsequent uses of the same Intent. That is, the exact same instance could be used, or a new instance could be created. Once the PendingIntent object is created, it can be assigned to the RemoteViews object via a call to the setOnClickPendingIntent() method. You need to add the code for this must before the call to the updateAppWidget() method:

```
Intent launchAppIntent =
    new Intent(context, QuizMenuActivity.class);
PendingIntent launchAppPendingIntent =
    PendingIntent.getActivity(context, 0, launchAppIntent,
    PendingIntent.FLAG_UPDATE_CURRENT);
remoteView.setOnClickPendingIntent(
    R.id.widget_view, launchAppPendingIntent);
```

The view identifier that the PendingIntent is added to via the call to the setOnClickPendingIntent() method is the RelativeLayout object from the widget.xml layout file. Now when the App Widget is clicked, QuizMenuActivity is launched; this happens to be the normal launch activity of the Been There, Done That! application. (Note that any activity could be launched, such as the high scores, but this one makes the most sense.)

> When you create a dynamic App Widget, individual views could have their own PendingIntent objects assigned. This way, the actions they send cause an updateAppWidget() method call to change the look of the App Widget in response to the click.

Working with Widget Background Operations

You might think that because the App Widget doesn't run within the application process, you don't have to worry about operations taking too long. You might also think that because the App Widget is a BroadcastReceiver object, it will automatically perform its actions in the background. In both cases, you'd be wrong.

For lengthy operations, the general solution is to launch a separate thread to handle things. However, for App Widgets, this isn't feasible. Instead, you must create and launch an Android Service instance and then, from the service, you can launch a background thread. An Android service can provide two useful operations: It can provide background processing, and it can provide an interface to a remote object, such as providing access to extensions or software libraries.

Why can't a `Thread` class be used directly from an App Widget? Although the full details are beyond the scope of this book, the simple answer is that when processing returns from the `onUpdate()` method, the App Widget process may go away, destroying any running threads. An Android `Service` instance won't go away, though, so you can use it to run background operations.

By the Way

You can see all the services currently running on an Android handset or emulator by selecting Settings, Applications, Running Services. From here, you can choose to stop services, as well. Figure 18.3 shows the Running Services screen.

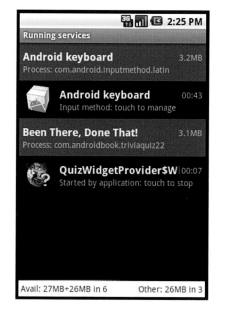

FIGURE 18.3
The Running Services screen.

Creating a Service

A `Service` object is created by extending the `Service` class, overriding three primary methods, and defining the service within the `AndroidManifest.xml` file. For the Been There, Done That! App Widget, you must define the `Service` object within `QuizWidgetProvider`. Then you can move the bulk of the `onUpdate()` code to the `onStartCommand()` method of the `Service` object and create a `Thread` object to do the work so the App Widget and service are responsive.

At this point, put the following code in to the `QuizWidgetProvider` class:

```java
public static class WidgetUpdateService extends Service {
    Thread widgetUpdateThread = null;
    private static final String DEBUG_TAG = "WidgetUpdateService";

    @Override
    public int onStartCommand(Intent intent, int flags, final int startId) {
        widgetUpdateThread = new Thread() {
            public void run() {
                // code moved from onUpdate() method
            }
        };
        widgetUpdateThread.start();
        return START_REDELIVER_INTENT;
    }

    @Override
    public void onDestroy() {
        widgetUpdateThread.interrupt();
        super.onDestroy();
    }

    @Override
    public IBinder onBind(Intent intent) {
        // no binding; can't from an App Widget
        return null;
    }
}
```

This is the service implementation, as it would appear after moving the code from the `onUpdate()` method to the `run()` method of the thread created in the `onStartCommand()` method.

Now the Android manifest file needs to be updated so the system knows about this service. To do this, add a `<service>` block to the `<application>` section of the manifest file, like this:

```
<service
    android:name="QuizWidgetProvider$WidgetUpdateService" />
```

This tells the system that there is a service and where to find it.

Controlling the Service

You now need to start the service from within the App Widget onUpdate() method. You can start a service in one of two ways: either through a call to the Context.startService() method or through a call to the Context.bindService() method. In this case, you use the startService() method by replacing the onUpdate() method with the following code:

```
@Override
public void onUpdate(Context context,
    AppWidgetManager appWidgetManager, int[] appWidgetIds) {
    Intent serviceIntent = new Intent(context, WidgetUpdateService.class);
    context.startService(serviceIntent);
}
```

When a service has finished, it's a good idea to stop it to free up valuable resources. The App Widget will update only once every three hours. Although you could leave the service around—doing nothing—you might as well stop it until it is needed again. This is accomplished by placing the following call at the end of the run() method of the Thread class you use to perform the background tasks:

```
if (!WidgetUpdateService.this.stopSelfResult(startId)) {
    Log.e(DEBUG_TAG, "Failed to stop service");
}
```

This call to the stopSelfResult() method tells the service to stop itself and returns whether or not the call was successful. If you don't care about the result, simply call the stopSelf() method instead. This method call is made when the processing is finished within the thread since there is no reason for the service to keep running, as it has no further actions to perform, in this case. The service can be launched again the next time the App Widget updates which, for this App Widget, is after three hours have elapsed.

If the App Widget is removed from its host, such as the Home screen, while an update is taking place, the service will need to be terminated in a different way. To accomplish this, put the following code for the onDeleted() method into the AppWidgetProvider implementation:

```
@Override
public void onDeleted(Context context, int[] appWidgetIds) {
    Intent serviceIntent = new Intent(context, WidgetUpdateService.class);
    context.stopScrvice(serviceIntent);
    super.onDeleted(context, appWidgetIds);
}
```

The call to the `stopService()` method triggers a call to the `onDestroy()` method of the `Service` class implementation, which then attempts to interrupt the thread to stop it.

> The example in this hour is pretty simple. It will work fine for a single instance of the App Widget. However, if you want to support multiple instances of the App Widget running simultaneously, further code is needed to handle the differentiation between instances.

Summary

In this hour, you built a simple App Widget for the Been There, Done That! application to display the user's avatar, nickname, and score. This hour covered all the implementation details of App Widget development, including designing the layout and defining the App Widget properties. You also added some simple event handling, allowing the user to click the App Widget to launch the Been There, Done That! application. Finally, you used a background service to handle processing of App Widget events and updates.

Q&A

Q. *Is the Home screen the only place I can include App Widget controls?*

A. No. Any App Widget host can hold App Widget controls. The Home screen is simply the place you'll most commonly see App Widgets used. See the documentation for `AppWidgetHost` and `AppWidgetHostView` for more details.

Q. *How do I add more interactive features, such as* `Button` *controls, to an App Widget?*

A. If you want to add configuration controls to an App Widget and allow the user to trigger updates to the App Widget content, you need to define each event separately and implement the appropriate click handlers to send specific event commands, via `PendingIntent` objects, to a registered receiver of the `Intent` objects. Then the App Widget application needs to receive the commands and process them accordingly, updating the App Widget content as necessary. You can find a complete example of an interactive App Widget provided in our article "Handling User Interaction with Android App Widgets," available at http://www.developer.com/ws/article.php/3837531/Handling-User-Interaction-with-Android-App-Widgets.htm.

Q. *Can I have multiple instances of an App Widget?*

A. Having multiple instances doesn't make sense with the App Widget you implemented for the Been There, Done That! application. However, in certain instances, it might make sense to allow the user to have multiple instances of an App Widget with different configurations. One way to accomplish this is to allow the user to configure each App Widget instance using the configuration activity defined for the App Widget. Then, the application must keep track of the differences between the instances by keeping track of the user configuration activity for each App Widget identifier. We also cover this advanced topic in our article "Handling User Interaction with Android App Widgets" (see the previous Q&A for details).

Workshop

Quiz

1. True or False: App Widgets can reside only on the Home screen.

2. Which of the following is an example of a `View` widget that cannot be used with an App Widget?

   A. `Button`

   B. `WebView`

   C. `ProgressBar`

3. True or False: Although App Widgets are defined in pixels, their size must correspond directly to a certain number of cells.

4. For what reason is a service used in an App Widget?

   A. To handle lengthy background operations

   B. To handle drawing directly on the screen

   C. To access private data

Answers

1. False. App Widgets can reside within an application that implements an `AppWidgetHost` object.

2. B. Both `Button` and `ProgressBar` can be used, but not `WebView`.

3. True. Each cell is typically defined as 74 pixels, but when adding up the number for multiple cells, 2 pixels are subtracted. Thus, 2 cells wide would be (74×2) – 2, or 146 pixels.

4. A. An App Widget runs in another process so must be responsive to requests. A `thread` can't be used because it might be killed when the App Widget returns. Therefore, a service is started to perform background processing.

Exercises

1. Modify the App Widget in the Been There, Done That! application to show information about a friend. (The XML returned for the friend's scores contains the nickname, score, rank, and avatar URL.)

2. Add a configuration activity that allows the user to choose which friend to show.

3. Continuing with the previous two exercises, modify the App Widget to allow multiple instances, one showing the user's data and the other showing a friend's data.

Internationalizing Your Application

What You'll Learn in This Hour:

▶ Languages supported by the Android platform

▶ Managing strings and other resources

▶ Localized formatting utilities

▶ Other internationalization concerns

The mobile marketplace is global—serving a variety of users in many countries and many locales. Developers need to keep this in mind when designing and developing applications for the Android platform; applications will likely be used by foreign-speaking users. In this hour, you learn about the localization features of the Android platform and the Android Market.

By the Way

> In Hour 24, "Publishing on the Android Market," you'll learn how your application can be made available for distribution within the Android Market.

General Internationalization Principles

With a global marketplace, developers can maximize profits and grow their user base by supporting a variety of different languages and locales. Let's take a moment to clarify some terms. While you likely know what we mean by *language*, you may not be aware that each language may have a number of different locales. For example, the Spanish spoken in Spain is quite different from that spoken in the Americas, the French spoken in Canada differs from that of Europe and Africa, and the English spoken in the United States differs from that spoken in Britain. English is a *language*, while English (United States), English (United Kingdom), and English (Australia) are *locales* (see Figure 19.1).

FIGURE 19.1
People who speak the same language often have localized dialects.

Applications are made up of data and functions (behavior). For most applications, the behavior is the same, regardless of the locale. However, the data must be localized. This is one of the key reasons resource files exist—to externalize application data.

The most common type of application data that requires localization is the strings of text used by the application. For example, a string of data might represent a user's name, but the text label for that value on an application screen would need to be shown in the proper language (for example, Name, Nom, Nombre).

Development platforms that support internationalization typically allow for string tables, which can be swapped around so that the same application can target different languages. The Android platform is no exception.

**Watch
Out!**

> Do not hard code string information into an application (that is, the Java source file) unless absolutely necessary. Doing so hinders internationalization efforts.

How Android Localization Works

Compared to other mobile platforms, the Android SDK provides reasonably extensive support for internationalization. However, this is a fairly complex topic with lots of caveats—and the Android documentation in this area is virtually nonexistent.

Android localization considerations fall into three main categories:

▶ The languages and locales supported by the Android platform (an extensive list—the superset of all available languages)

▶ The languages and locales supported by a specific Android handset (a list that varies—a subset of languages chosen by a handset manufacturer or operator)

▶ The countries, languages, and locales supported by the Android Market application (the countries and locales where Google can sell legally; this list grows continuously)

The specific locales supported by Android (as of this writing) are shown in Table 19.1.

TABLE 19.1　Languages and Regions Supported in Android

Language	Regions
Chinese (zh)	PRC (zh_CN)
	Taiwan (zh_TW)
Czech (cs)	Czech (cs_CZ)
Dutch (nl)	Netherlands (nl_NL)
	Belgium (nl_BE)
English (en)	United States (en_US)
	Britain (en_GB)
	Canada (en_CA)
	Australia (en_AU)
	New Zealand (en_NZ)
	Singapore (en_SG)
French (fr)	France (fr_FR)
	Belgium (fr_BE)
	Canada (fr_CA)
	Switzerland (fr_CH)
German (de)	Germany (de_DE)
	Austria (de_AT)
	Switzerland (de_CH)
	Liechtenstein (de_LI)
Italian (it)	Italy (it_IT)
	Switzerland (it_CH)
Japanese (jp)	Japan (jp_JP)
Korean (ko)	South Korea (ko_KR)
Polish (pl)	Poland (pl_PL)
Russian (ru)	Russia (ru_RU)
Spanish (es)	Spain (es_ES)

Did you
Know?

> The locales are likely to be enhanced. The latest list of locales can be viewed at http://developer.android.com/sdk/android-2.1.html#locs.

How the Android Operating System Handles Locale

Much like other operating systems, the Android platform has a system setting for locale. This setting has a default setting that can be modified by the mobile operator. For example, a German mobile operator might make the default locale Deutsch (Deutschland) for its shipping handsets. An American mobile operator would likely set the default locale to English (American) and also include an option for the locale Español (Estados Unidos)—thus supporting American English and Spanish of the Americas.

A user can change the system-wide setting for locale in the Settings application. The locale setting affects the behavior of applications installed on the handset.

▼   **Try It Yourself**

To change the locale on a handset, perform the following steps:

  1. From the Home screen, click the Menu button and choose Settings.

  2. From the Settings menu, select the Language & Keyboard option.

  3. Choose Select Locale and select a locale. The Android platform immediately changes the locale on the system. For example, if you choose Español, you see that many of the menus on the Android platform are now in Spanish.

  Take care to remember these steps, as you will have to navigate back to the locale settings in the foreign language you chose.

▲

How Applications Handle Locales

Now let's look at how the system-wide locale setting affects each Android application. When an Android application uses a project resource, the Android operating system attempts to match the best possible resource for the job at runtime. In many cases, this means checking for a resource in the specific language or regional locale. If no resource matches the required locale, the system falls back on the default resource.

Developers can specify specific language and locale resources by providing resources in specially named resource directories of the project. Any application resource can be localized, whether it is a string resource file, a drawable, an animation sequence, or some other type.

Specifying Default Resources

So far, every resource in the Been There, Done That! application is a default resource. A default resource is simply a resource that does not have specific tags for loading under different circumstances.

Default resources are the most important resources because they are the fallback for any situation when a specific, tailored resource does not exist (which happens more often than not). In the case of the Been There, Done That! application, the default resources are all in English.

Specifying Language-Specific Resources

To specify strings for a specific language, you must supply the resource under a specially named directory that includes the two-letter language code provided in ISO 639-1 (see www.loc.gov/standards/iso639-2/php/code_list.php). For example, English is en, French is fr, and German is de. Let's look at an example of how this works.

Say that you want the Been There, Done That! application to support English, German, and French strings. You would take the following steps:

1. Create a `strings.xml` resource file for each language. Each string that is to be localized must appear in each resource file with the same name, so it will be programmatically loaded correctly. Any strings you don't want to localize can be left in the default (English) `/res/values/strings.xml` file.

2. Save the French `strings.xml` resource file to the `/res/values-fr/` directory.

3. Save the German `strings.xml` resource file to the `/res/values-de/` directory.

Android can now grab the appropriate string, based on the system locale. However, if no match exists, the system falls back on whatever is defined in the `/res/values/` directory. This means that if English (or Arabic, or Chinese, or Japanese, or an unexpected locale) is chosen, the default (fallback) English strings will be used.

Similarly, you could provide a German-specific drawable resource to override one in the default `/res/drawable/` directory by supplying one with the same name in the `/res/drawable-de/` directory.

Specifying Region-Specific Resources

You may have noticed that the previous example specifies high-level language settings only (English, but not American English versus British English vs. Australian English). Don't worry! You can specify the region or locale as part of the resource directory name as well.

To specify strings for a specific language and locale, you must supply the resource under a specially named directory that includes the two-letter language code provided in ISO 639-1 (see http://www.loc.gov/standards/iso639-2/php/code_list.php), followed by a dash, then a lowercase r, and finally the ISO 3166-1-alpha-2 region code (see http://www.iso.org/iso/country_codes/iso_3166_code_lists/english_country_names_and_code_elements.htm). For example, American English is en-rUS, British English is en-rGB, and Australian English is en-rAU. Let's look at an example of how this works.

If you wanted the Been There, Done That! application to support these three versions of English, you could do the following:

1. Create a `strings.xml` resource file for each language. Any strings you don't want to localize can be left in the default (American English) `/res/values/strings.xml` file.

2. Save the British English `strings.xml` resource file to the `/res/values-en-rGB/` directory.

3. Save the Australian English `strings.xml` resource file to the `/res/values-en-rAU/` directory.

To summarize, you start with a default set of resources—which should be in the most common language your application will rely on. Then you add exceptions—such as separate language and region string values—where needed. This way, you can optimize your application so it runs on a variety of platforms.

Did you Know?

> For a more complete explanation of how the Android operating system resolves resources, check out the Android developer website: http://developer.android.com/guide/topics/resources/resources-i18n.html#best-match.

How the Android Market Handles Locales

The Android Market supports a subset of the locales available on the Android platform. Because the Android Market uses the Google Checkout system for payments, only countries where this online marketplace is legal can be supported for paid applications.

For a complete list of the countries and languages supported by the Android Market, see http://market.android.com/support/bin/answer.py?hl=en&answer=138294. Note that the Android Market differentiates between countries that allow only free applications and countries where developers can distribute fee-based applications.

> Developers must register to sell applications on the Android Market. A complete list of countries where developers of free Android apps may reside (which is different from where they may publish) is available at http://market.android.com/support/bin/answer.py?hl=en&answer=136758.

Did you Know?

Android Internationalization Strategies

Don't be overwhelmed by the permutations available to developers when it comes to internationalizing an application. Instead, give some thought to how important internationalization is to your application during the design phase of your project. Develop a strategy that suits your specific needs and stick to it.

Here are some basic strategies to handle Android application internationalization:

- ▶ Forgo internationalization entirely.
- ▶ Limit internationalization.
- ▶ Implement full internationalization for target audiences.

Now let's talk about each of these strategies in more detail.

Forgoing Application Internationalization

Whenever possible, save your development and testing teams a lot of work—don't bother to internationalize your application. This is the "one size fits most" approach to mobile development, and it is often possible with games and other simple, graphic-intensive applications. If your application simple enough to work smoothly with internationally recognized graphical icons (such as play, pause, stop, and so on) instead of text labels, or "Sims" language (garbled mumbles that get the point across to speakers of any language) then you may be able to forgo internationalization entirely. However, this works only for a subset of applications. If your application requires a help screen, for example, you're likely going to need at least some localization for your application to work well all over the world.

Some of the pros of this strategy are the following:

▶ Simplified development and testing

▶ Smallest application size (only one set of resources)

Some of the cons of this strategy are the following:

▶ For text- or culture-dependant applications, this approach greatly reduces the value of the application. It is simply too generic.

▶ This strategy automatically alienates certain audiences and limits your application's potential marketplaces.

Limiting Application Internationalization

Most applications require only some light internationalization. This often means internationalizing string resources only, but other resources, such as layouts and graphics, remain the same for all languages and locales.

Some of the pros of this strategy are the following:

▶ Modest development and testing requirements

▶ Streamlined application size (specialized resources kept to a minimum)

Some of the cons of this strategy are the following:

▶ Application may still be too generic for certain types of applications. Overall design (especially screen design) may suffer from needing to support multiple target languages. For example, text fields might need to be large enough to support verbose languages such as German but look odd and waste valuable screen real estate in less verbose languages.

▶ Because you've headed down the road of providing language-specific resources, your users are more likely to expect other languages you haven't supported. In other words, you're more likely to start getting requests for your app to support more languages if you've supported some. That said, you've already built and tested your application on a variety of languages, so adding new ones should be straightforward.

Implementing Full Application Internationalization

Some types of applications require complete internationalization. Providing custom resources for each supported language and locale is a time-intensive endeavor, and you should not do it unless you have a really good reason to do so because the size of the application grows as you include more resources. This approach often necessitates breaking the individual languages into separate APK files for publication, resulting in more complex configuration management. However, this allows a developer to tailor an application for each specific marketplace to a fine degree.

Some of the pros of this strategy are the following:

▶ The application is fully tailored and customized to individual audiences; this strategy allows for tweaks to individual locales.

▶ It builds user loyalty by providing users with the best, most customized experience. (This is also a technique used by Google.)

Some of the cons of this strategy are the following:

▶ It is the most lengthy and complicated strategy to develop.

▶ Each internationalized version of the application must be fully tested as if it were a completely different application (which it may well be, if you are forced to split it into different APK files due to application size).

Beware of over-internationalizing an application. The application package size will grow as you add language- and locale-specific resources. There is no reason to head down this road unless you have a compelling reason to do so—and unless you have the development, testing, and product team to manage it. Having a poorly localized version of an application can be worse to your image than having no localization at all.

Watch Out!

Using Localization Utilities

The Android SDK includes support for handling locale information. For example, the Locale class (`java.util.Locale`) encapsulates locale information.

Determining System Locale

If you need to modify application behavior based on locale information, you need to be able to access information about the Android operating system. You can do this by using the getConfiguration() method of the Context object, as follows:

```
Configuration sysConfig = getResources().getConfiguration();
```

One of the settings available in the `Configuration` object is the locale:

```
Locale curLocale = sysConfig.locale;
```

You can use this locale information to vary application behavior programmatically, as needed.

Formatting Strings Like Dates and Times

Another aspect of internationalization is displaying data in the appropriate way. For example, U.S. dates are formatted MM/DD/YY and December 8, 1975, whereas much of the rest of the world uses the formats DD/MM/YY and 8 December, 1975. The Android SDK includes a number of locale-specific utilities. For example, you can use the `DateFormat` class (`android.text.format.DateFormat`) to generate date and time strings in the current locale, or you can customize date and time information as needed for your application.

> You can use the `TimeUtils` class (`android.util.TimeUtils`) to determine the time zone of a specified country by name.

Handling Currencies

Much like dates and times, currencies and how they are formatted differ by locale. You can use the standard java `Currency` class (`java.util.Currency`) to encapsulate currency information. You can use the `NumberFormat` class (`java.text.NumberFormat`) to format and parse numbers based on locale information.

Summary

In this hour, you reviewed basic internationalization principles such as externalizing project resources and knowing your target markets. You learned how the Android platform handles different countries, languages, and locales. Finally, you learned how to organize Android application resources for a variety of different countries and regions, for maximum profit, using a number of different internationalization strategies.

Q&A

Q. *Which languages and locales should I target in my Android applications?*

A. The answer to this question depends on a variety of factors and is something of a numbers game. The short answer is this: the fewest you can get away with. The number of mobile users who use a specific language should not be the only factor in deciding which languages to support. For example, there are many more Spanish- and Chinese-speaking mobile users than English-speaking ones, but generally, English market users are willing to pay much higher prices for applications. The answer really boils down to knowing your user audience(s)—which should be part of your business plan to begin with.

Q. *Why does my Android handset show only a subset of the languages and locales listed in this hour?*

A. While the Android platform supports a variety of languages and locales, mobile handset manufacturers and operators can customize the locale support available on specific devices. This may be done for resource efficiency. For example, a phone available through a U.S. operator might support only English (American) and Spanish (Americas).

Q. *What language should I use for default resources such as strings?*

A. Your default resources should be in the language/locale used by your largest target audience—the most generic/likely values that will appeal to the most users. If you're targeting the world at large, the choice is often English, but it need not be. For example, if your application allows turn-based directions anywhere in China, then you'd probably want your default language/locale to be one of the Chinese options (and even within China, different locale settings are more widely used than others)—unless you were targeting business types who are visiting China, in which case, you're back to using English, which is still the international language of business" (at least, for now).

Q. *I changed the locale to Spanish. Why are some applications still displaying in English?*

A. If an application has its default strings in English and has no Spanish resources available, then the defaults will be used, regardless of the language chosen.

Workshop

Quiz

1. True or False: An Android application can support multiple languages within a single APK file.

2. True or False: The number of languages supported by the Android platform and the Android Market is fixed.

3. What language should your default resources be?

   A. English

   B. Chinese

   C. The language that appeals most to your target audience

   D. Another language

Answers

1. True. An application can be compiled with resources in several different languages. The Android platform can switch between these resources on-the-fly, based upon the locale settings of the handset.

2. False. Android language support is being updated continuously. New languages and locales are being added all the time.

3. C. Your default resources should be the ones that are most likely to load and be used. Therefore, it makes sense to design these resources to be in the language and locale that appeals to the most number of users.

Exercises

1. Add a new set of string resource values to the Been There, Done That! application in the language or locale of your choice. Test the results in the Android emulator and on a real handset (if it supports the language/locale you chose).

2. Change the Been There, Done That! application so that it loads a custom drawable or color resource for a specific language or locale. For example, change the planet graphic on the main menu to something more specific to that language/locale. Test the results in the Android emulator and on a real handset (if it supports the language/locale you chose).

HOUR 20

Developing for Different Devices

What You'll Learn in This Hour:

▶ Designing for different handset configurations

▶ Handling screen orientation changes

▶ Working with different Android SDK versions

The Android platform is maturing at an accelerating rate. We're seeing revisions of the Android SDK rolling out every few months, with new handsets showing up all the time. In this hour, you learn how to develop Android applications for different targets. Android devices vary in terms of hardware and software features, as well as the version of the Android SDK they run.

Configuration Management for Android

Developers must try to support the widest possible range of devices, without biting off more than they can chew in terms of maintenance and configuration management. The following are some factors to consider when determining target platforms:

▶ What hardware features will the application require? Does the application require a touch screen? A hardware keyboard? A directional pad? Specific screen dimensions?

▶ What software features will the application require? Does the application support different screen orientations?

▶ What Android SDK does the application require?

While some of these decisions necessitate changes in the project libraries and the Android manifest file, many can be handled using the same resource directory qualifier strategy used for application internationalization.

Resource directories can be qualified to provide resources for a number of different application configurations (see Table 20.1). You can apply these directory name qualifiers to the resource subdirectories, such as /res/values/. Qualifiers are concatenated onto the existing subdirectory name, in a strict order, shown in precedence order in Table 20.1. You can combine multiple qualifiers by separating them with dashes. Qualifiers are always lowercase, and a directory can contain only one qualifier of each type. Custom qualifiers are not allowed.

TABLE 20.1   Important Resource Directory Qualifiers

Directory Qualifier Type	Values	Comments
Language	`en, fr, es, zh, ja, ko, de,` and so on	ISO 639-1 two-letter language codes
Region/locale	`rUS, rGB, rFR, rJP, rDE,` and so on	ISO 3166-1-alpha-2 region code in ALL UPPERCASE, preceded by a lowercase *r*
Screen dimensions	`small, normal, large`	Screen size and density ratio
Screen orientation	`port, land`	Portrait mode, landscape mode
Screen pixel density	`ldpi, mdpi, hdpi, nodpi`	Screen density that the resource is for
Touch screen type	`notouch, stylus, finger`	No Touch screen, Stylus-only, Finger Touch screen
Is keyboard available	`keysexposed, keyshidden, keyssoft`	Keyboard available, Keyboard not available to user, resources used only with software keyboard
Are navigation keys available	`navexposed, navhidden`	Whether navigational keys are available or hidden because phone keypad is shut

Directory Qualifier Type	Values	Comments
Primary non-touch screen navigation method	`nonav, dpad, trackball, wheel`	Four-key directional pad, trackball, scroll wheel
SDK version	`v1, v2, v3, v4, v5, v6, v7, and so on`	The SDK version's API level (for example, v1 is Android SDK 1.0, while v7 represents Android SDK 2.1)

You can concatenate together resource directories by using dashes. Here are some good examples of properly qualified directories:

```
/res/values-en-rUS-port-finger
/res/drawables-en-rUS-land
/res/values-en-qwerty
```

The following are some incorrectly qualified directories:

```
/res/values-en-rUS-rGB
/res/values-en-rUS-port-FINGER
/res/values-en-rUS-port-finger-custom
```

For an exhaustive list of the qualifiers available for resource customization (mobile country code, carrier, screen size, and so on), see the Android developer website: http://developer.android.com/guide/topics/resources/resources-i18n.html#AlternateResources.

Handling Different Screen Orientations

Android applications can run in landscape or portrait mode, depending on how the user tilts the handset screen. Besides internationalization, one of the most common situations in which applications might want to customize resources is to handle screen orientation changes.

Adding a Custom Layout for Landscape Mode

Thus far, you have been developing and testing the Been There, Done That! application in portrait mode. Launch it now and change to landscape mode before launching the application. Review each screen. You'll note that some screens display fine (they have flexible layouts that work well in either landscape or portrait mode) and some screens, such as the game screen (see Figure 20.1), could use some work.

FIGURE 20.1
The game
screen in land-
scape mode
(default layout
used).

Modifying how a screen displays based on the orientation of the device is as simple as adding a new set of layout resource files. To do this, you need to do the following:

- Use all currently defined layout resources as the defaults.

- Design a new version of each layout that also looks nice in landscape mode.

- Add these new landscape-specific layouts to the /res/layout-land/ directory.

Let's give this a shot by providing two different versions of the game screen in the Been There, Done That! application—one for portrait mode (the default) and one for landscape mode.

By the Way

The full layout implementation for the landscape mode changes and handset differences discussed in this hour is available on the book's website, http://www.informit.com/title/9780321673350.

First, let's review the design of the existing game.xml layout file, shown in Figure 20.2.

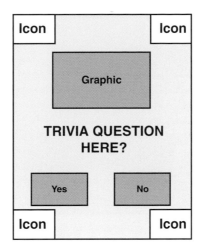

FIGURE 20.2
The game
screen design
(default layout
version).

In landscape mode, you just don't have enough vertical space for the ImageView, TextView, and Button controls. To streamline this layout for landscape mode, you might consider putting the TextView control to the right of the ImageView control. You could also modify the size of the graphic or the buttons if you needed to. The same controls (with the same names) are defined in both versions of the layout file; they're just rearranged in the landscape version (see Figure 20.3).

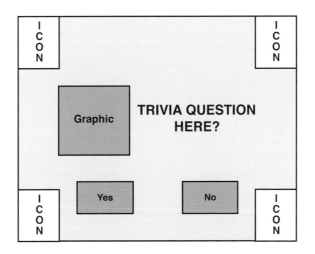

FIGURE 20.3
The game
screen design
(custom land-
scape layout
version).

The resulting screen looks much nicer when you switch to landscape mode, as shown in Figure 20.4.

Because screen orientation changes cause the current activity to be restarted, any processing tasks such as image decoding or network operations begin again unless you implement the onRetainNonConfigurationInstance() method of the Activity class. For more information on this type of situation, see the write-up at the Android developer website: http://developer.android.com/resources/articles/faster-screen-orientation-change.html.

Listening for Screen Orientation Changes

Applications can register to listen for screen orientation events. To do this, you request SensorManager by using the getSystemService() method. You can then query SensorManager for the current orientation, using the getOrientation() method. Alternatively, you can implement the OrientationEventListener class (android.view.OrientationEventListener) and override onOrientation Changed() to register for orientation changes.

However, listening for orientation changes is necessary only when applications require special internal handling of orientation. An application that defines a land-scape layout resource in the /res/layout-land/ directory and a default portrait layout resource in the /res/layout/ directory will work seamlessly, without the need for a listener.

You can toggle the orientation of the emulator by pressing Ctrl+F11 and Ctrl+F12.

Strategies for Handling Screen Orientation

The best way to support different orientations is to design simple enough layouts that work in either portrait or landscape mode, without modifications. For example, the settings screen of the Been There, Done That! application works fine in both landscape and portrait modes because each setting is stacked in a `LinearLayout` control, within a scrolling area that can scale well to any size. However, some layouts, such as the splash or game screen, may need some special tweaking for each orientation.

There are many strategies for supporting different screen sizes and orientations. Here are some tips for developing layouts that work for multiple types of screens:

- ▶ Don't crowd screens. Keep them simple.

- ▶ Use scalable container views such as `ScrollView` and `ListView`.

- ▶ Scale and grow screens in only one direction (vertically or horizontally), not both.

- ▶ Don't hard code the positions of screen elements. Instead, use relative positions and layouts, such as `RelativeLayout`.

- ▶ Avoid `AbsoluteLayout` and other pixel-specific layout settings.

- ▶ Use stretchable graphics, such as Nine-Patch.

- ▶ Keep resources as small as possible, so they load fast when the screen orientations change.

> The Android developer website contains a helpful set of guidelines for supporting multiple screens: http://developer.android.com/guide/practices/screens_support.html.

Supporting Different Screen Characteristics

Android devices come with a wide variety of display settings, including different screen sizes, densities, aspect ratios, and resolutions. Also, different devices have different default settings for display purposes, including themes and styles. Make sure you run your application on all target platforms prior to release. Your application will likely behave and display slightly differently on each device. Screen characteristics are major design factors to consider when developing user interfaces.

> You can create specific AVD profiles to mimic the behavior of specific screen characteristics in the emulator using the Android SDK and AVD Manager.

Figure 20.5 shows how the same layout might appear different on different screens. On the left, we have a generic medium density HVGA screen and on the right, we have the Motorola Droid, which has a high density WVGA854 screen. Note the rather marked differences.

FIGURE 20.5
A layout may display differently on different devices.

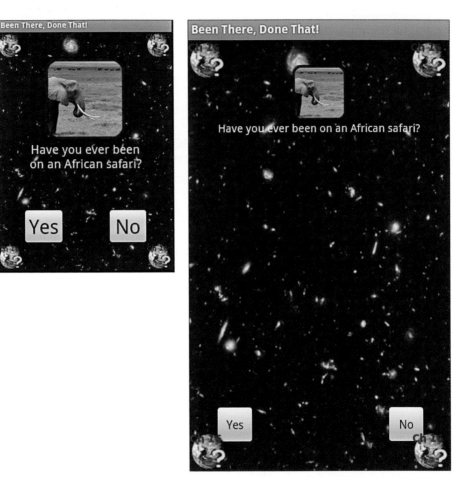

Don't despair, though. Fixing these sorts of problems is straightforward. Some ways to prevent display problems associated with screen density and the like in the first place include the following:

- ▶ Only set attributes you require (no unnecessary settings to maintain).

- ▶ Keep all dimension values in a dimension value resource file, not in individual layout files.

- ▶ Specify font sizes in dp or sp, as opposed to pt.

▶ Specify pixel dimensions in dp, as opposed to px.

▶ Add custom alternative resources when needed (but sparingly).

By making these changes to the Been There, Done That! project, we see that the application now displays properly on a wider variety of devices, including the Motorola Droid.

Supporting Different Handset Features

As you saw in Table 20.1, developers can provide custom resource files for a number of different handset configuration situations. A game might customize certain resources if the handset has no hardware keyboard or if the handset has a specific type of touch screen or navigation pad. Graphics files may be enlarged for very capable handsets with high-resolution screens, whereas on basic handsets they may be reduced to save space. In extreme cases, a game may be 2D on one handset and 3D on another.

Developing for Different Android SDKs

At the time of this writing, there are six different versions of the Android SDK in users' hands: Android 1.1, Android 1.5, Android 1.6, Android 2.0, Android 2.0.1, and Android 2.1. The upcoming releases (codenamed Froyo and Gingerbread) will add to this list. From time to time, Google publishes a breakdown of the usage of various Android versions on handsets:

▶ 0.1% of users are using Android SDK 1.1.

▶ 38.0% of users are using Android SDK 1.5.

▶ 31.6% of users are using Android SDK 1.6.

▶ 0.3% of users are using Android SDK 2.0.

▶ 2.7% of users are using Android SDK 2.0.1.

▶ 27.3% of users are using Android SDK 2.1.

This data was collected and provided online by the Android developer website during the two weeks prior to April 4, 2010. You can check for updated statistics at the following Android developer website: http://developer.android.com/resources/dashboard/platform-versions.html. One particularly interesting factor is that some versions of the SDK are effectively skipped by most devices, such as 2.0, because they are quickly replaced, and updates (like 2.0.1 and 2.1) are pushed out to users. This data can be invaluable for reducing testing load to just platforms where it matters.

It may not be feasible for certain phones, especially older models, to receive the latest firmware updates. As you can see, if you want to hit the broadest range of users, you may need to develop for several different versions of the SDK. This data can be invaluable for reducing the testing load to only those platforms where it matters.

Looking for new data, watching the market news, and surveying your target users will all ultimately help you determine which devices to target.

Choosing an Application's Target Platform

To appeal to the most users, you need to give some thought to your target platform before you develop any Android application. Will your application support some of the older, more established handsets or just the newest ones? Do some market research and determine what versions of the SDK your target users are using in the field.

> Backward compatibility in the Android platform is not guaranteed. Developers have experienced some rough patches when classes in the latest SDK are changed or deprecated. For example, some applications written for Android SDK 1.5 were broken by the Android 1.6 release, and then they worked again in Android 2.0. This can be very frustrating to developers and users.

Specifying a Project's Target SDK

You can specify an application's SDK support by compiling against the appropriate SDK version, which is set in the project settings, as well as the Android manifest file. You can also specify certain application resources to work with certain SDK versions, by using the appropriate resource directory qualifiers listed in Table 20.1.

Designing Applications for Backward Compatibility

To target the largest number of handsets, you need to target multiple versions of the SDK. However, setting required SDK versions in the Android manifest file limits the versions of the SDK on which your application can be installed.

There is a workaround here, though. Because Java uses reflection, you can query classes and methods without including them in the import statements. You could therefore set the minimum SDK version to the lowest possible version that your application can reasonably use. Then application logic can be used—by determining what's actually available at runtime—to enhance any functionality or features that are available. This method can also be used on devices that include specialized features or functions not found on other devices but that your application may want to leverage when they are available.

A great example of how to use reflection to support multiple Android SDK versions is available at http://developer.android.com/resources/articles/backward-compatibility.html.

Detecting the Android SDK Programmatically

You can programmatically determine the version of Android by using the `Build` class (`android.os.Build`). Specifically, you can check the `Build.VERSION` class's `SDK_INT` value, as defined in `android.os.Build.VERSION_CODES`.

Defining Android SDK–Specific Application Resources

Much as developers can provide resources for specific language, region, and handset configuration options in applications, they can also provide resources for specific versions of the Android SDK. Recall from Table 20.1 that resource paths can also specify a particular Android API level number.

Summary

In this hour, you learned how to customize application resources for a variety of handset configurations, including hardware and software requirements. You also learned how to design applications to smoothly handle orientation changes. Finally, you learned how to develop applications for a variety of Android SDK versions.

Q&A

Q. *A firmware upgrade broke my application. What can I do?*

A. First, dry your tears and delete that angry ranting email you were about to send off to the Android development team. This kind of thing is annoying and sometimes downright embarrassing, but it happens—a lot. In some cases, you can avoid surprises like this by testing your application against the open source project for the upcoming Android SDK release, but there's no guarantee that a specific handset (or operator) won't modify the firmware release, adding and removing features at will. Sometimes, you won't know there's a problem until you get a complaint from someone in Sao Paulo or Beijing or, perhaps most cringe-worthy, from your boss. Here, a solid response plan is a must. Designate someone (poor sod) in advance to stay on top of Android SDK releases—to fix bugs and to publish application updates to users.

Q. *How can I listen for orientation changes and load the appropriate portrait or landscape layout so my application screens always look nice?*

A. Your application does not have to listen for orientation changes to do this. Instead, just make sure you have the appropriately qualified layout resources (using the `port` or `land` qualifier). The Android operating system will automatically load the appropriate layout whenever the orientation of the device changes. As with any other resource, make sure the portrait and landscape resources contain the same child views (so you don't run into cases where a referenced view is undefined in one orientation).

Workshop

Quiz

1. True or False: The following is a correctly qualified resource directory name: `/res/drawables-rUS-en`.

2. For which of the following handset configurations can resources be defined?

    A. Language and region/locale

    B. Input methods, such as keyboards, touch screens, and navigation keys

    C. Screen size, resolution, and orientation

    D. Whether the keyboard and navigation keys are hidden

    E. All of the above

Answers

1. False. The region must follow the language. Therefore, the directory would appropriately be named `/res/drawables-en-rUS`.

2. E. All these qualifiers are available for application resources. There are also others. For a complete list, see the list at the Android developer website (http://developer.android.com/guide/topics/resources/resources-i18n.html#AlternateResources).

Exercises

1. Test the Been There, Done That! application on a handset. Change to landscape mode and ensure that all screens of the application display correctly. Add landscape-specific layout resources where needed (the splash screen and game play screen, at a minimum).

2. Compile the Been There, Done That! application for a variety of target SDK versions and test them on handsets or the emulator with the appropriate AVD.

HOUR 21

Diving Deeper into Android

What You'll Learn in This Hour:

▶ Exploring more advanced Android features
▶ Designing advanced user interfaces
▶ Working with multimedia
▶ Managing and sharing data
▶ Accessing underlying device hardware

When you are becoming familiar with a new mobile platform, it can be very helpful to know what is feasible and what is not. This hour provides a crash-course in some of the more advanced features of the Android SDK. Specifically, you will learn more about using core application features, designing advanced user interfaces, using multimedia, managing storage and data, and accessing the underlying device hardware.

Exploring More Core Android Features

Twenty-four hours is certainly not enough time to cover all the interesting and useful features of the Android platform and Android SDK. You've already packed tons of features into the Been There, Done That! application over the course of this book. In this hour, you will learn about many of the advanced features of the Android platform.

Declaring and Enforcing Application Permissions

As you know, applications must register the appropriate permissions they require within the Android manifest file. Applications can also declare and enforce their own custom permissions with the <permission> tag. Each permission must be defined in the Android manifest file and can be applied to specific components—notably an activity or a service—within the application. You can also apply permissions at the method level.

Alerting the User with Notifications

An application can alert the user even when the application isn't actively running in the foreground using a notification. For example, a messaging application might notify users when a new message is delivered, as shown in Figure 21.1.

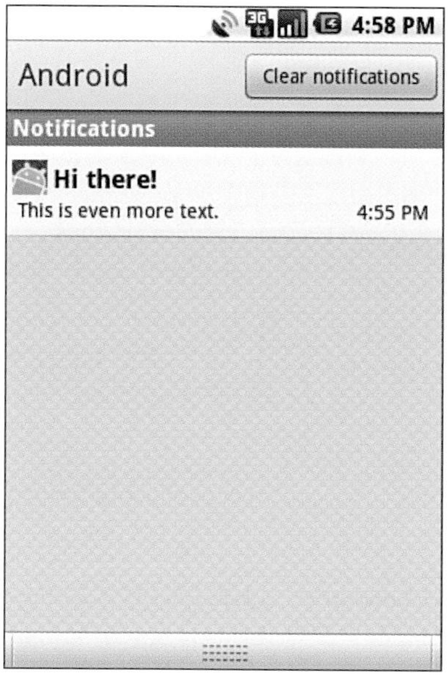

FIGURE 21.1
A notification in
the status bar.

Notifications come in a variety of forms. An application can use several different kinds of notifications, provided that it has the appropriate permissions registered in the Android manifest file:

- ▶ Display a text notification on the status bar.

- ▶ Play a sound.

- ▶ Vibrate the device.

- ▶ Change the indicator light color and blinking frequency.

**Watch
Out!**

Not all devices support every notification type. For example, some devices might not have the ability to vibrate or play sounds, or have an indicator light.

Notifications are created and triggered using the `NotificationManager` system service (`android.app.NotificationManager`). Once it is requested, you can create a `Notification` object (by setting the appropriate notification text, vibration, light, and sound settings) and use the `notify()` class method to trigger the notification.

> Take special care to use notifications appropriately, so as not to be a nuisance to the user. Some notification methods, such as vibration, must be tested on the device because the Android emulator does not simulate this type of action.

Watch Out!

Designing Advanced User Interfaces

The best and most popular applications on the Android platform have one thing in common: Each has an excellent, well-designed user interface. You've worked with many of the common user interface features of Android, such as layouts and user interface controls. However, the Android SDK has many other exciting user interface features, including the following:

- The ability to apply consistent settings across many controls or entire screens using styles and themes
- The ability to design and reuse custom user interface components
- A powerful input method framework
- The ability to detect various screen gestures
- A text-to-speech (TTS) engine
- Speech recognition support

Using Styles and Themes

The Android SDK provides two powerful mechanisms for designing consistent user interfaces: styles and themes. You can use themes and styles to make application screens consistent and easy to maintain.

A style is a grouping of common `View` attribute settings that can be applied to any number of `View` controls. For example, you might want all `View` controls in your application, such as `TextView` and `EditText` controls, to use the same text color, font, and size. You could create a style that defines these three attributes and apply it to each `TextView` and `EditText` control within your application layouts.

A theme is a collection of one or more styles. Whereas you apply a style to a specific control, such as a `TextView` control, you apply a theme to all `View` objects within a specified activity. Applying a theme to a set of `View` objects all at once simplifies making the user interface look consistent; it can be a great way to define color schemes and other common `View` attribute settings across an application. You can specify a theme programmatically by calling the `Activity` class's `setTheme()` method. You can also apply themes to a specific activity in the Android manifest file.

Did you Know?

The Android SDK includes a number of built-in themes, which can be found in the `android.R.style` class. For example, `android.R.style.Theme` is the default system theme. There are themes with black backgrounds, themes with and without a title bar, themes for dialog controls, and more.

Designing Custom `View` and `ViewGroup` Controls

You are already familiar with many of the user interface controls, such as `layout` and `View` controls, that are available in the Android SDK. You can also create custom controls. To do so, you simply start with the appropriate `View` (or `ViewGroup`) control from the `android.view` package and implement the specific functionality needed for your control or layout.

You can use custom `View` controls in XML layout files, or you can inflate them programmatically at runtime. You can create new types of controls, or you can simply extend the functionality of existing controls, such as `TextView` or `Button` controls.

For more information on implementing custom `View` controls, see http://developer.android.com/guide/topics/ui/custom-components.html.

Working with Input Methods

The Android platform provides a user-friendly software keyboard (see Figure 21.2) for devices that do not have hardware keyboards. The Android SDK also includes powerful text input method support for predictive text and downloadable input method editors (IMEs).

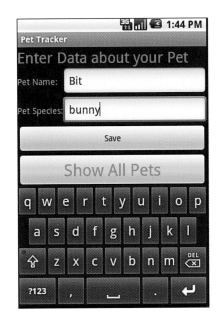

FIGURE 21.2
The Android
software key-
board.

Handling User Gestures

You already know how to listen for click events. You can also handle gestures, such as flings, scrolls, and taps, by using the GestureDetector class (android.view.GestureDetector). You can use the GestureDetector class by implementing the onTouchEvent() method within an activity.

The following are some of the gestures an application can watch for and handle:

- ▶ onDown—Occurs when the user first presses the touch screen

- ▶ onShowPress—Occurs after the user first presses the touch screen but before the user lifts up or moves around on the screen

- ▶ onSingleTapUp—Occurs when the user lifts up from the touch screen as part of a single-tap event

- ▶ onSingleTapConfirmed—Called when a single-tap event occurs

- ▶ onDoubleTap—Called when a double-tap event occurs

- ▶ onDoubleTapEvent—Called when an event within a double-tap gesture occurs, including any down, move, or up action

▶ onLongPress—Similar to onSingleTapUp but called if the user has held his or her finger down just long enough to not be a standard click but also didn't move the finger

▶ onScroll—Called after the user has pressed and then moved his or her finger in a steady motion and lifted up

▶ onFling—Called after the user has pressed and then moved his or her finger in an accelerating motion just before lifting it

In addition, the android.gesture package allows an application to recognize arbitrary gestures, as well as store, load, and draw them. This means almost any symbol a user can draw could be turned into a gesture with a specific meaning. Some versions of the SDK have a Gesture Builder application that can simplify the process of creating gestures for applications that don't have a gesture-recording feature.

For more information about the android.gesture package, see http://developer.android.com/resources/articles/gestures.html.

Converting Text to Speech

The Android platform includes a TTS engine (android.speech.tts) that allows devices to perform speech synthesis. You can use the TTS engine to have your applications "read" text to the user. You may have seen this feature used frequently with Location-Based Services (LBS) applications that allow for hands-free directions. Other applications use this feature for users who have reading or sight problems.

The Android TTS engine supports a variety of languages, including English (in American or British accents), French, German, Italian, and Spanish.

The synthesized speech can be played immediately or saved to an audio file, which can be treated like any other audio file.

Watch Out!

> To provide TTS services to users, an Android device must have both the TTS engine (available in Android SDK 1.6 and higher) and the appropriate language resource files. In some cases, the user must install the appropriate language resource files (assuming that the user has space for them) from a remote location. The users can do this themselves by going to Settings, Text-to-speech, Install Voice Data. You may also need to do this on your devices. Additionally, the application can verify that the data is installed correctly or trigger the installation if it's not. See the documentation for the android.speech.tts package.

Converting Speech to Text

You can enhance an application with speech recognition support by using the speech recognition framework (android.speech.RecognizerIntent). You use this intent to record speech and send it to a recognition server for processing, so this feature is not really practical for devices that don't have a reasonable network connection.

On Android SDK 2.1 and later, speech recognition is built in to most pop-up keyboards. Therefore, an application may already support speech recognition, to some extent, without any changes. However, directly accessing the recognizer can allow for more interesting spoken word control over applications.

Working with Multimedia

Mobile devices are increasingly being used as multimedia devices. Many Android devices have built-in cameras, microphones, and speakers, allowing playback and recording of multimedia in a variety of formats. The Android SDK provides comprehensive multimedia support, allowing developers to incorporate audio and visual media (still and video) into applications. These APIs are part of the android.media package.

The Android emulator cannot record audio or video. Testing of audio and video recording must be done using a real Android device. Also, the recording capabilities of a given device may vary based upon the hardware and software components used. For instance, Android devices that aren't phones may be lacking microphones and, more frequently, do not feature cameras.

Playing and Recording Audio

The Android SDK provides mechanisms for audio playback and recording in various formats. Audio files may be resources, local files, or URI objects to shared or network resources. The MediaPlayer class (android.media.MediaPlayer) can be used to play audio, and the MediaRecorder class (android.media.MediaRecorder) can be used to record audio. Recording audio requires the android.permission.RECORD_AUDIO permission.

Playing and Recording Video

You can use the VideoView control to play video content on a screen. You can use the MediaController control to provide the VideoView control with basic video controls, such as play, pause, and stop (see Figure 21.3).

As with audio recording, you can use the MediaRecorder class to record video content using the built-in camera. Applications that access the camera hardware must have the android.permission.CAMERA permission registered, and those that record audio using MediaRecorder must register the android.permission.RECORD_AUDIO permission in the Android manifest file. Thus, to record video, which uses the microphone and camera, both permissions should be added to the Android manifest file.

Working with 2D and 3D Graphics

If you're familiar with computer graphics programming, you will be pleased to note that Android has fairly sophisticated graphics capabilities for a mobile device.

Using the Android Graphics Libraries

The Android SDK comes with the android.graphics package, which includes a number of handy classes for drawing on the screen (see Figure 21.4). Some features of the Android graphics package include bitmap graphics utilities and support for typefaces, fonts, paints, gradients, shapes, and animation. There are also helper classes, such as the Matrix class that can help perform graphics operations.

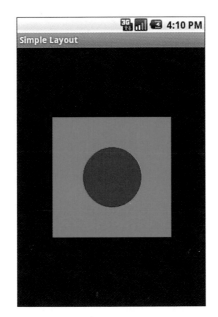

FIGURE 21.4
A simple two-dimensional graphic created with Android.

Using the OpenGL ES Graphics API

For more advanced graphics, Android uses the popular OpenGL ES graphics API (1.0), and it provides limited support for OpenGL ES 1.1. Applications can use Android's OpenGL ES support to draw, animate, light, shade, and texture graphical objects in three dimensions (see Figure 21.5).

FIGURE 21.5
An OpenGL ES
graphic created
with Android.

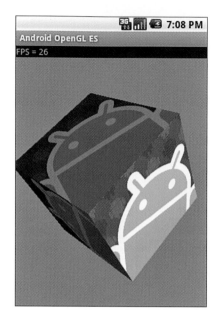

Personalizing Android Devices

Personalization of a device involves allowing the user to change the look and behavior of their user experience. From the software side, personalization involves configuring features such as the wallpaper, ringtone, and such. Android allows a deep level of customization and personalization. Alternate home screens, themes, graphics, and sounds can be modified. Android applications can provide many of these personalization features to users. For instance, a branded application might allow the users to set ringtones and wallpapers that support the brand.

Setting the Ringtone

An application can change the handset ringtone by using the `RingtoneManager`. To modify the ringtone, an application must have the appropriate permission (`android.permission.WRITE_SETTINGS`) registered in the Android manifest file. You can also launch the ringtone picker by using the `ACTION_RINGTONE_PICKER` intent.

Setting the Wallpaper

An application can set a wallpaper for the background of the Home screen by using the `WallpaperManager` class. Various methods are provided to retrieve the current wallpaper and set a new one using a bitmap, a resource, or another form of wallpaper.

In addition to using static images as wallpapers, Android supports the notion of live wallpapers. These are essentially animated wallpapers but can contain almost anything an application can draw on a surface. For example, you could create a wallpaper that visually shows the current weather, time of day, information about music playing, a slideshow, or some sort of video or animated demonstration. Live wallpapers are similar to widgets in that they are surfaces; however, the implementation details are different.

For more information on wallpapers, see the Android SDK documentation related to the `android.service.wallpaper` package.

Creating a Live Wallpaper

In addition to still image wallpapers, Android supports the notion of a live wallpaper. Instead of displaying a static image, such as a JPEG, a live wallpaper can display anything that can be drawn on a surface using the full graphical capabilities of the device and the Android SDK (as described in the section on 2D and 3D graphics we discussed earlier in this hour).

A live wallpaper is similar to an Android Service, but its result is a surface that the host can display. You can create a live wallpaper as complex as you like, but handset responsiveness and battery life should be taken in to account. Some examples of live wallpapers include

- ▶ A 3D display showing an animated scene portraying abstract shapes

- ▶ A service that animates between images found on an online image sharing service

- ▶ An interactive pond with water that ripples with touch

- ▶ Wallpapers that change based on the actual season, weather, and time of day

---

By the Way

To learn more about how to implement live wallpapers, see the article on live wallpapers at the Android documentation site (http://bit.ly/bngiaP) and the Cube Live Wallpaper sample application included with the Android SDK.

Managing and Sharing Data

You are already familiar with some of the ways applications can store data persistently:

▶ They can store simple, primitive data types within `SharedPreferences` at the application and activity levels.

▶ They can store data on a remote application server.

Applications can also store and share data by doing the following:

▶ They can leverage the file and directory structure on the device to store private application files in any format.

▶ They can store structured data in private SQLite databases.

▶ They can access data within other applications that act as content providers.

▶ They can share internal application data by becoming content providers.

You already know how to work with `SharedPreferences` and how to store data on a network application server, so let's talk about other ways of managing and sharing data.

Working with Files and Directories

Each Android application has its own private application directory and files. You can use the standard java file I/O package called `java.io` to manipulate files and directories.

Android application files are stored in a standard directory hierarchy on the Android file system. Android application data is stored on the Android file system in the following top-level directory:

`/data/data/<package name>/`

Several special-purpose subdirectories are created beneath the top-level application directory to store databases, preferences, and files. You can also create private directories and files here, as needed, using the appropriate methods of the application's `Context` object. The following are some of the important file and directory management methods of the `Context` class:

▶ `openFileInput()`—Opens an application file for reading in the `/files` subdirectory

- openFileOutput()—Creates or opens an application file for writing in the /files subdirectory

- deleteFile()—Deletes an application file by name from the /files subdirectory

- fileList()—Lists all files in the /files subdirectory

- getFilesDir()—Retrieves a File object for the /files subdirectory

- getCacheDir()—Retrieves a File object for the /cache subdirectory

- getDir()—Creates or retrieves a File object for a subdirectory by name

> You can browse the Android file system (of the emulator or a connected device) by using the DDMS File Explorer.

Did you Know?

Storing Structured Data in a SQLite Database

Android applications can have a locally accessible, private application database powered by SQLite. SQLite relational databases are lightweight and file based—ideal for mobile devices. The Android SDK includes a number of useful SQLite database management classes. The SQLite support available on the Android platform is found in the android.database.sqlite package. Here, you'll find utility classes for the following:

- Creating, versioning, and managing databases

- Building proper SQL queries

- Iterating through query results with Cursor objects

- Processing database transactions

- Handling specialized database exceptions

> Android has built-in SQLite support. However, you will also find generic database classes within the android.database package.

Did you Know?

In addition to programmatically creating and using SQLite databases, developers can use the sqlite3 command-line tool, which is accessible through the ADB shell interface for debugging purposes.

Sharing Data with Other Applications

An application can leverage the data available within other Android applications if they expose that data by becoming content providers. You can also enable your application to share data within other applications by making it a content provider.

Using Content Providers

The Android platform ships with some useful applications—such as a contacts application and a browser application—that expose some or all of their data by acting as content providers. An application can access the content of these applications by using the content provider data interface. Some content providers provide only "read" access to data, while others allow applications to create, update, and delete records, such as contacts.

Most access to content providers comes in the form of queries to specific predefined `URI` object contained addresses. Once formulated, a query might return a list of contacts or missed calls, or it might return a specific record, such as all contact information for John Smith. Applications can access content provider interfaces much as they would access any database.

You can think of a URI as an address to the location where content exists. You can use the `managedQuery()` method to retrieve data from a content provider and then iterate through the query results by using a cursor, just as you would any database query result.

Exploring Some Commonly Used Content Providers

The content providers included with Android can be found in the `android.provider` package. Here are some of the most useful content providers:

- `MediaStore`—Used to access media (audio, video, and still images) on the phone and on external storage devices

- `CallLog`—Used to access information about dialed, received, and missed phone calls

- `Browser`—Used to access the user's browsing history and bookmarked websites

- `Contacts`—Used to access the user's contacts database

- `UserDictionary`—A dictionary of user-defined words for use with predictive text input

You can bind data from a database or content provider cursor directly to user interface View controls such as ListView. To do so, use a data Adapter control, such as ArrayAdapter or CursorAdapter, and a View control derived from AdapterView, such as a ListView or Spinner control.

Acting as a Content Provider

An application can expose internal data to other applications by becoming a content provider. To share information with other applications, an application must implement a content provider interface and register as a content provider within the Android manifest file.

Organizing Content with Live Folders

A live folder is a special type of object that, when clicked, shows data from an application acting as a content provider. For example, a music application might allow the user to create live folders for specific music playlists, which could be placed on the Home screen (via a long-click on the home screen, then choosing Folders). To create a live folder, an application must create an Activity class that responds to the intent action ACTION_CREATE_LIVE_FOLDER and have a corresponding ContentProvider object for the data contents of the live folder. See the documentation for the android.provider.LiveFolders package for more details.

Integrating with Global Search

Android allows applications to be searchable at a system-wide level. This is done by configuring the application and providing custom Activity classes that handle the various commands required to handle the search actions and search results. Additionally, applications can provide search suggestions that will display when a user is typing their search criteria in the search field (the Quick Search Box).

If your application is content rich, either with content created by users or with content provided by you, the developer, then integrating with the global search mechanism of Android can provide many benefits and add value to the user. The application data becomes part of the overall handset experience, is more accessible, and your application may be presented to the user in more cases than just when they launch it.

To learn how to incorporate global search functionality into Android applications, see the documentation for SearchManager (android.app.SearchManager) and the Searchable Dictionary sample application found with the Android SDK.

Accessing Underlying Device Hardware

Android developers have unprecedented access to the underlying hardware on a device. In addition to hardware such as the camera and LBS services, the Android SDK has a variety of APIs for accessing low-level hardware features on the handset, including the following:

▶ Reading raw sensor data (such as the magnetic and orientation sensors)

▶ Accessing Wi-Fi and Bluetooth sensors

▶ Monitoring battery usage and power management

Not all sensors and hardware are available on each Android device. Many of these features are optional hardware.

The sensors available on a given device vary in terms of availability and sensitivity. Some sensors provide raw sensor data, while others are backed by services or software to provide useful data to the application.

Reading Raw Sensor Data

The following are some of the device sensors that the Android SDK supports:

▶ **Accelerometer**—Measures acceleration in three dimensions

▶ **Light sensor**—Measures brightness (which is useful for camera flashes)

▶ **Magnetic field sensor**—Measures magnetism in three dimensions

▶ **Orientation sensor**—Measures a device's orientation

▶ **Temperature sensor**—Measures temperature

▶ **Proximity sensor**—Measures the distance from the device to a point in space

The Android emulator does not simulate any device sensors natively, but OpenIntents provides a handy sensor simulator (www.openintents.org/en/node/23). This tool simulates accelerometer, compass, and orientation sensors, as well as a temperature sensor, and it transmits data to the emulator. You can also test sensor functionality on the target device.

The SensorManager object is used to gather data from the device sensors. You can retrieve an instance of SensorManager by using the getSystemService() method.

Working with Wi-Fi

Applications with the appropriate permissions (ACCESS_WIFI_STATE and CHANGE_WIFI_STATE) can access the built-in Wi-Fi sensor on a device by using the WifiManager object. You can retrieve an instance of WifiManager by using the getSystemService() method.

The Android SDK provides a set of APIs for retrieving information about the Wi-Fi networks available to a device as well as Wi-Fi network connection details. This information can be used for tracking signal strength, finding access points, or performing actions when connected to specific access points.

The emulator does not emulate Wi-Fi support, so you need to perform all testing of Wi-Fi APIs on a device.

Watch Out!

Working with Bluetooth

The Android SDK includes Bluetooth support classes in the android.bluetooth package. Here, you'll find classes for scanning for Bluetooth-enabled devices, pairing, and handling data transfer.

Managing Power Settings and Battery Life

Most mobile devices operate primarily using battery power. To monitor the battery, an application must have the BATTERY_STATS permission, register to receive Intent.ACTION_BATTERY_CHANGED BroadcastIntent, and implement BroadcastReceiver to extract the battery information and take any actions required. The following are some of the battery and power settings that can be monitored:

- ▶ Whether a battery exists
- ▶ The battery health, status (charging state), voltage, and temperature
- ▶ The battery charge percentage and associated icon
- ▶ Whether the device is plugged in via AC or USB power

An application can use the information about the device power state to manage its own power consumption. For example, an application that routinely uses a lot of processing power might disable features that use a lot of power in a low-power situation.

Summary

In this hour, you learned about more advanced features of the Android platform. You learned about some of the more advanced architectural components of Android applications, such as how services and notifications can be used and how applications can define and enforce their own permissions. You learned how to design consistent user interfaces by using styles and themes. You now know that Android devices have many powerful multimedia features, including the ability to play and record audio and video, and that it is feasible to develop 3D graphics-intensive applications by using OpenGL ES. Android applications can take advantage of the handy SQLite database features and can share data with other applications by accessing a content provider or by becoming a content provider. Finally, applications can access and interact with myriad underlying hardware sensors on a device.

Q&A

Q. *What multimedia formats are supported on the Android platform?*

A. Different Android devices support different formats. The platform supports a number of core formats, but specific devices may also extend this list as they see fit. For a complete list of supported formats, see the Android documentation at http://developer.android.com/guide/appendix/media-formats.html.

Q. *Where can I see code examples of the advanced features covered in this chapter?*

A. The implementation details of the features discussed in this chapter are beyond the scope of this book. However, we have written an advanced Android book titled *Android Wireless Application Development*. You can also find many Android SDK examples on the Android developer website, http://developer.android.com.

Workshop

Quiz

1. True or False: Content providers always require an Android application to declare permissions in the Android manifest file.

2. Which multimedia features are feasible on Android?

    A. Ability to play audio

    B. Ability to play video

    C. Ability to record audio

    D. Ability to record video

    E. All of the above

3. True or False: The indicator light on an Android device is accessible using the Android SDK.

4. True or False: This chapter covers all additional features of the Android SDK not covered elsewhere in this book.

Answers

1. False. Content providers may require specific permissions. However, the enforcement of permissions depends on the content provider. Check the specific content provider documentation for what specific permissions are required to access its provider interface.

2. E. The android.media package includes support for playing and recording audio and video in a variety of formats. Different Android devices have different hardware available, so check specific target devices to make sure they support the multimedia features an application requires.

3. True. You can use the NotificationManager class to access the LED indicator light on an Android device.

4. False. The Android SDK has many more features and nuances. In addition, the framework is being updated and enhanced very rapidly. Various resources, blogs, articles, and developer guides can be found at http://developer.android.com. Also see our blog for tips, tricks, guides, and pointers to other resources: http://androidbook.blogspot.com.

Exercises

1. Think of three different ways a local SQLite database could be used to enhance the Been There, Done That! application.

2. Review the various system services that can be requested by using the `getSystemService()` method. The various services are defined in the `android.content.Context` class.

3. Review the Been There, Done That! application and identify three functional areas where you could design and use custom `View` controls. What would those custom controls do?

4. Many Android applications have the same look because they rely on the default theme provided by the platform. Add theme definitions to the layout screens in the Been There, Done That! application. This way, the application will have a custom look that will be consistent across Android devices, regardless of what their default theme is.

HOUR 22

Testing Android Applications

What You'll Learn in This Hour:

▶ Best practices for testing mobile applications
▶ Developing a mobile test framework
▶ Handling other testing concerns

Every mobile developer dreams of developing a "killer app." Many people think that if they could just come up with a great idea, they'd be home free. Wrong. The truth is, anyone can come up with a great idea. The trick is to act on the idea with a clear vision, a concise "pitch" to users, an intuitive user interface, and you have to get that app out to users quickly—before someone else does! A killer app must have the right mix of these ingredients, but a poor implementation of an excellent idea isn't going to become a killer app, so it's important to test an application thoroughly before you publish it. In this hour, you learn how to test mobile applications in a variety of ways.

Testing Best Practices

Mobile users expect a lot from today's mobile applications. They expect the applications they install to be stable, responsive, and secure. *Stable* means that the application works and doesn't crash or mess up the user's phone. *Responsive* means the phone always responds to key presses, and long operations use progress bar indicators. *Secure* means that the application doesn't abuse the trust of the user, either intentionally or unintentionally. Users expect an application to have a reasonably straightforward user interface, and they expect the application to work 24/7 (especially when it comes to networked applications with a server side).

It might seem like users expect a lot for an application that might be priced at $0.99, but really, do any of these expectations seem unreasonable? We don't think so. However, they do impose significant responsibilities on a developer in terms of testing and quality control.

Whether you're a team of one or one hundred, every mobile development project can benefit from a good development process with a solid test plan. The following are some quality measures that can greatly improve the development process:

► Coding standards and guidelines

► Regular versioned builds

► A defect tracking system with a process for resolving defects

► Systematic application testing (using a test plan)

You can outsource application testing to a third party. Keep in mind that the success of any outsourced project depends heavily on the quality of the documentation you provide (for example, functional specifications, use cases) to the outsourcing facility.

Developing Coding Standards

When developers have and follow some guidelines, their code is more cohesive and easy to maintain. Developing a set of well-communicated coding standards for development can help drive home some of the important requirements of mobile applications. For example, developers might want to do the following:

► Discuss and come up with a common way for all developers to implement error and exception handling.

► Move lengthy or process-intensive operations off the main UI thread.

► Release objects and resources that aren't actively being used.

► Practice prudent memory management and track down memory leaks.

► Use resources appropriately. For example, don't hard-code data in code or layout files.

Performing Regular Versioned Builds

Implementing a reproducible build process is essential for a successful Android project. This is especially true for any application that plans to support multiple Android SDK versions, handsets, or languages. To perform regular, versioned builds, do the following:

▶ Use a source control system to keep track of project files.

▶ Version project files at regular intervals and perform builds.

▶ Verify (through testing) that each build performs as expected.

There are many wonderful source control systems out there for developers, and most that work well for traditional development will work fine for a mobile project. Many popular source control systems—such as Perforce, Subversion, and CVS—work well with Eclipse.

Because of the speed at which mobile projects tend to progress, iterative development processes are generally the most successful strategies for mobile development. Rapid prototyping gives developers and quality assurance personnel ample opportunities to evaluate an application before it reaches users.

Did you Know?

Using a Defect Tracking System

A defect tracking system provides a way to organize and keep track of application bugs, called *defects*, and is generally used along with a process for resolving these defects. Resolving a defect generally means fixing the problem and verifying that the fix is correct in a future build.

With mobile applications, defects come in many forms. Some defects occur on all handsets, while others occur only on specific handsets. Functional defects—that is, features of an application that are not working properly—are only one type of defect. You must look beyond these and test whether an application works well with the rest of the Android operating system in terms of performance, responsiveness, usability, and state management.

Developing Good Test Plans

Testers must rely heavily on an application's functional specification, as well as any user interface documentation, to determine whether features and functionality have been properly implemented. The application features and workflow must be thoroughly documented at the screen level and then validated by testing. In larger teams, it is not uncommon for interpretive differences to exist between the functional specification, the developer's implementation, and the tester's resulting experience. These differences must be resolved as part of the defect-resolution process.

Testers of Android applications have a variety of tools at their fingertips. While some manual testing is essential, there are now numerous opportunities for automated testing to be incorporated into testing plans.

Test plans need to cover a variety of areas, including the following:

▶ **Functional testing**—This testing ensures that the features and functions of the application work correctly, as detailed in the application's functional specification.

▶ **Integration testing**—This testing ensures that the software integrates well with other core device features. For example, an application must suspend and resume properly, and it must gracefully handle interruptions from the operating system (for example, incoming messages, calls, powering off).

▶ **Client/server testing**—Networked mobile applications often have greater testing requirements than stand-alone applications. This is because you must verify the server-side functionality in addition to the mobile client.

▶ **Upgrade testing**—Android phones receive frequent firmware updates, necessitating application upgrades. When possible, perform application upgrade testing of both the client and the server to ensure that any upgrades go smoothly for users.

▶ **Internationalization testing**—This testing ensures internationalization support—especially language support—early in the development process. If an application is supporting multiple languages, you're likely to run into some problems in this area related to screen real estate as well as issues such as date formatting.

▶ **Usability testing**—This testing identifies any areas of the application that lack visual appeal or are difficult to navigate or use. It verifies that the application's resource consumption model matches the target audience. For example, gamers might accept shorter battery life for graphic-intensive games, but productivity applications should not drain the battery unnecessarily.

▶ **Performance testing**—This testing uses the debugging utilities of the Android SDK to monitor memory and resource usage; it also identifies performance bottlenecks as well as dangerous memory leaks and fixes them.

▶ **Conformance testing**—This testing reviews any policies, license agreements, and terms that an application must conform to and verifies that the application complies.

▶ **Edge-case testing**—An application must be robust enough to handle random and unexpected events. We've all forgotten to lock our phones on occasion, only to find that the phone has received random key presses, launched random apps, or made unnecessary phone calls from the comfort of our pocket. An application must handle these types of events gracefully. That is to say, it shouldn't crash. You can use the Exerciser Monkey tool that comes with the Android SDK to stress-test an application.

Maximizing Test Coverage

While 100% test coverage is unrealistic, the goal is to test as much of an application as possible. To do this, you are likely to need to perform tests on the emulator as well as on target handsets, and you might want to consider using both manual and automated testing procedures.

Managing the Testing Environment

Don't assume that mobile applications are simpler to test just because they are "smaller" than desktop applications or have fewer features. Testing mobile applications poses many unique challenges to testers, especially in terms of configuration management.

Identifying and Acquiring Target Handsets

The earlier you can decide on and get your hands on the target handsets, the better. Sometimes, this is as easy as going to the store and grabbing a new phone with a new service plan; other times, it's more complicated.

> Some companies run developer programs with phone labs. Here, developers can rent time on specific handsets—by mail, remotely (via the Internet), or by traveling to the lab. This gives developers access to a wide variety of handsets on many different networks, without requiring them to own each and every one. Some labs are even staffed with experts to help iron out handset-specific problems.

For preproduction handsets, it can take months to get the hardware in-hand from the manufacturer or operator through developer program loaner services. Cooperating with carrier handset loaner programs and buying handsets from retail locations is frustrating but sometimes necessary. Don't wait until the last minute to gather the test hardware you need.

> There is no guarantee that a preproduction handset will behave exactly the same as the production model that eventually ships to consumers. Features are often cut at the last minute to make the production deadline.

Dealing with Device Fragmentation

One of the biggest challenges a mobile application tester faces is the explosion of new Android devices on the market. This problem—called handset fragmentation—makes the task of keeping track of the devices available—running the different versions of the Android SDK and having different screen sizes, features, and hardware increasingly complex (see Figure 22.1).

FIGURE 22.1
Handset frag-
mentation.

Managing a Handset Database

It is a good idea to use a database to keep track of handset information for development, testing, and marketing purposes. Such a database might contain information
such as the following:

▶ Handset information (models, features, SDK versions, hardware specifics such
as whether a handset has a camera or built-in keyboard)

▶ Which handsets you have on hand (and where they are, if they are owned or
loaned, and so on)

▶ Which handsets you want to target for a given application

▶ The handsets on which your applications are selling best

Testing on the Emulator

A test team cannot be expected to set up testing environments on every carrier or in
every country where users will use an application. There are times when using the
Android emulator can reduce costs and improve testing coverage. The following are
some of the benefits of using the emulator:

▶ Rapidly testing when a target handset is not available (or is in short supply).

▶ Simulating handsets when they are not yet available (for example, preproduction phones).

▶ Testing difficult or dangerous scenarios that are not feasible or recommended
on live handsets (such as tests that might somehow break a phone or invali-
date a service agreement).

The emulator provides a useful but limited simulation of a generic Android device. By using AVD configuration options, you can customize an emulator to closely represent a target handset. However, an emulator does not rely on the same hardware—or software—implementation that will be found on an actual handset. An emulator simply pretends. The more hardware features an application relies on (for example, making calls, networking, LBS, the camera, Bluetooth), the more important it is to test on an actual device.

Watch Out!

Testing on Target Handsets

Here is a mobile mantra that is worth repeating: *Test early, test often, test on the actual device.*

It's important to get target handsets in-hand as soon as you can. This cannot be said enough: *Testing on the emulator is helpful, but testing on the handset is essential.* In reality, it doesn't really matter if your application works on the emulator; users run the applications on handsets.

It's important to test application assumptions early and often, on the target handset(s). This is called *feasibility testing*. It is disheartening to design and develop an application and then find that it doesn't work on the actual handset. Just because your application works on the emulator does not guarantee that it will work on the handset.

Watch Out!

Testing on a target handset is the safest way to ensure that an application works correctly because you are running the application on the same hardware that your users are going to use. By mimicking the environment your users will use, you can ensure that your application works as expected in the real world.

While it can be convenient to test with the handset plugged in, this is not the way most users will use your application. They will generally use battery power only. Be sure to unplug the handset and test an application the way users will most likely encounter it.

Watch Out!

Performing Automated Testing

Collecting application information and building automated tests can help you build a better, more bulletproof application. The Android SDK provides a number of packages related to code diagnostics. Application diagnostics fall into two categories:

- ▶ Logging application information for performance or usage statistics
- ▶ Automated test suites based on the JUnit framework

Logging Application Information

At the beginning of this book, you learned how to leverage the built-in logging class `Log` (android.util.Log) to implement different levels of diagnostic logging. You can monitor the output of log information from within Eclipse or by using the LogCat utility provided with the Android SDK.

> Don't forget to strip any diagnostic information, such as logging information, from the application before publication. Logging information and diagnostics can negatively affect application performance.

Automated Testing with JUnit and Eclipse

The Android SDK includes extensions to the JUnit framework for testing Android applications. Automated testing is accomplished by creating test cases, in Java code, that verify that the application works the way you designed it. This automated testing can be done for both unit testing and functional testing, including user interface testing.

This discussion is not meant to provide full documentation for writing JUnit test cases. For that, look to online resources, such as http://www.junit.org, or books on the subject.

Did you Know?

> Some people follow a paradigm of creating the test cases first, and then writing code that causes the test cases to pass. This method can work well in an environment where all application results and behavior are known before coding begins and will change little or not at all.

Automated testing for Android involves just a few straightforward steps:

1. Create a test project.
2. Add test cases to the new project.
3. Run the test project.

The following sections walk you through how to perform each of these steps to test a specific feature of the Been There, Done That! settings screen.

Creating the Test Project

Recall from Hour 1, "Getting Started with Android," when you first created a project using Eclipse, that the wizard has an option for creating a test project. You're now going to leverage that option to get up and running quickly with creating test cases.

Conveniently, the option for creating a test project is also available after a project already exists. To create a test project for an existing Android project in Eclipse, follow these steps:

1. Choose File, New, Project.

2. Under the Android option, choose Android Test Project.

3. In the section labeled Test Target, choose An Existing Android Project and click the Browse button.

4. Find the project you want to test and select it. The wizard fills in the rest of the fields with reasonable default values, as shown in Figure 22.2.

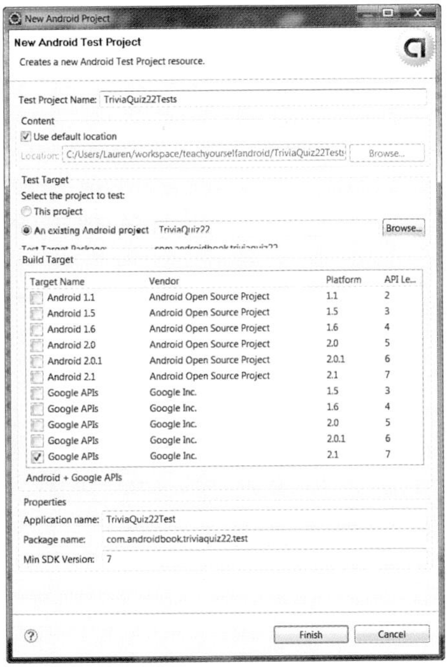

FIGURE 22.2
Test Application Project Wizard defaults in Eclipse.

5. Click Finish. Your new test project is created.

Creating a Test Case

When you have your test project in place, you can write test cases. You will now create a test case that tests the behavior of the Nickname field of the settings screen controlled by the QuizSettingsActivity class. To do this, first follow these steps to create the empty test case file:

1. Right-click the package name within the src folder of your test project.

2. Choose New, JUnit Test Case.

3. Modify the Name field to say `QuizSettingsActivityTests`.

4. Modify the Superclass field to say `android.test.ActivityInstrumentation TestCase2<QuizSettingsActivity>`. (Ignore the warning that says "Superclass does not exist.")

5. Modify Class Under Test to say `com.androidbook.triviaquiz22. QuizSettingsActivity`.

6. Click Finish.

7. In the newly created file, manually add an import statement for `QuizSettingsActivity` (or organize your imports).

8. Finally, add the following constructor to the newly created class:

```
public QuizSettingsActivityTests() {
    super("com.androidbook.triviaquiz22", QuizSettingsActivity.class);
}
```

Now that your test case file is ready, you can test the Nickname field and make sure it matches the value of the nickname in `SharedPreferences` and that it updates after a new string is entered. You first need to modify the `setUp()` method to perform some common behavior. You get the nickname `EditText` object for use in the other two tests. The following code does just that:

```
@Override
protected void setUp() throws Exception {
    super.setUp();
    final QuizSettingsActivity settingsActivity = getActivity();
    nickname =
        (EditText) settingsActivity.findViewById(R.id.EditText_Nickname);
}
```

The method call for `getActivity()` retrieves the activity being tested. Within the `ActivityInstrumentationTestCase2` class, the activity is created as it would normally be when the activity is launched.

Normally, you would also override the `tearDown()` method. However, for these tests, you have no lingering items that need to be cleaned up.

JUnit tests must begin with the word `test`. So, to write specific tests, you need to create methods that begin with the word `test`, followed by what you are testing. First,

make sure the displayed Nickname field is consistent with the stored value in
`SharedPreferences`. Add the following code to `QuizSettingsActivityTests` to
implement this test:

```
public void testNicknameFieldConsistency() {
    SharedPreferences settings =
        getActivity().getSharedPreferences(QuizActivity.GAME_PREFERENCES,
            Context.MODE_PRIVATE);
    String fromPrefs =
        settings.getString(QuizActivity.GAME_PREFERENCES_NICKNAME, "");
    String fromField = nickname.getText().toString();
    assertTrue("Field should equal prefs value",
        fromPrefs.equals(fromField));
}
```

The first few lines are all standard Android code that you should be familiar with.
By using the Android testing framework, you are enabling using the various
Android objects within the testing code. The last line, however, is where the real test
is performed. The `assertTrue()` method verifies that the second parameter actually
is true. If it's not, the string is output in the results. In this case, the two strings are
compared. They should be equal.

The next test is to verify that editing the field actually updates the `Shared
Preferences` value. Add the following code to `QuizSettingsActivity` to test that
this is true:

```
private static final String TESTNICK_KEY_PRESSES = "T E S T N I C K ENTER";
// ...
public void testUpdateNickname() {
    Log.w(DEBUG_TAG, "Warning: " +
        "If nickname was previously 'testnick' this test is invalid.");
    getActivity().runOnUiThread(new Runnable() {
        public void run() {
            nickname.setText("");
            nickname.requestFocus();
        }
    });
    sendKeys(TESTNICK_KEY_PRESSES);
    SharedPreferences settings =
        getActivity().getSharedPreferences(QuizActivity.GAME_PREFERENCES,
            Context.MODE_PRIVATE);
    String fromPrefs =
        settings.getString(QuizActivity.GAME_PREFERENCES_NICKNAME, "");
    assertTrue("Prefs should be testnick", fromPrefs
        .equalsIgnoreCase("testnick"));
}
```

As before, most of this is standard Android code that you should be familiar with.
However, notice that this code is performing a couple calls on the UI thread. This is
required for these particular calls; if you remove those calls from the UI thread, the
test case fails.

To run an entire test method on the UI thread, add the `@UiThreadTest` annotation before your method implementation. But note that this won't work in the example shown here because the `sendKeys()` method can't be run on the main thread. (You get the "This method cannot be called from the main application thread" exception error.) Instead, just portions of the test can be run on the UI thread, as shown.

Running Automated Tests

Now that your tests are written, you need to run them to test your code. There are two ways of doing this. The first method is the most straightforward and provides easy-to-read results right in Eclipse: You simply select Debug, Debug As, Android JUnit Test. The Console view of Eclipse shows the typical installation progress for both the test application and the application being tested (see Figure 22.3).

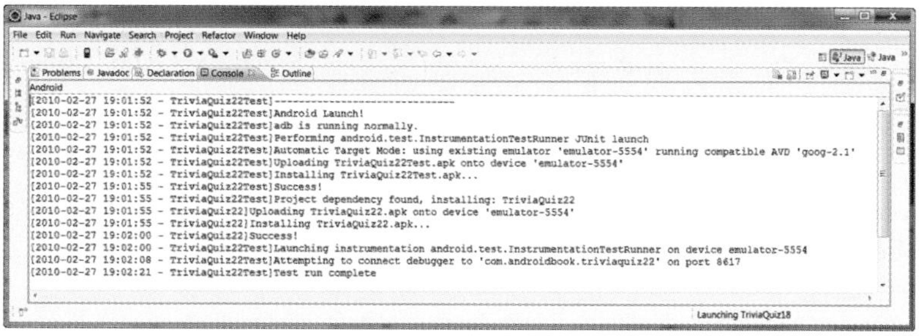

FIGURE 22.3
Eclipse console output while running JUnit tests on Android.

If the test project is not selected, Eclipse may try to run a regular application as a JUnit test application, resulting in a bunch of warnings and errors. To avoid this problem, right-click on the project name in the Package Explorer pane of Eclipse, choose Debug As, and then choose Android JUnit Test. Alternately, you can go to the Debug Configurations menu, double-click on Android JUnit Test to create a new test configuration, and then fill in the details.

With the LogCat view, you see the normal Android debug output as well as new output for the tests that are performed. In this way, you can better debug problems or errors that result from failures, or even find new failures that should be tested for.

The JUnit view, though, may be the most useful. It summarizes all the tests run and how long each one takes, and it includes a stack trace for any failures found. Figure 22.4 shows what this looks like in Eclipse.

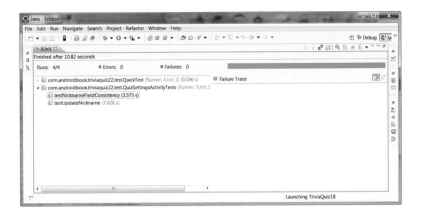

FIGURE 22.4
Eclipse JUnit
view running
Android tests.

The second way of running the tests is available only in the emulator. To use this method, launch the Dev Tools app and then choose Instrumentation. If you've followed along and don't have any other tests installed, you'll likely see `android.test.InstrumentationTestRunner` as the only item shown. Clicking this launches the tests. When you use this method, the only way to see results (other than a visual indication during user interface tests) is to watch the LogCat output.

The description of the item in the list can be changed. In the `AndroidManifest.xml` file of the test app, in the instrumentation section, modify it to read as follows:

```
<instrumentation
    android:targetPackage="com.androidbook.triviaquiz22"
    android:name="android.test.InstrumentationTestRunner"
    android:label="TriviaQuiz22 Tests" />
```

Now when you launch Dev Tools and go to the Instrumentation section, you see the text of the label rather than the name.

Adding More Tests

Now you have all the tools you need to add more unit tests to your application. The Android SDK includes a variety of classes that can be implemented for performing a wide range of tests specific to Android. Among these are the following:

- ▶ `ActivityUnitTestCase`—Similar to the example testing in the preceding section in that it tests on `Activity`, but at a lower level. This class can be used to unit test specific aspects of an activity, such as how it handles `onPause()`, when it has called `onFinished()`, and so on. This is a great way to test the life cycle of an activity.

- ▶ `ApplicationTestCase`—Like `ActivityUnitTestCase`, this class allows testing of `Application` classes in a fully controlled environment.

▶ ProviderTestCase2—Performs isolated testing on a content provider.

▶ ServiceTestCase—Performs isolated testing on a service.

In addition to these test case objects, there are helper classes for providing mock objects (that is, objects that aren't the real ones but can be used to better trace calls to the real objects), helper classes for simulating touch screen events, and other such utilities. You can find full documentation on these classes in the android.test package.

Summary

In this hour, you learned about the many different ways in which an Android application can be tested and improved, resulting in a higher-quality product that users will appreciate. You learned many best practices for testing mobile applications, including the importance of creating a solid, complete testing plan. You learned about some of the ways you can acquire handsets for testing purposes. You also learned how to create automated tests using the Android JUnit framework. Finally, you learned about some other specialized testing concerns that should be part of any good product test plan.

Q&A

Q. *Are there any certification programs for Android applications?*

A. There are currently no certification programs for Android applications. However, providers, operators, and certain mobile marketplaces may impose their own application quality standards, as they see fit.

Q. *Where can I find out more about creating automated test suites with JUnit?*

A. Visit the JUnit organization website, at www.junit.org, or find one of the many books on JUnit.

Workshop

Quiz

1. True or False: Developers can create automated tests to exercise Android applications programmatically.

2. Which of the following should be considered an application defect or bug?

    A. An application takes a long time to start up.

    B. An application crashes when there is an incoming call.

    C. German text is too long to display onscreen and overflows.

    D. Buttons are too small or close together to push with a finger.

    E. An application enters an infinite loop when certain criteria are reached.

    F. All of the above.

3. True or False: Automated testing for Android applications can be performed only on the emulator.

4. The JUnit framework included with Android can be used for testing many things. Which of the following can it not do?

    A. Run repeated tests all day long, without tiring

    B. Test on old devices

    C. Move the handset around the country to test GPS signals

    D. Test behavior on multiple carriers/operators

Answers

1. True. The Android SDK includes a variety of packages for developing test suites for automated application testing.

2. F. These are all defects of different kinds—performance, integration, internationalization, usability, and functional defects. (A) An application that takes too long to start up is a serious performance issue that may cause the Android operating system to kill the app—which is not good. (B) Most Android devices are phones first; an application must interact well with the rest of the system, which means gracefully handling incoming calls and text messages. (C) A well-written application does not short-change users in foreign languages by

providing a substandard user interface. (D) A well-done user interface is essential to the success of an application. (E) A functional defect—that is, a problem with the core application logic—is always a defect, no matter how unlikely the event.

3. False. Automated tests can be performed on any Android device that can be connected for debugging.

4. C and D. Unfortunately, the JUnit framework alone can't physically move handsets around the world. In addition, it can't simulate nuances to specific carriers around the world. However, emulator options can be used to mimic certain network performance characteristics but not the specifics of a different networking environment.

Exercises

1. Develop a high-level test plan for the Been There, Done That! application.

2. Write a test case for validating that a user's avatar uploads correctly.

3. Review the various agreements you have encountered in beginning to develop Android applications (such as the Android SDK License Agreement and Google Maps API Terms and Conditions). Identify any test cases that might be required for compliance with these agreements.

HOUR 23

Getting Ready to Publish

What You'll Learn in This Hour:

- ▶ Preparing for application publication
- ▶ Testing and verifying a release build
- ▶ Packaging and signing your application for release

An application may be functionally complete, but you need to take one final step before you can publish: You must package the application so that it can be deployed to users. In this hour, you will learn how to prepare and package an application for release on the most popular Android publishing program: the Android Market.

Understanding the Release Process

Preparing and packaging an application for publication is called the *release process* (Figure 23.1). The release process is an exciting time: The application is humming, all those troublesome bugs have been resolved (within reason, at least), and you're ready to put your app in front of users.

The final build you perform—the build you expect to deliver to users—is called the *release candidate build*. The release candidate build should be rigorously tested and verified before it reaches users' hands. If the release candidate build passes every test, it becomes the *release build*—the official build for publication.

FIGURE 23.1
An overview of
the release
process.

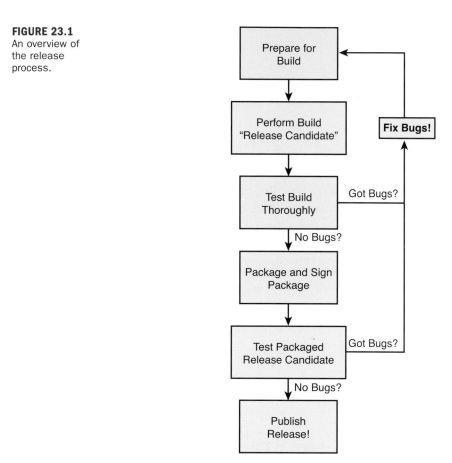

Different people use different terminology for the release process. Different software methodologies impose different terms. Some companies have code names
for such events, such as "going gold." Over the years, we've settled on *release*
and *release candidate* because, regardless of the methodology of choice, the
terms are pretty self-explanatory to most developers.

To publish an Android application, take the following steps:

1. Prepare and perform a release candidate build of the application.

2. Test the application release candidate thoroughly.

3. Package and digitally sign the application.

4. Test the packaged application release thoroughly.

5. Publish the application.

Let's explore each of these steps in more detail.

Preparing the Release Candidate Build

It's important to polish your application and make it ready for public consumption. This means you have to resolve any open or outstanding problems or issues with the application that might block the release. All features must be implemented and tested. All bugs must be resolved or deferred. Finally, you need to remove any unnecessary diagnostic code from the application and verify that the application configuration settings in the Android manifest file are appropriate for release.

Here's a short prerelease checklist for a typical Android application:

☐ Sufficiently test the application as described in the test plan, including testing on target handsets.

☐ Fix and verify all defects and bugs in the application.

☐ Turn off all debugging diagnostics for release, including any extraneous logging that could affect application performance.

Preparing the Android Manifest File for Release

Before release, you need to make a number of changes to the application configuration settings of the Android manifest file. Some of these changes are simply common sense, and others are imposed by marketplaces such as the Android Market.

You should review the Android manifest file as follows:

☐ Verify that the application icon (various sizes of PNG) is set appropriately. This icon will be seen by users and is often used by marketplaces to display the application.

☐ Verify that the application label is set appropriately. This represents the application name as users will see it.

☐ Verify that the application version name is set appropriately. The version name is a friendly version label that developers (and marketplaces) use.

> The Android SDK allows the `android:versionName` attribute to reference a string resource. The Android Market does not. You will see an error during the upload process when your package is validated. The package will not be accepted.

☐ Verify that the application version code is set appropriately. The version code is a number that the Android platform uses to manage application upgrades. Consider incrementing the version code for the release candidate in order to differentiate it from the prerelease version of the application.

☐ Confirm that the application uses-sdk setting is set correctly. You can set the minimum, target, and maximum Android SDK versions supported with this build. These numbers are saved as the API level of each Android SDK. For example, Android 2.1 is API level 7.

> The Android Market filters applications available to specific users based on the information provided in each application's manifest file, including the information provided in the uses-sdk settings.

☐ Disable the `debuggable` option.

☐ Confirm that all application permissions are appropriate. Request only the permissions the application needs with `uses-permission`, and make sure to request permissions the application uses, regardless of handset behavior without them.

Readying Related Services for Release

If the Android application relies on any external technologies or services, such as an application server, then these must also be readied for release.

Many large projects have a "mock" application server (often called a *sandbox*) as well as a real "live" server. The release build needs to be tested against the live server, just the way users would use it.

Testing the Application Release Candidate

Once you have addressed all the prerelease issues discussed earlier, you're ready to perform the release candidate build. There is nothing particularly special about the general build process here, except that you need to launch Run Configuration, rather than Debug Configuration, in Eclipse.

You should test the release candidate as rigorously as possible. In addition to any regular testing, you should verify that the application meets the criteria of the application marketplaces (such as the Android Market) that where you want to publish to the app.

If you find any defects or issues with the release candidate build, you must decide whether they are serious enough to stop the release process. If you decide that an issue is serious enough to require another build, you simply start the release process over again (see Figure 23.2).

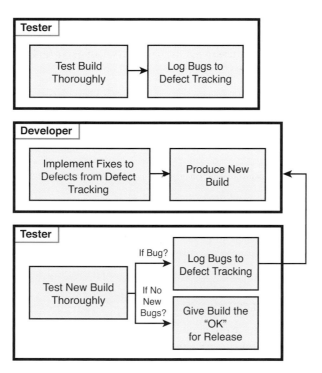

FIGURE 23.2
The release candidate testing cycle.

Packaging and Signing an Application

Now that you have a solid release candidate build that's tested and ready to go, you need to package the application for publication. This process involves generating the Android package file (the .apk file) and digitally signing it.

The process of packaging and signing an application has never been easier. The newest improvements to the Android plug-in for Eclipse include a wizard for doing just that!

Digitally Signing Applications

Android application packages must be digitally signed for the Android package manager to install them. Throughout the development process, Eclipse has used a debug key to manage this process. However, for release, you need to use a real digital signature—one that is unique to you and your company. To do this, you must generate a private key.

A private key identifies the developer and is critical to building trust relationships between developers and users. It is very important to secure private key information.

The private key can be used to digitally sign the release package files of your Android application, as well as any upgrades. This ensures that the application (as a complete entity) is coming from you, the developer.

By the Way

You don't need to use a certificate authority, such as Verisign, Equifax, or any of the other companies that will certify that you are who you say you are before providing a certificate. Self-signing is standard for Android applications, which simply means that you aren't proving who you are, but the next time you publish something, if the keys match, then users (and Android) will know it's been signed by the same person or entity. So don't share your private key!

Application updates must be signed with the same private key. For security reasons, the Android package manager does not install the update over the existing application if the key is different. This means you need to keep the key corresponding with the application in a secure, easy-to-find location for future use.

Did you Know?

The Android platform tests the digital signature only at install time. Therefore, if the signature expires after installation, the application will continue to run.

Exporting and Signing the Package File

You are now ready to export and sign your Android package file. To do this using the wizard provided as part of the Eclipse plug-in, perform the following steps:

1. In Eclipse, right-click the appropriate application project and choose the Export option.

2. Under the Export menu, expand the Android section and choose Export Android Application.

3. Click the Next button.

4. Select the project to export. (The one you right-clicked before is the default.)

5. On the keystore selection screen, choose the Create New Keystore option and enter a file location (where you want to store the key) as well as a password for managing the keystore. (If you already have a keystore, choose browse to pick your keystore file, then enter the correct password.)

Make sure you choose strong passwords for the keystore. Remember where the keystore is located, too. The same one is required to publish an upgrade to your application. If it's checked in to a revision control system, the password will help protect it, but consider adding an extra layer of privilege required to get to it.

6. Click the Next button.

7. On the Key Creation screen, enter the details of the key, as shown in Figure 23.3.

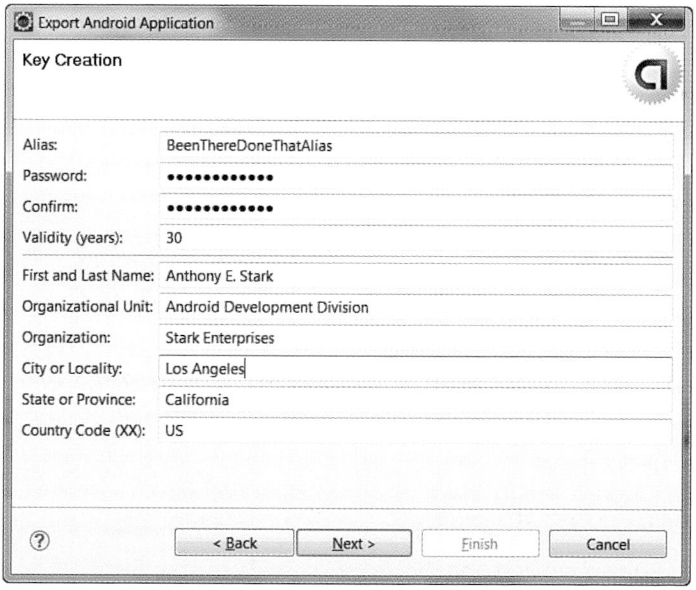

FIGURE 23.3
Exporting an Android application using the Eclipse plug-in.

The Android team recommends that you use a key validity of 25 years or more. In fact, the Android Market will reject any application with a key that is not valid until at least October 22, 2033, so 25 years covers this requirement as well.

8. Click the Next button.

9. On the "Enter destination and key/certificate checks" screen, enter a destination for the application package file.

10. Click the Finish button.

You have now created a fully signed and certified application package file.

You can also use the `keytool` and `jarsigner` applications available within the JDK in addition to the `zipalign` utility provided with the Android SDK to create a suitable key and sign an application package file (.apk). Although `zipalign` is not directly related to signing, it optimizes the package for more efficient use on Android. The ADT plug-in for Eclipse runs `zipalign` automatically after the signing step.

Testing the Signed Application Package

Now that you have signed and packaged an application, and now that it's ready for production, you should perform one last test cycle, paying special attention to subtle changes to the installation process for signed applications.

Installing the Signed Application Package

Up until now, you've allowed Eclipse to handle the packaging and delivery of the application to handsets and emulators for debugging purposes. Now you have the application release version sitting on your hard drive, and you need to load it and test it.

Before installing the release version of your application on the emulator or handset, you should uninstall the debugging version completely. You can do this on the handset (or emulator) from the Home screen by clicking Menu, Settings, Application, Manage Applications, choosing the application from the list, clicking the Uninstall button, and verifying that you want to uninstall the application. Note that files or data in shared locations, such as images stored in the gallery, may be left behind. Private files and data, including preferences, will be removed, though.

The simplest way to manually install (or uninstall) an application package (.apk) file on a handset or the emulator is to use the adb command-line tool. The following is the command for installing a package using adb:

```
adb install <path_to_apk>
```

If there is only one device or emulator, this command works. However, if you have multiple devices and emulators floating around, you need to direct the installation command to a specific one. You can use the `devices` command of the `adb` utility to query for devices connected to your computer:

```
adb devices
```

The list this command returns includes any emulators or handsets attached to the computer. The results might look like this:

```
$ adb devices
List of devices attached
emulator-5554  device
HT9CSP801234   device
```

You can then target a specific device on which to install the application package file by using the `-s` option. For example, to install the `BeenThereDoneThat.apk` application package file on the emulator, you use the following:

```
adb -s emulator-5554 install BeenThereDoneThat.apk
```

For more information about the `adb` command-line tool, see the website http://developer.android.com/guide/developing/tools/adb.html.

Verifying the Signed Application

You're almost done. Now it is time to perform a few last-minute checks to make sure the application works properly:

▶ Verify smooth installation of the signed application package.

▶ Verify that all debugging features have been disabled.

▶ Verify that the application is using the "live" services as opposed to any "mock" services.

▶ Verify that application configuration data such as the application name and icons, as well as the version information, displays correctly.

If you find any issues with the signed application functionality, you must decide whether they are serious enough to stop the release process and begin again. Once you've tested the application package thoroughly and are confident that users will have a positive experience using your application, you are ready to publish!

Summary

In this hour, you learned how to prepare an application for publication. Specifically, you learned about the steps to take to verify that your application is ready for publication, such as stripping debugging information and verifying application configuration settings. You then learned to export an unsigned application package file, generate a private key, and digitally sign the application for publication.

Q&A

Q. *Will the release process described in this hour work for any Android application marketplace?*

A. Generally speaking, yes. We have focused on the Android Market requirements. For details on the requirements imposed by other marketplaces, see those specific developer programs. Typically, any differences are in the requirements imposed on the application's Android manifest file and the specifics of the digital signature that accompanies the application.

Q. *Why must the key be valid until October 22, 2033?*

A. The digital signature of an application may persist through various application upgrades. By enforcing a date far in the future, trust relationships between the application provider and third parties (including users) can be established and maintained for the long term.

Q. *Can I programmatically obtain information about an application package?*

A. Yes, you can use the `getPackageInfo()` method of the `PackageManager` class to obtain information about an application package. This method returns a `PackageInfo` object, which contains all the information of that application's manifest file, from configuration details to the list of specific activities and permissions of the application.

Workshop

Quiz

1. True or False: The release process is important only for big projects.

2. Which version fields in the application's Android manifest file should you verify for release purposes?

    A. `android:versionCode`

    B. `android:versionLabel`

    C. `android:versionName`

    D. `android:version`

    E. All of the above

3. True or False: You cannot publish an application that includes a debug signature.

Answers

1. False. Whether you're a hobbyist working on your own or a member of a large development team, taking the time to verify whether an application is ready for release is important to the success of the application.

2. A and C. The Android platform uses the version code to perform upgrades, and the version name is a string field that developers and markets use for product support purposes.

3. True. The Android package manager installs only applications that have been properly signed.

Exercises

1. Choose one of the Been There, Done That! builds from this book (from any hour). Export the APK package file and digitally sign it.

2. Install the Been There, Done That! application package on a handset by using the adb command-line utility.

HOUR 24

Publishing on the Android Market

What You'll Learn in This Hour:

▶ Selling Android applications to the Android Market
▶ Exploring Android application publishing options
▶ Protecting your intellectual property

Congratulations! You've made it to the final hour, and you've learned how to build and test an Android application. The next logical step is to publish your application. In this hour, you learn how to publish an Android application on the popular Android Market and explore other publishing options.

Unlike other mobile platforms, Android supports paid distribution, free distribution, and even self-distribution options. This gives a developer wonderful flexibility for getting applications into the hands of users, with fewer hurdles than most platforms and a greater number of choices for users.

Selling on the Android Market

At this time, the Android Market is the primary mechanism for distributing Android applications. This is where typical users purchase and download applications. As of this writing, the Android Market is available on most Android handsets. Therefore, in this hour, we show you how to check a package for preparedness, sign up for a developer account, and submit your application for sale on the Android Market.

Signing Up for a Developer Account

To publish applications through the Android Market, you must register as a developer. Registering as a developer verifies who you are to Google and signs you up for a Google Checkout account, which the Android Market uses to disperse revenue from applications sales back to developers.

To sign up for Android Market, follow these steps:

1. Browse to http://market.android.com/publish/signup, as shown in Figure 24.1.

2. Sign in with the Google Account you want to use. (At this time, you can't change the associated Google Account, but you can change the contact email addresses for applications independently.)

3. Enter you developer information, including your name, email address, and website, as shown in Figure 24.2.

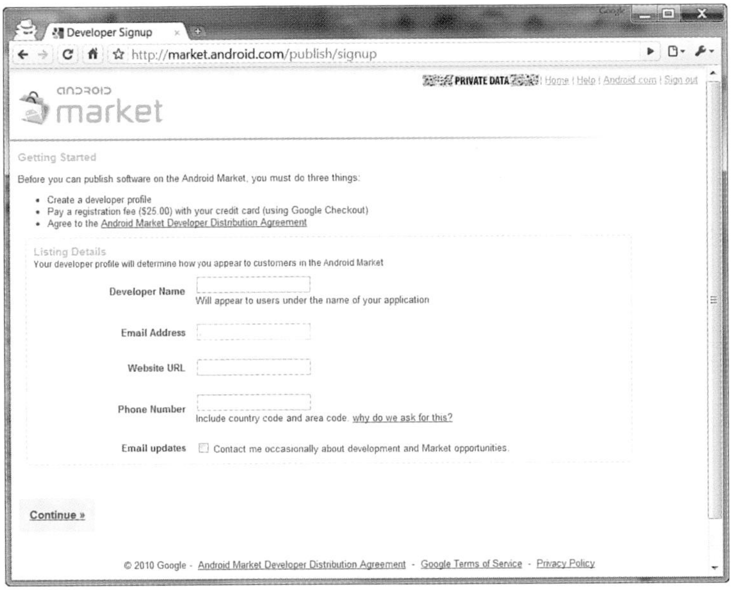

FIGURE 24.2
The Android
Market publish-
er profile page.

4. Confirm your registration payment (as of this writing, $25 USD). Note that Google Checkout is used for registration payment processing.

5. Provide information for a Google Checkout Merchant account. This is mandatory when signing up and paying to be an Android Developer.

6. Agree to link your credit card and account registration to the Android Market Developer Distribution Agreement.

When you successfully complete these steps, you are presented with the home screen of the Android Market, which also confirms that the Google Checkout Merchant account was created.

Uploading an Application to the Android Market

Now that you have an account registered for publishing applications through Android Market and a signed application package, you are ready to upload it. From the main page of the Android Market website, sign in and click the Upload Application button, as shown in Figure 24.3.

FIGURE 24.3
Android Market
listings.

You now see a form, as shown in Figure 24.4A, for uploading the application package.

FIGURE 24.4A
Uploading an
application
form.

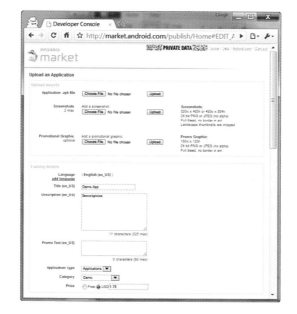

Figure 24.4B shows the screen allowing the developer to choose which countries to ship the application to. All countries that do not allow paid applications to be exported to are disabled.

FIGURE 24.4B
Choosing the
countries to
export your
application to.

The following is some of the information you must enter on this form:

▶ **Application title and description in several languages**—English is the
default language.

▶ **Countries (locations) where the application will be published**—These locations are subject to export compliance laws, so choose your locations carefully.
As of this writing, nearly 50 locations are available, and new locations are
being added regularly. In addition, you can choose specific carriers for each
location to further limit application distribution. Alternatively, you can
choose All Locations to include any future locations supported by the market.
For a complete list of locations where Android applications can be sold or
published for free, see http://market.android.com/support/bin/
answer.py?hl=en&answer=138294.

▶ **Application type and category**—Spend the time to set these fields appropriately, as defined by the Android Market, so that your application reaches its
intended audience. Incorrectly categorized applications do not sell well.

▶ **Application price**—The Android Market currently supports only one pricing
model: single payment. No subscription model pricing exists yet within the
Android Market. You must find other mechanisms in you're interested in
recurring payment pricing. Note that the Android Market currently imposes a
30% transaction fee for hosting applications within the Android Market. Prices

can range from $0.99 to $200 USD, and similar ranges are available in euros and UK pounds.

▶ **Copy protection information**—Choosing this option may help prevent the application from being copied from the device and distributed without your knowledge or permission.

▶ **Support contact information**—This option defaults to the information you provided for the developer account. You can change it on an app-by-app basis, though, which allows for great support flexibility when you're publishing multiple applications.

▶ **Consent**—You must click the checkboxes to agree to the terms of the current (at the time you click) Android Content Guidelines as well as the export laws of the United States, regardless of your location or nationality.

Watch Out!

Be sure to carefully read the details pages (follow the Learn More link) for the export compliance rules. There, Google also links to a couple of U.S. government web pages that provide enough information to know if you'll run afoul of these laws.

The application package is uploaded and verified while you fill out the form.

Did you Know?

Once an application package has been successfully uploaded, the previous information can be saved as a draft, which is great for verification before final publishing. Also, the application icon, name, version, localization information, and required permissions are shown so you can verify that you have configured the Android Manifest file properly.

Publishing on the Android Market

After you click the Publish button, the application appears in the Android Market almost immediately. Once your app is published, you can see statistics including ratings, reviews, downloads, active installs, and so on in the Your Android Market Listings section of the main page on your developer account. These statistics aren't updated as frequently as the publish action, and you can't see review details directly from the listing.

By clicking the application listing, you can edit the various fields. Although some details can be edited, pricing information can't be changed. For example, if your app starts as a free application, it will remain that way. You can always upload a different version for a paid version of the application with new features. Paid application pricing can be changed at any time but must fall within certain limits. (In USD, this is from 99 cents to $200, but it varies depending on the currency in use.)

Understanding Billing

Unlike some other mobile platforms you may have used, Android does not currently provide built-in billing APIs that work directly from within applications or charge directly to the user's cell phone bill. Instead, Android Market uses Google checkout for processing payments. Once an application is purchased, the user owns it.

If your application requires a service fee or sells other goods within the application (for example, ringtones, music, ebooks), you need to develop a custom billing mechanism. Most Android devices can leverage the Internet, so using online billing services and APIs—PayPal, Google, and Amazon, to name a few—is likely to be the common choice. Check with your preferred billing service to make sure it specifically allows mobile use.

Currently, the Android Market agreement does not allow for collecting payments within an application. Although there are applications available on the market that leverage this sort of thing for enhancing the appeal and user experience of the applications, this is technically in violation of the current Android Market Developer Distribution Agreement. Other forms of application distribution, though, may not be subject to these limitations.

Watch Out!

Another method for making money from users is to have an ad-supported mobile business model. This is a relatively new model for use within applications, as many older application distribution methods specifically disallowed it. However, Android has no specific rules against using advertisements within applications. This shouldn't come as too much of a surprise, considering the popularity of Google's AdSense.

Understanding the Android Market Application Return Policy

Although it is a matter of no small controversy, the Android Market has a 24-hour refund policy on applications. That is to say, a user can use an application for 24 hours and then return it for a full refund. As a developer, this means that sales aren't final until after the first 24 hours. However, this only applies to the first download and first return. If a particular user has already returned your application and wants to "try it again," he or she must make a *final* purchase—and can't return it a second time. Although this limits abuse, you should still be aware that if your application has limited reuse appeal or if all its value can come from just a few hours (or less) of use, you might find that you have a return rate that's too high and need to pursue other methods of monetization.

Removing Your Application from the Android Market

You can use the unpublish action in your developer account to remove an application from the Android Market. The unpublish action has an immediate effect but may take a few moments to become unavailable across the entire system.

Using Other Developer Account Benefits

Having a registered Android developer account enables you to manage your applications on the Android Market. In addition, if you have a developer account, you can purchase development versions of Android handsets. These handsets are useful for general development and testing but may not be suitable for final testing on actual target handsets because some functionality may be limited, and the firmware version may be different than that found on consumer handsets.

Exploring Other Android Publishing Options

The Android platform is an open platform, and publishing options are also very open. You've learned how to publish on the Android Market, but there are other options available as well. You might want to take advantage of these alternatives to target handsets and devices that do not come with the Android Market, distribute handsets to a narrower target audience, distribute applications that don't comply with the Android Market rules, or simply control distribution on your own.

Did you Know?

There are alternative markets for Android devices such as the ARCHOS 5 Internet Tablet. Applications developed especially for these types of devices are generally (but not always) marketed separately from applications developed for Android handsets.

Selling Your Application on Your Own Site

You can distribute Android applications directly from your own website or server. This method is most appropriate for vertical market applications, content companies developing mobile marketplaces, and big-brand websites wishing to drive users to their branded Android applications. It can also be a good way to get beta feedback from end users.

Although self-distribution is perhaps the easiest method of application distribution, it may also be the most difficult in terms of marketing and protect your application and making money. The only requirement for self-distribution is to have a place to host the application package file.

The downside of self-distribution is that the end user must configure his or her device to allow packages from unknown sources. This setting is found under the Application Settings section of the device Settings application, as shown in Figure 24.5.

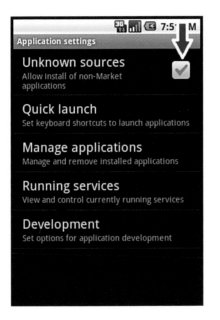

After that, the user must enter the URL of the application package into the web browser on the handset and download the file (or click a link to it). Once the file is downloaded, the standard Android installation process occurs, during which the user needs to confirm the permissions and, optionally, confirm an update or replacement of an existing application if a version is already installed.

Not all devices include the option for enabling installation from unknown sources. For instance, the ARCHOS 5 Internet Tablet does not include this option, but (luckily) automatically has this functionality turned on so users can install applications from any source they choose. Keep in mind such device differences when providing instructions for users.

Watch Out!

Selling Your Application Using Other Alternatives

The Android Market is not the only consolidated market available for selling Android applications. Because Android is an open platform, there is nothing preventing a handset manufacturer or an operator (or even you) from running an Android marketplace website or building an Android application that serves as a market.

Here are a few marketplaces where you might consider distributing your Android applications:

▶ **PocketGear**—This site distributes mobile applications across a wide range of devices, using various billing models (http://www.pocketgear.com).

▶ **SlideME**—This is an Android-specific distribution community for free and commercial applications, using an on-device store (http://slideme.org).

▶ **AndAppStore**—This site offers Android-specific distribution for free applications, using an on-device store (http://www.andappstore.com).

▶ **SHOP4APPS**—This application store run by Motorola targets China (http://developer.motorola.com/shop4apps/).

▶ **MobiHand**—This site distributes mobile applications for a wide range of devices for free and commercial applications (http://www.mobihand.com).

This list is not complete, and we don't specifically endorse any one market over another, but it is important to note that there are a number of alternative distribution mechanisms available to developers. Application requirements vary by store. In addition to these, many manufacturers and wireless operators have their own stores, especially for devices that don't include the "Google experience" (that is, devices that don't include Google apps, such as the Android Market).

Third-party application stores are free to enforce whatever rules they want on the applications they accept, so carefully read the fine print at each site. A particular site may enforce content guidelines, require additional technical support, and enforce digital signing requirements. Only you and your team can determine which sites are suitable for your specific needs.

Did you Know?

Anyone can develop a new Android application store and market applications on his or her own terms. That's one of the benefits of an open and free platform.

Summary

In this final hour, you learned how to publish an Android application for the world to see and use. You now know there are several different publishing avenues, including self-publishing from your website as well as a variety of third-party application stores that can help you sell your work (usually for a cut of the profit). You also learned how to set up a developer account with the Android Market, one of the most popular application stores, and can now begin to sell your own applications there.

Perhaps you already have some great app ideas in mind. Fire up Eclipse and start coding! When you start building applications, drop us a note and tell us about them. (Our contact information is available in Appendix C, "Supplementary Materials.") We'd love to hear from you!

Q&A

Q. *What languages are supported by the Android Market?*

A. The Android Market currently supports over a dozen languages, and more are added all the time. The following are some of the languages currently supported by the Android Market:

- American English (en_US)

- French/français (fr_FR)

- German/Deutsch (de_DE)

- Italian/italiano (it_IT)

- Spanish/Español (es_ES)

- Dutch/Nederlands (nl_NL)

- Polish/polski (pl_PL)

- Czech/čeština (cs_CZ)

- Portugese/português (pt_PT)

- Taiwanese/中文（繁體）(zh_TW)

- Japanese/日本語 (ja_JP)

- Korean/한국어 (ko_KR)

- Russian/русский (ru_RU)

Q. *How can I protect my hard work from software piracy?*

A. After you spend time, money, and effort building a valuable Android application, it makes sense to protect yourself against reverse engineering of trade secrets and software piracy. Because Android applications are compiled for the Dalvik virtual machine, most traditional Java obfuscation tools won't work. Some tools, such as ProGuard (http://proguard.sourceforge.net) do support Android. The Android Market application publication screen also includes a mysterious (undocumented) check box for copy protection when publishing your application.

Workshop

Quiz

1. True or False: You don't need an account to sell on the Android Market.

2. Which of the following statements are true?

   A. The Android Market allows for paid and free applications.

   B. The Android Market allows developers to sell applications only in the United States.

   C. The Android Market is the only Android application store available.

   D. The Android Market imposes a 30% transaction fee on applications sold.

   E. All of the above.

3. True or False: You can sell Android applications from your own website.

4. Before submitting an application to the Android Market, which of the following must you do?

   A. Certify your application through an approved, expensive certification program.

   B. Provide a notarized Statement of Testing Completeness, proving you've tested every single aspect of the application in all scenarios.

   C. Sign your application package with a well-known certificate authority approved for use with the Android Market.

   D. Record a video of your application in action.

E. Provide a Word document with thorough documentation of application flows and a complete user manual.

F. Get certified carrier and operator approval from each and every carrier you plan on launching on before uploading your application package.

Answers

1. False. You must create an authenticated developer account with Google before you can publish Android applications on the Android Market.

2. A and D. The Android Market, the most popular Android application store, allows developers to publish free and paid applications in a number of different countries, and it takes a 30% transaction fee for hosting applications.

3. True. You can sell your Android applications from a number of application shops, including your own site. Keep in mind that users need to enable installation of applications from unknown sources to install applications from unknown websites.

4. None! Although none of these are required, some of them, such as thoroughly testing your application, are advisable. Others might be useful for marketing purposes. However, none are actually required by the Android Market. It's very open!

Exercises

1. Create a developer account for yourself on the Android Market.

2. Browse through the Android Market (on a handset or on the Android Market website). Think of an idea for an application and determine what category and price range for that application in the Android Market.

3. Go write a fabulous and exciting application, and then share it with the world.

APPENDIX A

Configuring Your Android Development Environment

This appendix walks you through the steps needed to install and configure all the appropriate tools you need to get started developing Android applications:

▶ The appropriate Java Development Kit (JDK)

▶ The Eclipse integrated development environment (IDE)

▶ The Android Software Development Kit (SDK) and tools

▶ Any drivers required by specific Android devices

These software packages are available free of charge from their vendors' websites.

Development Machine Prerequisites

Android developers may use a number of different operating systems and software configurations. This appendix walks you through the installation of the tools used in this book. If you're installing from scratch, you will want to choose the latest versions of the software packages required for development.

For a complete list of software and system requirements, see the Android developer website, http://developer.android.com/sdk/requirements.html.

Supported Operating Systems

Android applications can be written on the following operating systems:

▶ Windows XP or later

▶ Mac OS X 10.5.8 or later (x86 only)

▶ Linux

Available Space

You need around 2GB of space to safely install all the tools you need to develop Android applications. This includes installing the JDK, the Eclipse IDE, the Android SDK, and the tools and plug-ins.

Installing the Java Development Kit

Android applications can be developed using Sun's JDK 5 or JDK 6. You can read the license agreement and download the latest version of the Java Standard Edition JDK at Sun's website, http://java.sun.com/javase/downloads/. For specific installation for your operating system, see the documentation available with the installation package you choose.

Installing the Eclipse IDE

Most developers use the popular Eclipse IDE for Android development; this IDE is available for Windows, Mac, and Linux operating systems. You can develop Android applications using either Eclipse 3.4 (Ganymede) or Eclipse 3.5 (Galileo).

> If this is your first time using Eclipse, you'll probably want to choose the Eclipse IDE for Java EE Developers. This version of the Eclipse IDE includes the Eclipse Java Development Tools (JDT) plug-in and the optional Web Tools Platform (WTP).

You can read the license agreement and download the Eclipse IDE for Java EE Developers at www.eclipse.org/downloads/.

The Eclipse package comes as a compressed zip file. There is no installer. You unzip the package into the desired folder and then follow the specific instructions in the following sections for your target operating system.

Notes on Windows Installations

Once you've installed the files in the appropriate location, navigate to the Eclipse.exe executable and create a shortcut on your desktop. Edit the shortcut and modify the target field with any command-line arguments you desire.

Notes on Mac OS X Installations

If you are installing Eclipse on a Mac OS X system, make sure to review the README.html file included with the Eclipse package. This readme file covers how to pass command-line arguments to Eclipse using the eclipse.ini file and how to run more than one instance of Eclipse so that you can work with multiple project workspaces simultaneously.

> If you don't want to use Eclipse, you can find more information about configuring your computer for Android development with other IDEs at the Android website: http://developer.android.com/guide/developing/other-ide.html.

Did you Know?

Installing the Android SDK

You need to install the Android SDK to develop Android applications. The Android SDK includes the Android JAR file (Android application framework classes) as well as Android documentation, tools, and sample code.

The Android SDK is available from the Android Developer website, at http://developer.android.com/sdk/index.html. You need to agree to the Android license agreement prior to installing the developer package.

Newer versions of the Android SDK have a helpful installer. You simply download the compressed file, unzip it into the desired folder, and launch the setup. The compressed SDK files require about 25MB of hard drive space and uncompress to a size of approximately 40MB.

The Android tools and SDK versions are componentized. This means that instead of installing one large package for development for all supported versions of Android, you can pick and choose the Android SDK versions you want to install and work with using the Android SDK and AVD Manager. This tool allows developers to easily upgrade their development environment when a new version of Android comes out (which, historically, has happened quite frequently). In addition to various Android target versions to choose from, other tools and support can be downloaded, such as USB drivers for Windows.

You need to use the Android SDK and AVD Manager to install the tools.

Notes on Windows Installations

To update your PATH variable to include the Android tools directory, right-click Computer and choose Properties. In Vista, you also need to click Advanced System Settings. You continue by clicking the Advanced tab of the System Properties dialog and clicking the Environment Variables button.

In the System Variables section, edit the PATH variable and add the path to the tools directory.

Notes on Mac OS X Installations

To update your PATH variable to include the Android tools directory, you need to edit your .bash_profile file in your Home directory.

Notes on Linux OS Installations

To update your PATH variable to include the Android tools directory, you need to edit your ~/.bash_profile, ~/.bashrc, or ~/.profile file.

Installing and Configuring the Android Plug-in for Eclipse (ADT)

The Android Plug-in for Eclipse allows seamless integration with many of the Android development tools. If you're using Eclipse, it's highly recommended that you install the in, as it will make your life much easier. The Plug-in includes various wizards for creating and debugging Android projects.

To install the Android Plug-in for Eclipse (ADT), you must launch Eclipse and install a custom software update. The steps required depend on the version of Eclipse you use. For complete instructions, see the Android developer website, http://developer.android.com/sdk/eclipse-adt.html.

To install Android Plug-in on Eclipse 3.5 (Galileo), follow these steps:

1. Launch Eclipse.

2. Select Help, Install New Software.

3. Select the Available Software tab.

4. Click the Add button.

5. Add the remote site https://dl-ssl.google.com/android/eclipse/. If this site fails, try http://dl-ssl.google.com/android/eclipse/.

6. On the Available Software tab, check the box next to Developer Tools box. (Also check the boxes for Android DDMS and Android Development Tools.)

7. Click the Next button and follow the wizard for installing the tools. Accept the terms of the license agreement and click the Finish button.

8. After the software update completes, restart Eclipse.

After you install the Android SDK Eclipse plug-in, update your Eclipse preferences to point at the Android SDK you previously downloaded. To do this, launch Eclipse and choose Window, Preferences (or Eclipse, Preferences in Mac OS X). Select the Android preferences and set the path to where you installed the Android SDK. Once you have set the path appropriately, you will see a number of target SDK versions (Android 1.0, 1.5, 1.6, 2.0, 2.01, 2.1, and so on) listed below SDK Location in the Android Preferences dialog in Eclipse.

Upgrading the Android SDK

The Android SDK is currently in development, which means you will inevitably have to upgrade the version of the SDK on your machine. Changes to the Android SDK may include addition, update, and removal of features; package name changes; and tool updates.

With each new version of the SDK, Google provides the following useful documents:

- **An Overview of Changes**—A brief description of major changes to the SDK

- **An API Diff Report**—A complete list of specific changes to the SDK

- **Release Notes**—A list of known issues with the SDK

To update the Android SDK, you launch the Android SDK and AVD Manager (by clicking the little icon that looks like a phone, or under Window, Android SDK and AVD Manager) and update all packages and check for new ones. Upgrading the Android SDK involves updating the Android targets (and AVD) within Eclipse, updating path variables, and reconfiguring existing Android development tools, as needed. After you upgrade the development environment, you need to port your Android applications to the new SDK.

Configuring Development Hardware for Device Debugging

Each Android phone model may have different debugging configurations. Your Android device must be enabled for debugging via a USB connection.

Enabling USB Debugging on an Android Device

To enable USB debugging, from the Home screen of the Android device, select Menu, Settings, Applications, Development and enable the USB Debugging option. Different devices may have this option in different places. For instance, on the Archos 5 Internet tablet, it is found under Device Storage & USB connection, USB Connection Mode, and then choose Debug Bridge (ADB) to enable USB debugging.

> During long debugging sessions, your phone might often go to sleep. To prevent this from happening, select the option to have the phone stay awake while charging, found in the development settings. You should see this option in the development settings, usually labeled "Stay Awake" or the likes.

Configuring Your Operating System for Device Debugging

To install and debug Android applications on hardware such as the T-Mobile G1, Motorola Droid, or Nexus One, you might need to configure your operating system to access the phone via USB. This is especially true of Windows machines. The Android SDK ships with drivers for some devices, and you can simply point the Device Manager at the directory where you installed the Android SDK and then plug in the phone via USB, and it will show up when you launch an application via Eclipse.

Notes on Windows Installations

You need to install Android USB drivers. You will find them as one of the packages in the Android SDK and AVD Manager, under USB Driver Package. Alternatively, you can download them separately from http://developer.android.com/sdk/win-usb.html. After you unzip the drivers, connect your phone to your computer via the USB cable and select the drivers you want to install.

Notes on Mac OS X Installations

On a supported Mac, all you have to do is plug in the USB cable to the Mac and the device. There is no additional configuration needed.

Notes on Linux OS Installations

Ubuntu Linux installations require a rules file, using the following steps:

1. Log in as root administrator.

2. Create the file /etc/udev/rules.d/50-android.rules.

3a. For Gutsy (7.10)/Hardy (8.04) Ubuntu Linux installations, the file should contain `SUBSYSTEM=="usb"`, `SYSFS{idVendor}=="0bb4"`, `MODE="0666"`.

3b. For Dapper (6.06) Ubuntu Linux installations, the file should contain `SUBSYSTEM=="usb_device"`, `SYSFS{idVendor}=="0bb4"`, `MODE="0666"`.

4. Enter `chmod a+rx /etc/udev/rules.d/50-android.rules`.

APPENDIX B

Eclipse IDE Tips and Tricks

In this appendix, a variety of tips and tricks for Eclipse are offered for your enjoyment and benefit. These tips and tricks are geared toward tasks performed frequently while developing Android applications but may also apply to other Java development in Eclipse.

> Do you have your own tips or tricks for Android development in Eclipse? If so, email them to us (with permission to publish them) at androidwirelessdev@gmail.com, and they may be included on our blog at http://androidbook.blogspot.com. Get your moment of geekly fame!

Creating New Classes and Methods

You can quickly create a new class and corresponding source file by right-clicking the package to create it and choosing New, Class. Then you enter the class name, pick a superclass and interfaces, and choose whether to create default comments and method stubs for the superclass for constructors or abstract methods.

Along these lines, you can quickly create method stubs by right-clicking a class or within a class in the editor and choosing Source, Override/Implement Methods. Then you choose the methods to create stubs for, where to create them, and whether to generate default comment blocks.

Organizing Imports

When referencing a class in your code for the first time, you can hover over the newly used class name and choose "Import 'Classname' (package name)" to have Eclipse quickly add the proper import statement.

In addition, the Organize imports command (Ctrl+Shift+O in Windows or Cmd+Shift+O on a Mac) causes Eclipse to automatically organize your imports. Eclipse removes unused imports and adds new ones for packages used but not already imported.

If there is any ambiguity in the name of a class during automatic import, such as with the Android Log class, Eclipse prompts you with the package to import.

Finally, you can configure Eclipse to automatically organize the imports each time you save a file. This can be set for the entire workspace or for an individual project. Configuring this for an individual project allows better flexibility when you're working on multiple projects and don't want to make changes to some code, even if they are an improvement. To configure this, perform the following steps:

1. Right-click the project and choose Properties.

2. Expand Java Editor and choose Save Actions.

3. Check Enable Project Specific Settings, Perform the Selected Actions on Save, and Organize Imports.

Documenting Code

Regular code comments are useful (when done right). Comments in Javadoc style appear in code completion dialogs and other places, thus making them even more useful. To quickly add a Javadoc comment to a method or class, simply press Ctrl+Shift+J in Windows (or Cmd+Alt+J on a Mac). Alternatively, you can choose Source, Generate Element Comment to prefill certain fields in the Javadoc, such as parameter names and author, thus speeding up the creation of this style of comment.

Using Auto-Complete

Auto-complete is a great feature that speeds up text entry. If this feature hasn't appeared for you yet or has gone away, you can bring it up by pressing Ctrl+spacebar.

Auto-complete not only saves time in typing but can be used to jog your memory about methods—or find a new method. You can scroll through all the methods of a class and even see the associated Javadocs with them. You can easily find static methods by using the class name or the instance variable name. You follow this name with a dot (and maybe Ctrl+spacebar) and then scroll through all the names. Then you can start typing the first part of a name to filter the results.

Editing Code Efficiently

Sometimes, you might find that the editor window is just too small, especially with all the extra little metadata windows and tabs surrounding it. Try this: Double-click the tab of the source file that you want to edit. Boom! It's now nearly the full Eclipse window size! Just double-click to return it to normal.

Ever wish you could see two source files at once? Well, you can! Simply grab the tab for a source file and either drag it over to the edge of the editor area or to the bottom. You then see a dark outline, showing where the file will be docked—either side-by-side with another file or above or below another file. This creates a parallel editor area where other file tabs can be dragged, as well.

Ever wish you could see two places at once in the same source file? You can! Right-click the tab for the file in question and choose New Editor. A second editor tab for the same file comes up. With the previous tip, you can now have two different views of the same file.

Ever feel like you get far too many tabs open for files you're no longer editing? I do! There are a number of solutions to this problem. First, you can right-click a file tab and choose Close Others to close all other open files besides the chosen one. You can quickly close specific tabs by middle-clicking with a mouse on each tab. (This even works on a Mac with a mouse that can middle click, such as one with a scroll wheel.) Finally, you can use the Eclipse setting that limits the number of open file editors:

1. Open Eclipse's Preferences dialog.

2. Expand General, choose Editors, and check Close Editors Automatically.

3. Edit the value in Number of Opened Editors Before Closing.

I find eight to be a good number to use for the Number of Opened Editors Before Closing option to keep the clutter down, but have enough editors open to still get work done and have reference code open. Note also that if you check Open New Editor under When All Editors Are Dirty or Pinned, more files will be open if you're actively editing more than the number chosen. Thus, this setting doesn't affect productivity when you're editing a large number of files all at once but can keep things clean during most normal tasks.

Renaming Almost Anything

Eclipse's Rename tool is quite powerful. It can be used to rename variables, methods, class names, and more. Most often, you can simply right-click the item you want to rename and then choose Refactor, Rename. Alternatively, after selecting the item, you can press Ctrl+Alt+R in Windows (or Cmd+Alt+R on a Mac) to begin the renaming process. If you are renaming a top-level class in a file, the filename will have to be changed as well. Eclipse usually handles the source control changes required to do this, if the file is being tracked by source control.

If Eclipse can determine that the item is in reference to the identically named item being renamed, all instances of the name will be renamed as well. Occasionally, this even means comments are updated with the new name. Quite handy!

Formatting Code

Eclipse has a built-in mechanism for formatting Java code. Formatting code with a tool is useful for keeping the style consistent, applying a new style to old code, or matching styles with a different client or target (such as a book or an article).

To quickly format a small block of code, select the code and press Ctrl-Shift+F in Windows (or Cmd+Shift+F on a Mac). The code is formatted to the current settings. If no code is selected, the entire file is formatted. Occasionally, you need to select more code—such as an entire method—to get the indentation levels and brace matching correct.

The Eclipse formatting settings are found in the Properties pane under Java Code Style, Formatter. You can configure these settings on a per-project or workspace-wide basis. Dozens of rules can be applied and modified to suite your own style.

Organizing Code

Sometimes, formatting code isn't enough to make it clean and readable. Over the course of developing a complex activity, you might end up with a number of embedded classes and methods strewn about the file. A quick Eclipse trick comes to the rescue: With the file in question open, make sure the outline view is also visible. Simply click and drag methods and classes around in the outline view to place them in a suitable logical order. Do you have a method that is only called from a certain class but available to all? Just drag it in to that class. This works with almost anything listed in the outline, including classes, methods, and variables.

Fun with Refactoring

Do you find yourself writing a whole bunch of repeating sections of code that look, for instance, like this:

```
TextView nameCol = new TextView(this);
nameCol.setTextColor(getResources().getColor(R.color.title_color));
nameCol.setTextSize(getResources().
    getDimension(R.dimen.help_text_size));
nameCol.setText(scoreUserName);
table.addView(nameCol);
```

This code sets text color, text size, and text. If you've written two or more blocks that look like this, your code could benefit from refactoring. Eclipse provides two very useful tools—Extract Local Variable and Extract Method—to speed up this task and make it almost trivial.

Follow these steps to use the Extract Local Variable tool:

1. Select the expression `getResources().getColor(R.color.title_color)`.

2. Right-click and choose Refactor, Extract Local Variable (or press Ctrl+Alt+L).

3. In the dialog that appears, enter a name for the variable and leave the Replace All Occurrences check box selected. Then click OK and watch the magic happen.

4. Repeat steps 1–3 for the text size.

The result should now look like this:

```
int textColor = getResources().getColor(R.color.title_color);
float textSize = getResources().getDimension(R.dimen.help_text_size);
TextView nameCol = new TextView(this);
nameCol.setTextSize(textSize);
nameCol.setText(scoreUserName);
nameCol.setTextColor(textColor);
table.addView(nameCol);
```

All repeated sections of the last five lines also have this change made. How convenient is this?

Now you're ready for the second tool. Follow these steps to use the Extract Method tool:

1. Select all five lines of the first block of code.

2. Right-click and choose Refactor, Extract Method (or choose Ctrl+Alt+M).

3. Name the method and edit the variable names anything you want. (Move them up or down, too, if desired.) Then click OK and watch the magic happen. By default, the new method is below your current one.

If the other blocks of code are actually identical, meaning the statements of the other blocks must be in the exact same order, the types are all the same, and so on, they will also be replaced with calls to this new method! You can see this in the count of additional occurrences shown in the dialog for the Extract Method tool. If that count doesn't match what you expect, check that the code follows exactly the same pattern.

Now you have code that looks like the following:

```
addTextToRowWithValues(newRow, scoreUserName, textColor, textSize);
```

It is easier to work with this code than with the original code, and it was created with almost no typing! If you had ten instances before refactoring, you've saved a lot of time by using a useful Eclipse tool.

Resolving Mysterious Build Errors

Occasionally, you might find that Eclipse is finding build errors where there were none just moments before. In such a situation, you can try a couple quick Eclipse tricks.

First, try refreshing the project: Simply right-click the project and choose Refresh or press F5. If this doesn't work, try deleting the R.java file, which is found under the gen directory under the name of the particular package being compiled. (Don't worry: This file is created during every compile.) If the Compile Automatically option is enabled, the file is recreated. Otherwise, you need to compile the project again.

Finally, you can try cleaning the project. To do this, choose Project, Clean and choose the projects you want to clean. Eclipse removes all temporary files and then rebuilds the project(s).

Creating Custom Log Filters

Every Android log statement includes a tag. These tags can be used with filters defined in LogCat. To add a new filter, click the green plus sign button in the LogCat pane. Name the filter—perhaps using the tag name—and fill in the tag you want to use. Now there is another tab in LogCat that will show messages that contain this tag. In addition, you can create filters that display items by severity level.

Android convention has largely settled on creating tags based on the name of the class. You see this frequently in the code provided with this book. Note that we create a constant in each class with the same variable name to simplify each logging call. Here's an example:

```
public static final String DEBUG_TAG = "MyClassName";
```

This convention isn't a requirement, though. Tags could be organized around specific tasks that span many activities or could use any other logical organization that works for your needs.

Moving Tabs Around

Eclipse provides some pretty decent layouts with the default perspectives. However, not everyone works the same way and, with Android, a few perspectives have poor default layouts for us.

For instance, the Properties tab is usually found on the bottom. For code, this works fine because this tab is only a few lines high. But for layouts in Android, this doesn't work so well.

Luckily, in Eclipse this is easy to fix: Simply drag the tab by left-clicking and holding on the tab (the title) itself and dragging it to a new location, such as the vertical section on the right side of the Eclipse window. This provides the much-needed vertical space to see the dozens of properties often found there.

You can experiment to find a tab layout that works well for you. Each perspective has its own layout, too, and the perspectives can be task oriented. If you completely mess up a perspective, or just want a clean start, you can simply choose Window, Reset Perspective.

Integrating Source Control

Eclipse has the ability to integrate with many source control packages through add-ons. This allows Eclipse to manage checking out a file—making it writable—when you first start to edit a file, checking a file in, updating a file, showing a file's status, and a number of other tasks, depending on the support of the add-on. Common source control add-ons are available for CVS, Subversion, Perforce, git, and many other packages.

Generally speaking, not all files are suitable for source control. For Android projects, any file with the bin and gen directories shouldn't be in source control.

To exclude these generically within Eclipse, go to Preferences, Team, Ignored Resources. Add *.apk, *.ap_, and *.dex by clicking the Add Pattern button and adding one at a time.

APPENDIX C

Supplementary Materials

A number of supplementary materials have been developed to accompany this book. These materials, such as source code for many of the examples provided in the book, are available online. There are also a number of other online resources available for Android developers.

Accessing the Publisher's Website

The source code that accompanies this book is available for download from the publisher's website (see Figure C.1), http://www.informit.com/title/9780321673350:

FIGURE C.1
The InformIT website.

Here's what you'll find on the publisher's website:

► A thorough description of this book

► Downloadable source code

▶ Errata and book updates

▶ InformIT users' reviews of the book

▶ Sample content

▶ Other related books

Accessing the Authors' Website

The authors' book website, at http://androidbook.blogspot.com, is a comprehensive guide for designing, developing, debugging, and distributing Android applications (see Figure C.2).

FIGURE C.2
The Android Mobile Application Development website.

Here's what you'll find on the authors' website:

▶ Information about Android SDK updates

▶ Market news and information related to Android and other mobile technologies

▶ Tips, tricks, and pitfalls of Android development

▶ Links to public reviews of this book

▶ Supplemental code examples

▶ Informal discussions of more advanced Android development topics

▶ Links to other Android materials written by the authors, including their more advanced Android book and technical articles available online

Contacting the Authors

Send the authors feedback at androidwirelessdev @gmail.com!

We welcome your feedback! If you have comments, questions, or concerns about the content of this book, you can email us (Lauren and Shane) at androidwirelessdev@gmail.com (see Figure C.3). We do our best to answer each and every query and often post commonly asked questions and their answers on the book website at : http://androidbook.blogspot.com.

FIGURE C.3
Send us feedback!

Leveraging Online Android Resources

The Android developer community is friendly and helpful. Here are a number of useful websites for Android developers and followers of the wireless industry in general:

▶ **Android Developer Website**—The Android SDK, developer reference site, and forums: http://developer.android.com

▶ **Open Handset Alliance**—Android manufacturers, operators, and developers: http://www.openhandsetalliance.com

▶ **Android Market**—Buy and sell Android applications: http://market.android.com/publish

▶ **OpenIntents**—An Android developer resource with a public intent registry as well as source for third-party Android libraries and extensions: http://openintents.org

▶ **anddev.org**—An Android developer forum: http://www.anddev.org

▶ **FierceDeveloper**—A weekly newsletter for wireless developers: http://www.fiercedeveloper.com

▶ **Stack Overflow: Android**—A collaborative site for programmers, with an official section for Android: http://stackoverflow.com/questions/tagged/android

▶ **Wireless Developer Network**—A daily news digest for the wireless industry: http://www.wirelessdevnet.com

▶ **Developer.com**—A developer-oriented site that publishes technical articles: http://www.developer.com

Index

O

P

The Complete, Start-to-Finish Guide to Android Development—From Concept to Market!

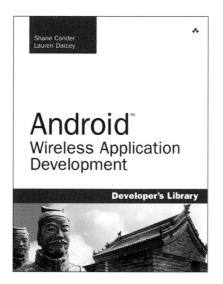

▶ **Covers application design, development, debugging, packaging, distribution, and much more**

▶ **Includes invaluable real-world tips from experienced mobile developers**

▶ **Unlike many competitive books, reflects the final Android SDK, not a beta**

ISBN-13: 9780321627094

Android Wireless Application Development is the comprehensive resource for developers who are new to Android—or to wireless development in general. Conder and Darcey cover all this, and much more:

▶ Mastering the Android development environment
▶ Quickly writing a basic Android application
▶ Understanding the entire Android application lifecycle
▶ Building effective user interfaces
▶ Using Android's APIs for networking, location-based services, data, storage, multimedia, telephony, graphics, and more
▶ Working with Android's optional hardware-specific APIs
▶ Designing more effective applications using Notifications and Services
▶ Developing and testing bulletproof Android applications

The book also provides valuable appendices on Android's Emulator, DDMS, Debug Bridge, and SQLite database, as well as a convenient glossary that demystifies the terminology of mobile development.

informIT For more information and to read sample material please visit
informit.com/title/9780321627094

  Title is also available at **safari.informit.com**

FREE Online Edition

Your purchase of **Sams Teach Yourself Android™ Application Development in 24 Hours** includes access to a free online edition for 45 days through the Safari Books Online subscription service. Nearly every Sams book is available online through Safari Books Online, along with more than 5,000 other technical books and videos from publishers such as Addison-Wesley Professional, Cisco Press, Exam Cram, IBM Press, O'Reilly, Prentice Hall, and Que.

SAFARI BOOKS ONLINE allows you to search for a specific answer, cut and paste code, download chapters, and stay current with emerging technologies.

Activate your FREE Online Edition at www.informit.com/safarifree

STEP 1: Enter the coupon code: YFEHTZG.

STEP 2: New Safari users, complete the brief registration form.
Safari subscribers, just log in.

If you have difficulty registering on Safari or accessing the online edition,
please e-mail customer-service@safaribooksonline.com